T0331088

SUSTAINABILITY AT WORK

Sustainability at Work is a compelling guide for anyone who seeks both a successful career and a career that makes a positive difference in society.

Containing career advice of great value to students and professionals, and explaining how one can integrate sustainability into future roles, this book's appeal extends far beyond those well versed in sustainability thinking. The text includes an easy-to-follow structure—the SURF Framework—that anyone wondering how they can make a difference in the workplace can apply. In this thoroughly revised new edition, Marilyn Waite builds upon recent career trends to include two all-important themes that are redefining sustainability: justice, equity, diversity, and inclusion and climate-related career pathways. In addition, practical advice for finding and creating roles that correspond to one's preferences and purpose is elaborated. The book explains how real people in a plethora of sectors can have a positive impact on people and planet. Professionals from a variety of backgrounds and locations explain how they brought a sustainability approach to various sectors, including agriculture, business, economics, and financial services, education and research, entertainment and media, health care, law and policy, and science and technology. The breadth of stories covers individuals working on five continents in various levels of responsibility.

Through inspiring narratives and a structured framework, *Sustainability at Work* illustrates how sustainability can be incorporated into every imaginable career to impact the quadruple bottom line: environment, economy, society, and future generations.

Marilyn Waite's vision is a world where sustainability values of social justice, environmental consciousness, intergenerational equity, and economic health drive decision-making and business practices. A sustainability expert and practitioner, she has addressed audiences globally on sustainability in careers, finance, textiles, climate change, water, and energy. Marilyn holds a Master's degree with distinction in Engineering for Sustainable Development from the University of Cambridge and a Bachelor of Science degree in Civil and Environmental Engineering from Princeton University. She serves on several boards and investment committees.

"*Sustainability at Work* is a great source to practically guide professionals on their career journey, providing frameworks and real-world stories of people in various sectors and professions. The content from the first edition has been used in our China MBA Program with the University of International Business and Economics (UIBE) in Beijing. This second edition is most welcome, as it expands the career narratives to include China and highlights roles to help curb climate change. It is a great addition to many university courses, and I would personally recommend it to my entourage."

Yanan Xu, *Assistant Provost, China, City University of Seattle*

"As China undergoes a rapid acceleration towards an ecological civilization based on shared prosperity, with a pledge to peak carbon emissions by 2030 and become carbon neutral by 2060, it is imperative that professionals gain an understanding of sustainability concepts and apply the tools to their work. The second edition of *Sustainability at Work* enables the reader to ground themselves in the present-day context of environmental, social, and governance (ESG) strategies as applied to various sectors and roles. I highly recommend *Sustainability at Work* for global curricula."

Junjie Zhang, *Professor, Nicholas School of the Environment, Duke University; Director, Initiative for Sustainable Investment, Duke Kunshan University; Chief Economist, Green Finance Forum of 60 (GF60)*

"As dean at INSEEC Master of Science business school, I've accompanied thousands of students in their career journey. Increasingly, the job market is demanding operational, entry-level staff in the fields of corporate sustainability, responsible investing, and environmental, social and governance (ESG) strategies. The second edition of *Sustainability at Work* is a timely read to gain the tools and insights needed to be successful in the growing application of ESG practice. I highly recommend *Sustainability at Work* for today's young professionals."

Ellen Kountz, *Dean of the Finance Department, Professor of Finance, INSEEC MSc business school, Paris Campus (OMNES Education group)*

"As a professor in France that teaches climate politics and climate negotiations, I help prepare students for a workforce that is increasingly centered on the global ecological transition. As such, I warmly recommend the second edition of *Sustainability at Work* with its new chapter on climate-related careers."

Carola Klöck, *Assistant Professor, Centre for International Studies (CERI), Sciences Po Paris*

"The second edition of *Sustainability at Work* is most welcome as law students and practicing legal professionals grapple with the complex intersections of environmental, social, and governance jurisprudence in the public and private domains. I therefore highly recommend this updated version to my network in Spain and Latin America."

Izabel Rigo Portocarrero, *Deputy Director of the Public Law Department, Faculty of Law, International University of La Rioja (UNIR Spain)*

"The second edition of *Sustainability at Work* has filled a gap in the social and environmental action nonfiction field. The volume serves as a useful guide to readers in incorporating the theory of sustainability into the workplace for various roles. I have found the book to be an invaluable resource for my students. I highly recommend the book for use in Latin America."

Mary Little, *Associate Professor of Justice, Resilience and Ecology, School for Field Studies, Atenas, Costa Rica*

SUSTAINABILITY AT WORK

Careers That Make a Difference

Second edition

Marilyn Waite

LONDON AND NEW YORK

Designed cover image: Eoneren © Getty

Second edition published 2024
by Routledge
4 Park Square, Milton Park, Abingdon, Oxon OX14 4RN

and by Routledge
605 Third Avenue, New York, NY 10158

Routledge is an imprint of the Taylor & Francis Group, an informa business

© 2024 Marilyn Waite

The right of Marilyn Waite to be identified as author of this work has been asserted in accordance with sections 77 and 78 of the Copyright, Designs and Patents Act 1988.

First edition published by Routledge 2016

British Library Cataloguing-in-Publication Data
A catalogue record for this book is available from the British Library

Library of Congress Cataloging-in-Publication Data
Names: Waite, Marilyn, author.
Title: Sustainability at work : careers that make a difference / Marilyn Waite.
Description: Second edition. | New York, NY : Routledge, 2024. |
Includes bibliographical references and index.
Identifiers: LCCN 2024001133 (print) | LCCN 2024001134 (ebook) |
ISBN 9781032615837 (hbk) | ISBN 9781032615820 (pbk) |
ISBN 9781032615844 (ebk)
Subjects: LCSH: Career development--Environmental aspects. |
Sustainable development. | Environmentalism.
Classification: LCC HF5381 .W159 2024 (print) | LCC HF5381 (ebook) |
DDC 650.14--dc23/eng/20240412
LC record available at https://lccn.loc.gov/2024001133
LC ebook record available at https://lccn.loc.gov/2024001134

ISBN: 978-1-032-61583-7 (hbk)
ISBN: 978-1-032-61582-0 (pbk)
ISBN: 978-1-032-61584-4 (ebk)

DOI: 10.4324/9781032615844

Typeset in Sabon
by Taylor & Francis Books

CONTENTS

ILLUSTRATIONS

Figures

Tables

FOREWORD

There are many stories that start with excitement. This is one of them. Something happened in the early twenty-first century. Many of a certain generation, now called Millennials or Generation Y, were attending institutions of higher education—wreaking havoc. Only this was the good sort of destruction. I completed my first university degree in 2006, and my professors noted how much new interest there was in environmental protection coupled with social consciousness. Students were challenging the notions of "business as usual" and looking forward to creating a future of purpose and positive impact.

The number of organizations, degrees, and programs dedicated to sustainability directly and indirectly has grown tremendously in the past few decades. The Association for the Advancement of Sustainability in Higher Education (AASHE) lists, as of this publication, 3,731 sustainability-focused academic programs across 30 countries. That's up from zero. There are record numbers of people attending sustainability conferences, developing and participating in social enterprise incubators, and serving as intrapreneurs or entrepreneurs in order to bring about a socially, environmentally, financially, and generationally sound change.

When I first talked about sustainability with people around me in the early 2000s, there was a great degree of hesitancy and unawareness. Today, the first has diminished and the latter replaced by more action and—given the climate crisis—urgency. This shift presents not only a great opportunity to spark conversations and plant the seeds of change in our personal discussions, but also a great opportunity to transform our careers and associated organizations.

It was in 2009 at the height of the financial crisis when I found myself in a spent fuel reprocessing plant in Normandy, France. As a trained engineer, manufacturing innovative products was exciting, and recycling nuclear fuel, dealing with the waste problem, so to speak, even more so. Nevertheless, many days on-site were challenging. One particular day stands out. I was working on shift in the nuclearized zone and speaking with a colleague on a coffee break. Without any hesitation, my colleague pursued a line of questioning omnipresent in many large industrial companies in France at that time—did I attend a *Grande-Ecole* (elite institution of higher education) and what did I study? Once I proceeded to explain my first degree in civil and environmental engineering and then my second in engineering for sustainable development, the reaction was along the lines of "What does engineering have to do with sustainable development?" It was then that I realized that "sustainable development" and "sustainability" were misunderstood among the general public, especially how the concepts relate to careers. The experience sparked an interest to uncover what was behind an apparent contradiction. On one hand, students and professionals had an overwhelming passion for creating a more sustainable world, and on the other hand, there was a misunderstanding of how sustainability could be incorporated into their everyday jobs.

I went to different corners of the globe—Asia, Europe, the Americas, and Africa—to speak with professionals in various sectors. My journey took me to emergency rooms and farms. To media studios and manufacturing facilities. The stories were fascinating. What I unraveled in my quest has become the central thesis of this book: *sustainability can be incorporated into every imaginable career.*

SECOND EDITION NOTES

The first edition of *Sustainability at Work: Careers That Make a Difference* was published in 2017. By 2023, it was clear that both the general context within which careers take place and the specificities around sustainability thinking had shifted. Remote work has become more of a norm for many professions. The demographics of the workplace in many countries has shifted towards the younger staff making up most staff. Globalization continues even while values and policies for local manufacturing and processes increase. More tools, frameworks, and approaches have been developed to help the individual and collective thrive under uncertainty and a multitude of crises.

The second edition of *Sustainability at Work: Careers That Make a Difference* is thus an effort to both update the content of the first edition and bring forth additional tools and perspectives that have become core to integrating sustainability into a career journey. Two chapters have been added to the line-up: one on climate-related careers and one on justice, equity, diversity, and inclusion (JEDI). Both additions reflect growing movements that intersect with one another and the broader discourse around sustainability and environmental, social, and governance (ESG) strategy. New narratives have been espoused that reflect a greater diversity of geographies, racial, ethnic, and class backgrounds, and lived experiences.

I'm excited to share this second edition with readers across the globe and hope it inspires new and continued direction for all who take up sustainability in various forms—full-time.

1

BACKGROUND

Four pillars of sustainable development

> My definition of sustainable development is "Meeting the needs of all generations, present and future, while improving their well-being through social, economic, environmental, and intergenerational efforts."
>
> *(Marilyn Waite)*

Introduction

Many people have been exposed to sustainable development or sustainability marketing, awareness campaigns, or even training through work, school, and extracurricular activities. The take-home messages often center on how individuals can contribute to the cause through concrete actions. These actions include:

- Investing in environmental and/or ethical companies or funds.
- Buying in-season, local, organic, and/or fair-trade products.
- Understanding labeling and logos to make informed consumer decisions.
- Finding alternatives to purchasing new material goods (repairing existing goods, buying recycled content, etc.).
- Buying high-quality, long-lasting products.
- Keeping informed on sustainable development indicators and trends.
- Eating less resource-intensive products such as meat.
- Voting or otherwise participating in a democratic process to bring forth more sustainability-related policies.

The individual is sometimes positioned as the "consumer" who must move from a more traditional purchasing policy (I will buy the least expensive product/service with a preference for good value for money) to a more sustainable purchasing policy (I will buy the best product/service, the one which provides

DOI: 10.4324/9781032615844-1

the most guarantee for its efficiency) (Baddache, 2008). Otherwise, the individual is positioned as a "constituent" who must navigate their political system to help drive more sustainability-related public policy. In our personal lives, there is a checklist for more sustainable living (examples in Figure 1.1). What is the checklist for our careers?

Whether at work or at home, there is no boundary to actively participate in sustainable development. Many of the choices to save water and energy that people make at home can be made at work. Company purchasing departments can also take into consideration the social and environmental impacts of their supply chains. The same health incentive that causes parents to choose plant-based cleaning materials to use around their three-year-old can also serve as a reason to use those products on an industrial scale. There is a series of remedies to our unsustainable path to development, which include behavioral, technological, managerial, and organizational fixes. Just as our everyday consumer choices bring us closer or further from sustainability, our career choices can as well. How does one define a sustainable job or a sustainable career? Is it only limited to those positions that contain the word "green," "ESG," "responsible," "environment," "social," or "sustainability" in the job title?

A series of United Nations conferences have dealt with the theme of sustainable development; in 2015, the UN announced what would follow the Millennium Development Goals: the Sustainable Development Goals (SDGs). There are 17 SDGs with 169 associated targets and a deadline of 2030. These goals range from ending poverty to promoting inclusive and sustainable industrialization.[1] In

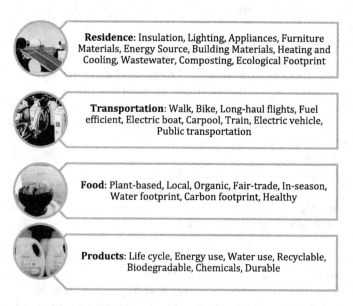

Residence: Insulation, Lighting, Appliances, Furniture Materials, Energy Source, Building Materials, Heating and Cooling, Wastewater, Composting, Ecological Footprint

Transportation: Walk, Bike, Long-haul flights, Fuel efficient, Electric boat, Carpool, Train, Electric vehicle, Public transportation

Food: Plant-based, Local, Organic, Fair-trade, In-season, Water footprint, Carbon footprint, Healthy

Products: Life cycle, Energy use, Water use, Recyclable, Biodegradable, Chemicals, Durable

FIGURE 1.1 Keywords representing conventional sustainability thinking

December 2015, countries under the UN Framework Convention on Climate Change (UNFCCC) adopted the Paris Agreement, which requires countries to submit national climate plans to curb climate change.

While the outcomes of such international meetings have mixed results, it's clear that intergovernmental collaboration alone cannot meet the demands of sustainable development. Since the bottom lines of some multinational corporations outnumber the gross domestic products (GDPs) of some countries, for-profit companies also have a responsibility. Integrating sustainability into careers in all sectors and jobs in all professions can be a large part of the solution. Sustainability thinking has its role to play in the most specialized to the most general careers. According to the UN Educational, Scientific and Cultural Organization (UNESCO):

> Both public sector and private sector employees should receive ongoing vocational and professional training infused with the practices and principles of sustainability, so that all the members of the labour force can access the knowledge and skills necessary to make decisions and work in a sustainable manner.
>
> *(UNESCO, 2012)*

We spend so much of our lives "working," either in school or the workplace, that our entire economies and ways of life are shaped by jobs and careers. In order to build a more environmentally, socially, intergenerationally, and economically sustainable society, we have to apply sustainability to our work and careers. As you will find through the narratives presented in this book, our careers may be in peril if we do not understand sustainability and how our particular professional role applies to sustainability; and in some cases, our careers will be given a significant boost by becoming an expert in the subject.

If the reader is already knowledgeable about the origins and definitions of sustainable development, the reader may choose to skip this chapter that serves mostly as background.

Origins of sustainable development

Before delving into the connection between sustainable development and careers, it is important to have a brief overview of the origins of sustainable development. There is a common misconception that the term "sustainable development" suddenly appeared with the World Commission on Environment and Development whose 1987 report *Our Common Future* brought to light the modern-day concerns, challenges, and endeavors in the sustainability realm. However, the foundations of sustainable development and sustainability are as old as our ancient civilizations. And the ideas of sustainable development have a long history in the economic development and environmental discourse.

We can turn to coastal West Africa in what is present-day Ghana for examples of how human beings adapt, rethink, and try to sustainably develop their economy. In the book *Between the Sea and the Lagoon: an Eco-social History of Southeastern Ghana*, author Emmanuel Kwaku Akyeampong traces the environmental history of the Anlo-Ewe from the nineteenth century. "As the Anlo became more familiar with their environment, they developed and adopted technologies that facilitated the intensive exploitation of their environment" (Akyeampong, 2001). This new industrialized phase of development also coincided with sea erosion; the Anlo thus faced flooding and erosion in their salt making and fishing efforts. "Many thoughtful Anlo wondered if their intrusive inscriptions on the natural world had resulted in this ecological imbalance" (Akyeampong, 2001). Sea erosion signaled permanent damage of the environment, and it caused the Anlo to examine their history and belief system for explanations and solutions (Akyeampong, 2001). The questioning of human impact on the environment and the ability to sustain needs for future generations was already at play in the 1800s on the African continent.

Throughout human history, people have been concerned about material progress and its impact on the resources used to fuel that progress. Underlying sustainable development are two ways of dealing with nature. One way is to develop new natures, such as developing artificial or lab-grown meat, manufacturing clean water, etc.; the other way is to limit or redress human intervention in nature, such as by conserving forests and recycling waste (Swyngedouw, 2007). Both of these approaches can manifest themselves in various careers.

Definitions of sustainable development

There are multiple understandings of sustainability. Let's clarify the terms "sustainable" or "sustainability." These words are void of "development" and thus suggest something finite or somehow finished. The adjective "sustainable" can be used to describe any noun—from the economy, employment, and "practices," to toys, shoes, and a kitchen cabinet. Used as an adjective, "sustainable" often presents the most controversy because it can appear as an oxymoron: sustainable growth and sustainable consumption come to mind. Some believe that growth and consumption must be limited or "slowed" in order for future generations to be able to meet their needs. Sustainability is a noun that implies an end goal; it is not a process like "development," but rather an end state. Sustainability is what we are trying to reach, and perhaps we can never get there; this is why the notion of sustainable development is important to set strategy and a general direction for where we as individuals, companies, and societies would like to head.

> My definition of sustainable development is "Meeting the needs of all generations, present and future, while improving their well-being through social, economic, environmental, and intergenerational efforts."

Introduction to the four pillars

The four pillars of sustainable development are the foundation for understanding how to apply sustainability to different professions in a very concrete manner. Independent of sector, geographical region, and job tasks, the four pillars of sustainable development underpin careers that move us along a sustainable path: intergenerational equity, society, the environment, and the economy. In order to find practical solutions to attain sustainability, sustainable development has traditionally been broken down into three pillars: society, economy, and environment (also referred to as the 3Ps: people, planet, and profit; or the 3Es: equity, economy, ecology). The challenge is to adequately address the three pillars when shaping policies, implementing projects, and transforming communities. The notion of the triple bottom line (TBP) arises from the need to equally weigh the environmental and social results of a business against the net profit "bottom line." However, the current mainstream discourse surrounding sustainable development often fails to underscore what this book will call the fourth pillar: *intergenerational equity*. It is this long-term thinking that sets sustainable development apart from previous social and environmental considerations. Even if the societal, economic, and ecological implications of a product, service, or decision are taken into account, they can still fail to meet sustainable development goals if only the short-term implications are considered.

So what constitutes the long-term or future generations? How far out a vision should be considered? This will often depend on the industry or topic at hand. In energy predictions, it is customary to think 50 years ahead. In 2024, the year 2030 is like yesterday, and it is not uncommon to think about 2060 for energy resources and energy mixes of different countries. When running a small restaurant business, 50 years may seem like a long-term outlook. A sustainable development framework requires us to push the limits of whatever the traditional time boundaries may be. Those reading this book who have children or grandchildren understand the idea of "future generations." However, sustainable development requires us to think about the unborn—what the future generations may need and want beyond what is tangible today. It is for that reason that this pillar is often met with unease in reflections about sustainability. Responses such as "I cannot predict the future" and "I do not know what the needs of tomorrow will be" can arise. The intergenerational equity dimension thus underlines the uncertainty in questions about the environmental, social, and economic needs of future generations.

Future generations dimension

The future generations dimension of sustainable development is often included as a backdrop to the other three pillars of social, environmental, and economic considerations. It deserves to stand on its own, for the idea of future planning is what makes sustainable development a more evolved principle than the

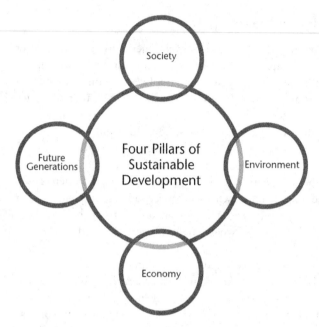

FIGURE 1.2 Quadruple bottom line (QBL) of sustainable development
Source: Waite (2013)

environmental, social welfare, or economic movements on their own. A food procurement manager may source agricultural products that do not destroy biodiversity that future generations will need; a chef may ensure that the food is healthy in order to help leave future generations with a legacy of healthy eating and healthy food choices. The future generations dimension is often difficult to quantify or qualify, since it entails various assumptions of current generations about future generations. Experience indicates that preferences change over time on the individual and collective levels (Anderson et al., 2012). The task is to balance intergenerational (across generations) and intragenerational (within a single generation or lifespan) needs and equity.

As Peter Cock, a member of the Moora Moora community of Australia (intentionally alternative community established in 1974), writes:

> Intergenerational conflicts are real ... The tendency is for a newer, younger generation to wish to do things or at least to be seen to do things differently. Each has a tendency to view the other generation as not being capable of meeting the needs of the present. The younger generation has the tendency to see the older as having had too much experience, that is seen as locked into the past. The older generation has the tendency to see the younger as lacking sufficient experience in matters of significance.
>
> *(Cock, 2009)*

Thus, the intergenerational component of sustainable development presents real challenges. One of Peter Cock's take-home lessons from his experience in this matter is that communities must be watchful of their age structure and keep it as varied as possible. This seems like common sense: to obtain intergenerational equity, as many generations as possible should be at the table. Sustainability does not mean keeping things the same for future generations; flexibility is an important component of intergenerational equity.

There are two principles that can be used to understand the future generations dimension: the principle of intergenerational neutrality and the freedom-as-capabilities approach. The principle of intergenerational neutrality says that we need to take into account the interests of generations who have not yet been born; it proposes that the citizens of every generation be treated equally. This principle can be derived from the classic Rawls' theory of justice and the idea of the "veil of ignorance." According to Rawls:

> no one knows his place in society, his class position or social status, nor does anyone know his fortune in the distribution of natural assets and abilities, his intelligence, strength, and the like. I shall even assume that the parties do not know their conceptions of the good or their special psychological propensities. The principles of justice are chosen behind a veil of ignorance.
>
> *(Rawls, 1971)*

Extrapolating from Rawls' social contract theory, intergenerational neutrality attempts to create outcomes for all generations based on a similar veil of ignorance.

The freedom-as-capabilities approach by Amartya Sen states that accounting for future generations should be based on one's ability to choose and pursue the goods that one values. This also entails freedom from any unwarranted constraints imposed by others (Bessant et al., 2011). Authors Stiglitz, Sen, and Fitoissi (2009) argue that the key question is to determine whether levels of human well-being can be sustained over time, understanding that this "depends on whether stocks of natural, physical, human, and social capital are passed on to future generations"; the elements of well-being that need to be assessed include material living standards, health, education, activities for work and leisure, governance, public voice, social connections and friendship, environmental quality, and various kinds of insecurity (Bessant et al., 2011).

Environmental dimension

Sustainable development recognizes that, fundamentally, people live and work in *places*. Those places are on Earth and must have certain characteristics to sustain human life—an adequate supply and quality of water, clean air, sustainable energy, healthy soil and agriculture, food, etc. Sustainable development encourages us to work, produce, consume, move, and eat while adopting practices that are the most favorable to the planet's health. For example, a food caterer may choose to purchase local, organic, and plant-based foods when possible to limit the environmental damage done through transportation (thus local), the health damage done through pesticides (thus organic), and the overall climate damage done through greenhouse gas emissions (thus plant-based).

The environmental dimension of sustainable development concerns the natural environment and how living creatures including human beings can live within the carrying capacity of the Earth. This is also known as ecological sustainability. The ecosystem (or *biocoenosis*) is a geographic area where flora and fauna, as well as weather and landscape, work together to form a life system. Ecosystems contain biotic (living parts) and abiotic factors (nonliving parts) (National Geographic, n. d.). According to author Michael Redclift, an ecologically sustainable society is one that conserves biodiversity and ecosystems, ensures that the use of renewable resources is sustainable, minimizes depletion of nonrenewable resources, and stays within the carrying capacity of supporting ecosystems (Redclift, 2005). This idea of carrying capacity is sometimes used to define sustainable development itself, which describes not surpassing the environment's maximum load for a given species.

There are various concepts, methods, and tools that pertain to environmental sustainability, including life cycle analysis, cradle-to-cradle, the circular economy, biomimicry, ecological footprint. Life cycle assessment or analysis (LCA) details the environmental impacts of a product, process, or service throughout its entire life (from raw materials to waste or recycling). Which is a more environmentally sustainable drinking receptacle: a paper cup or a polyfoam cup? Which is a more environmentally sustainable building material: wood or concrete? The answers sometimes yield unexpected results based on the subjective weighting included in LCA. Cradle-to-cradle is the concept that "waste" equals "food" in both natural and industrial processes.

The Industrial Revolution brought with it a cradle-to-grave process for technical materials that did not mimic that of nature. Cradle-to-cradle design provides a framework for creating products and industrial systems that turn materials into nutrients by (1) enabling the flow in the cyclical processes of nature and (2) enabling the circulation of valuable materials in closed-loop production, use, recovery, and reproduction (McDonough & Braungart, 2002). A similar concept to the cradle-to-cradle approach is the circular economy, which combines the concepts of regenerative design, industrial ecology, cradle-to-cradle, biomimicry, and the blue economy. The circular economy refers to a system "where materials never become waste and nature is regenerated; products and materials are kept in circulation through processes like maintenance, reuse, refurbishment, remanufacture, recycling, and composting" (Ellen MacArthur Foundation, 2023). Biomimicry uses the more than 3.8 billion years of experience of Earth's flora and fauna to create solutions to today's problems. The Biomimicry Institute defines biomimicry as, "an empathetic, interconnected understanding of how life works and ultimately where we fit in; it is a practice that learns from and mimics the strategies used by species alive today" (Biomimicry Institute, 2023).

The environmental dimension of sustainable development also includes various notions of the marks that human beings leave on the Earth—or "footprint." Carbon footprinting involves calculating the total amount of greenhouse gases that are emitted into the atmosphere by an entity (e.g., a person, organization, or financial institution). Carbon footprinting is used as an indicator for any previous climate change impact and can provide indications of what can be improved to reduce such an impact. Water footprinting comprises calculating the total volume of freshwater used to produce the goods and services consumed by an individual or community or produced by a business. Water use is measured in terms of water volumes consumed (evaporated or incorporated into a product) and/or polluted per unit of time (Hoekstra et al., 2011). Ecological footprinting measures how much land and water area a human population requires to produce the resources it consumes and to assimilate its wastes (including greenhouse gas emissions). Connected to the concept of ecological footprint is "Earthshare"—the bioproductive area of the world divided by its total population (estimated at 1.9 hectares in the early 2000s); if an entity is living within its Earthshare, it can be argued that it is living environmentally sustainably (Dawe et al., 2004).

Social dimension

The social dimension of sustainable development pertains to the well-being of people in society. This encompasses employment, compensation, working conditions, health care, education, civil liberties, diversity and inclusion, safety, and other items that can be categorized under wellness. A society cannot move along a sustainable development trajectory if its social problems are not addressed. As stated by Erik Swynge-douw (2007) in "Impossible 'Sustainability' and the Post-Political Condition," "Environmental transformation is not independent from class, gender, ethnic or other power struggles." When deciding whether or not a product or service is "socially sustainable," various questions linked to well-being must therefore be answered. These questions can be related to fair trade, child labor, slave labor, human rights, equity, equality, empowerment, and poverty. Referring to the food procurement manager example, this job requires social sustainability thinking throughout the planning, purchasing, and delivery stages. The food should be sourced so that the food preparers and providers are paid a livable wage all along the supply chain, so that workers' health and safety is not put in jeopardy, so that deals are made without corruption, so that there is intentionality of having diverse representation at all decision-making levels, and so that a culture of inclusion and belonging prevails.

There are many methods that attempt to quantify social sustainability, including indices and indicators that have been proposed by international organizations, academics, and individual countries alike. The Human Development Index (HDI) is a composite index that measures a country's progress in health, knowledge, and income. Health is measured by life expectancy at birth; knowledge is measured by a combination of adult literacy rates and school enrollment rates from primary- through university-level education; and income is measured by gross national income (GNI) per capita adjusted for purchasing power parity (United Nations Development Programme, 2011). There are other aspects of human development that are captured in other indices, such as the Gender Inequality Index, the Racial Equity Index, and the Multidimensional Poverty Index. The HDI uses mean values per country and therefore does not illustrate regional or demographic differences that may be critical factors in sustainable development.

Although the idea of using happiness as a measure of the well-being of a country is not new, the term "gross national happiness" (GNH) was coined by Jigme Singye Wangchuck, the Fourth King of Bhutan in 1972 (Ura et al., 2012). The 2008 Constitution of Bhutan calls for the country to promote conditions that will enable the pursuit of GNH. Happiness itself is not seen as a one-dimensional adjective, but rather a multidimensional state that covers nine domains: psychological well-being, time use, community vitality, cultural diversity, ecological resilience, living standard, health, education, and good governance. There are 33 indicators of the GNH index that fall under the nine domains.[2]

Economic dimension

As economist Herman Daly famously said, "The economy is a wholly owned subsidiary of the environment." When deciding whether a product or service is "economically sustainable," various questions linked to its economic viability are asked. These questions revolve around profit, value for money, capital efficiency, shareholder value, return on investment, and other indicators. Sustainable development promotes work, production, consumption, mobility and transportation, and lifestyle habits that adopt the best practices and use the best products that provide good value for money. This value for money should include the environmental and social costs (wages, water and energy use, pollution, land use, etc.). The food procurement manager must meet the laws of supply and demand in terms of food quantity, uphold food quality expectations, and ensure a long-term financial benefit for their financial well-being and that of other stakeholders.

Authors Pearce and Atkinson propose a formula for measuring sustainable development on a macroeconomic level. First, capital assets are divided into four categories: produced goods or *human-made capital* (K_M), human knowledge and skills or *human capital* (K_H), *natural capital* (K_N), and *social capital* (K_S). Natural capital is any natural asset yielding a flow of ecological services with economic values (includes all renewable resources and "quasi-renewables" such as the ozone layer) (Pearce, 1992). Social capital is defined as the relationships between individuals, between institutions, and between individuals and institutions (Pearce & Atkinson, 1998). Given this break down of capital assets, the condition for sustainable development can be expressed as:

$$\frac{dK}{dt} \geq 0, \text{ where } K = K_M + K_H + K_N + K_S$$

This equation illustrates that the change in overall capital assets, K, with time must be at least zero. The underlying assumption is that changes in individual K components can be traded off for each other. According to Pearce and Atkinson, "If some part of natural capital, K_M, is depleted then this is consistent with sustainability as long as *adequate* investment is made in other forms of wealth, such as human capital" (Pearce & Atkinsonf, 1998). However, since some forms of capital have no clear substitute, such as the ozone layer, the notion of weak sustainability and strong sustainability is derived.

For weak sustainability:

$$\frac{dK}{dt} \geq 0, \text{ where } K = K_M + K_H + K_N + K_S$$

For strong environmental sustainability:

$$dk/dt \geq 0 \;\; and \;\; dK_N/dt \geq 0$$

For strong social sustainability:

$$dk/dt \geq 0 \;\; and \;\; dK_S/dt \geq 0$$

Concluding thoughts

No single dimension of sustainable development can stand alone or can be fully explained without the other dimensions. Take the example of cycling to work. Cycling can be considered, *ceteris paribus*, (1) environmentally sustainable because of the absence of greenhouse gas emissions (lessens the impact on climate) and because a bicycle can be repaired, transferred to someone else at the end of its use, and/or parts recycled, (2) socially sustainable because cycling performs the valuable services of transportation and exercise, (3) economically sustainable because cycling is a relatively low-cost transportation method that still supports employment (materials, bicycle manufacturing, and support staff), and (4) intergenerationally sustainable because cycling is an activity that can be done by the young and elderly alike, and can be continued for generations.

Stratigraphers, those who study rock strata in order to determine their geological history, call the epoch in which we are now living "Anthropocene." This term was coined by Paul Crutzen, a Dutch chemist who suggested that the period began in the late eighteenth century with the onset of industrialization when carbon dioxide levels began a so-far uninterrupted increase; other scientist place the start of Anthropocene in the mid-twentieth century with the exponential rise in population growth and consumption (Kolbert, 2011). In the planet's history, Anthropocene presents a period of unprecedented human impact on the environment. Authors Steffen, Crutzen and McNeill categorize Anthropocene into two stages as follows:

- *Stage 1*: between 1800 and 1945 (Industrial Era), which marked an "enormous expansion in the use of fossil fuels, first coal and then oil and gas as well";
- *Stage 2:* between 1945 and 2015 (Great Acceleration), where human enterprise suddenly accelerated after the end of the Second World War; population doubled in just 50 years and the global economy increased by more than 15-fold.

(Steffen et al., 2007)

The Earth is moving into a less forested, less biologically diverse, and more climate extreme state—and rapidly; the term Anthropocene suggests that Earth has now left its natural geological epoch called Holocene.

The concepts of sustainable development and sustainability of today would most appropriately be preceded by "neo" (a prefix used to make it clear that the phenomenon is a revitalization of the original). Neo-sustainable development and neo-sustainability are characterized by marketing campaigns, online tools for reducing footprints, company corporate social responsibility (CSR) and sustainability reports, shareholder value, buzzwords, and a globalized economy.

According to the Brundtland Report, the pursuit of sustainable development requires:

- a political system that secures effective citizen participation in decision making;
- an economic system that is able to generate surpluses and technical knowledge on a self-reliant and sustained basis;
- a social system that provides for solutions for the tensions arising from disharmonious development;
- a production system that respects the obligation to preserve the ecological base for development;
- a technological system that can search continuously for solutions;
- an international system that fosters sustainable patterns of trade and finance;
- an administrative system that is flexible and has the capacity for self-correction.

(World Commission on Environment and Development, 1987)

These systems are driven by people who occupy jobs and build careers that make sustainability a reality. The political system is made up of policy makers and constituents. The economic system includes producers, consumers, and financial capital allocators. The social system includes community organizers, religious and spiritual practitioners, legal interpreters, and public workers across fields including education and health care. The technological system includes engineers, technicians, designers, and manufacturers. The international and administrative systems are made up of civil servants who perform a variety of tasks to support the political system and laws that come from it. So on and so forth. In other words, a single job or profession is an important component of the collective.

Careers are at the heart of neo-sustainability, yet many people are unaware of how understanding the issues of sustainable development can impact and even help their field, job, and career experience. Let's take a closer look at sustainable development and careers.

Notes

1 The 17 UN Sustainable Development Goals for 2030 are:
1. End poverty in all its forms everywhere;
2. End hunger, achieve food security and improved nutrition and promote sustainable agriculture;
3. Ensure healthy lives and promote well-being for all at all ages;
4. Ensure inclusive and equitable quality education and promote lifelong learning opportunities for all;
5. Achieve gender equality and empower all women and girls;
6. Ensure availability and sustainable management of water and sanitation for all;
7. Ensure access to affordable, reliable, sustainable and modern energy for all;
8. Promote sustained, inclusive and sustainable economic growth, full and productive employment and decent work for all;
9. Build resilient infrastructure, promote inclusive and sustainable industrialization and foster innovation;
10. Reduce inequality within and among countries;
11. Make cities and human settlements inclusive, safe, resilient and sustainable;
12. Ensure sustainable consumption and production patterns;
13. Take urgent action to combat climate change and its impacts;
14. Conserve and sustainably use the oceans, seas and marine resources for sustainable development;
15. Protect, restore and promote sustainable use of terrestrial ecosystems, sustainably manage forests, combat desertification, and halt and reverse land degradation and halt biodiversity loss;
16. Promote peaceful and inclusive societies for sustainable development, provide access to justice for all and build effective, accountable and inclusive institutions at all levels;
17. Strengthen the means of implementation and revitalize the global partnership for sustainable development.
(Source: https://sdgs.un.org/goals)

2 The GNH Index consists of nine domains:
1. Living standards: assets, housing, household per capita income;
2. Health: mental health, self-reported health status, healthy days, disability;
3. Psychological well-being: life satisfaction, positive emotions, negative emotions, spirituality;
4. Ecological diversity and resilience: ecological issues, environmental responsibility, wildlife damage, urbanization issues;
5. Time use: work, sleep;
6. Good governance: government performance, fundamental rights, services, political participation;
7. Education: literacy, schooling, knowledge, values;
8. Cultural diversity and resilience: speak native language, cultural participation, artistic skills, Driglam Namzha;
9. Community vitality: time/money donations, community relationship, family, safety.
(Source: www.gnhcentrebhutan.org/the-9-domains-of-gnh)

References

Akyeampong, E. K. (2001). *Between the Sea and the Lagoon: An Eco-Social History of the Anlo of Southeastern Ghana c. 1850 to Recent Times.* Athens, OH: Ohio University Press.

Anderson, M., Teisl, M., & Noblet, C. (2012). Giving voice to the future in sustainability: Retrospective assessment to learn prospective stakeholder engagement. *Ecological Economics* 84, 1–6.

Baddache, F. (2008). *Développement durable tout simplement.* Paris: Eyrolles.

Bessant, J., Emslie, M., & Watts, R. (2011). Accounting for future generations: Intergenerational equity in Australia. *Australian Journal of Public Administration* 70, 143–155.

Biomimicry Institute. (2023). https://biomimicry.org/what-is-biomimicry.

Cock, P. H. (2009). Community sustainability: The challenge of intergenerational change. *Communal Societies* 29, 286–299.

Dawe, G. F., Vetter, A., & Martin, S. (2004). An overview of ecological footprinting and other tools and their application to the development of sustainability process. *International Journal of Sustainability in Higher Education* 5(4), 340–371.

Ellen MacArthur Foundation. (2023). What is the circular economy?www.ellenmacarthurfoundation.org/topics/circular-economy-introduction/overview.

Hoekstra, A. C., Aldaya, M., & Mekonnen, M. (2011). *The Water Footprint Assessment Manual: Setting the Global Standard.* London: Routledge. https://doi.org/10.4324/9781849775526.

Kolbert, E. (2011). Enter the Anthropocene—Age of Man. National Geographic. www.nationalgeographic.com/magazine/article/age-of-man.

McDonough, W., & Braungart, M. (2002). *Cradle to Cradle: Remaking the Way We Make Things.* North Point Press.

National Geographic. (n.d.). Ecosystem. Encyclopedia. http://education.nationalgeographic.com/education/encyclopedia/ecosystem/?ar_a=1.

Pearce, D. (1992). *Are National Economies Sustainable? Measuring Sustainable Development.* Centre of Social and Economic Research on the Global Environment.

Pearce, D., & Atkinson, G. (1998). Concept of sustainable development: An evaluation of its usefulness 10 years after Brundtland. *Environmental Economics and Policy Studies* 1, 95–111. https://doi.org/10.1007/BF03353896.

Rawls, J. (1971). *A Theory of Justice.* Cambridge, MA: Harvard University Press.

Redclift, M. (2005). *Sustainability: Critical Concepts in the Social Sciences.* London: Routledge.

Steffen, W., Crutzen, P. J., & McNeill, J. R. (2007). The Anthropocene: Are humans now overwhelming the great forces of nature? *Ambio* 36(8), 614–621.

Stiglitz, J., Sen, A., & Fitoussi, J. (2009). *Report by the Commission on the Measurement of Economic Performance and Social Progress.* Paris: Commission on the Measurement of Economic Performance and Social Progress.

Swyngedouw, E. (2007). Impossible "Sustainability" and the Post-Political Condition. In R. A. Krueger (ed.), *The Sustainable Development Paradox: Urban Political Economy in the United States and Europe* (pp. 13–40). New York, NY: The Guilford Press.

UNESCO (United Nations Educational, Scientific and Cultural Organization). (2012). *Education for Sustainable Development Sourcebook 2012.* Paris: UNESCO.

United Nations Development Programme. (2011). Frequently Asked Questions (FAQs)—Human Development Index (HDI). www.undp.org/sites/g/files/zskgke326/files/migration/tr/UNDP-TR-EN-HDR-2019-FAQS-HDI.pdf.

Ura, K., Alkire, S., Zangmo, T., & Wangdi, K. (2012). *A Short Guide to Gross National Happiness Index*. Thimphu, Bhutan: The Centre for Bhutan Studies. https://opendocs.ids.ac.uk/opendocs/bitstream/handle/20.500.12413/11807/Short-GNH-Index.pdf;jsessionid=676EBDF0B1333D9ED4CB783B6C0E207B?sequence=1.

Waite, M. (2013). SURF Framework for sustainable development and the green economy. *Journal of Management and Sustainability* 3(4), 25–40.

World Commission on Environment and Development. (1987). *Our Common Future*. Oxford: Oxford University Press.

2

INTRODUCTION

Sustainability and careers

The emphasis is not on creating more sustainability or green officers within organizations, but to incorporate social, environmental, economic, and inter-generational equity principles into any job and career move.

Introduction

Careers today are in many ways without boundaries; they involve drastic shifts (geographical and content-based), improvisation, and the expression of personal values (Arnold, 2002). The definition of "career" has evolved with time, with career specialists still debating the term and its application in modern life. The human resources profession is an entire field of its own within both private and public institutions. Employees and the self-employed are concerned about how best to construct and manage their careers. Author John Arnold, in his article "Careers and Career Management," prefers the following definition of career, which allows for a broad interpretation of both the objective and subjective elements of a person's life including those activities outside of (but related to) employment:

> A career is the sequence of employment-related positions, roles, activities and experiences encountered by a person.
>
> *(Arnold, 2002)*

Employment can be defined as any money-earning work, including self-employment. The objective elements include compensation, formal titles, and functions in an organizational hierarchy, and avoiding involuntary unemployment. The subjective elements include job satisfaction, a certain expertise or mastery of a subject, and confidence of future career progression (Arnold,

DOI: 10.4324/9781032615844-2

2002). In careers today, people are encouraged to continually enrich their skills and competencies through continuing education programs, training, certifications, and other professional development activities. The boundaries are blurred between official employment and experiences that occur outside of that realm. For example, many people belong to professional organizations, attend conferences, and network, all of which may take place outside of the standard workplace. I use the aforementioned definition of career and interpret the term as a boundaryless concept throughout this book.

While this book does not focus on the practicalities of job hunting and soul searching, the premise of integrating sustainability into one's career is one that is closely aligned with design. In the book *Designing Your Life: How to Build a Well-Lived, Joyful Life,* authors Bill Burnett and Dave Evans describe a well-designed life as one that "makes sense; it's a life in which who you are, what you believe, and what you do all line up together" (Burnett and Evans, 2022). In that vein, if you value a better world, incorporating sustainability into your career design helps make your life make more sense. And better still, doing so will have a positive impact on more than just yourself.

In the forthcoming chapters, I elevate the stories of those who have integrated sustainability into a variety of fields and jobs, and provide practical tools for you to do the same. It is thus complementary to any foundational career-planning tools that you use. In this section, I will provide a few notions on the practical side of career development.

Career basics

Regardless of your specific location, field, and expertise (existing or being developed), it is worth noting that career choices, including shifts and pivots, are often centered around the following three elements: location (or geography), field (or sector), and role (or function). For example, one can work for a sustainability-focused fintech in Brazil as a marketing manager. One could also work for a pharmaceutical company in India as a chemist. While it is challenging to change all three aspects all at once in many career shifts, changing one out of the three is often feasible in the short term, two out of the three in the medium term, and all three in the long term.

Table 2.1 provides examples of some of the life- and career-coaching tools that help you understand who you are, what you value, how you show up, and your strengths. Irrespective of location, field, and role, it is important to have a grasp of these aspects of yourself as it is likely that you will be able to prototype opportunities more effectively with this foundational knowledge. In turn, you will shine, those around you will benefit, and you will be more impactful in your sustainability pursuits.

After understanding one's own strengths and criteria for a well-designed life, which is sometimes referred to as a self-inventory, the next step in

TABLE 2.1 Practical career resources for understanding and developing oneself

Tool or resource name	One-sentence summary
California Psychological Inventory™ (CPI™)	The CPI assessment indicates which of four different ways of living best describe the respondent, comparing an individual's responses to data on 5,600 managers and executives who participated in the Leadership Development Program at the Center for Creative Leadership.
DiSC	DiSC is an acronym that stands for the four main personality profiles described in the DiSC model: (D)ominance, (i)nfluence, (S)teadiness, and (C)onscientiousness, used to better understand oneself and those one interacts with—and then use this knowledge to reduce conflict and improve working relationships.
Emotional Quotient Inventory	The Emotional Quotient Inventory examines an individual's social and emotional strengths and weaknesses based on 15 key areas of emotional skill that have been proven to contribute to proficiency in complex business activities such as conflict resolution and planning.
Enneagram	The Enneagram identifies nine core personality types and reveals how each type views, engages in, and feels about the world.
Influence Style Indicator	The Influence Style Indicator helps one become aware of their influence style preferences and those of others, viewed from five distinct preferences: Rationalizing, Asserting, Negotiating, Inspiring, Bridging.
LIFO	LIFO (Life Orientations) is a method that identifies behavioral style preferences to promote individual and group productivity, beginning with identifying one's orientation to life and work.
LifeScore Assessment	Analyzes satisfaction with professional and personal domains of your life: body, mind, spirit, love, family, community, money, work, and hobbies in order to set better goals.
Myers-Briggs Type Indicator (MBTI®)	The MBTI® personality inventory attempts to translate the theory of psychological types described by C. G. Jung into a useful framework for one's life and career, based on four dichotomies and a total of 16 personality types.
Search Inside Yourself	Search Inside Yourself provides a mindfulness approach to work in the form of education activities and exercises, based on neuroscience.
StrengthsFinder	StrengthsFinder measures the intensity of one's talents in 34 themes that represent what people do best.
VIA Institute on Character Strengths	Provides a ranking of "character strengths," the strengths related to feeling authentic and engaged, based on 24 strengths in different degrees.

finding a new position is to begin the so-called job hunt. Approaches to job hunting include using affinity networking, school alumni networking and alumni services, sector-specific networking, Slack and similar forums for job listings and exchanges in a defined community, job club and career fellowship circles, internet job postings, professional journal and newspaper job listings, local and national government job services, private search firms, short-term contract and temp agencies, and short trainings where both exposure to new opportunities and new people can arise. These approaches vary in terms of success rate. In general, the more of a stranger one is to the hiring manager and their network, the less likely one is to be chosen for a particular position. This is partly why networking, conducting short informational interviews with people whose career or whose institution is of interest, and meeting people for virtual or in-person coffee/tea/culturally relevant beverage can be very helpful.

When thinking about incorporating sustainability in one's career, who you are and what you believe will serve as a filter for roles. That said, the sustainability-related and sustainability-adjacent career space is full of terms and acronyms, including the green economy, green collar, impact careers, corporate social responsibility, and environmental, social, and governance (ESG). Let's elucidate these connected concepts.

The green economy

According to the United Nations Environmental Programme (UNEP), a green economy is one that results in "improved human well-being and social equity, while significantly reducing environmental risks and ecological scarcities" (UNEP, 2013). While the notion of the green economy is not meant to replace that of sustainable development, it is quite apparent that sustainability is reached by greening the economy and all of the goods and services within it. Some jobs clearly cover the realm of sustainability, such as environmental engineer or sustainability officer. Others, while not so obvious, also lie in the realm of sustainable development: manufacturer (for renewable energy components), journalist (focusing on sustainability issues), and architect (specializing in zero-impact buildings).

But what if a job has not been branded as "green" or for the good of "sustainability"? Does that mean that one's role lies outside of sustainable development? Does that mean that one can safely consider oneself to be "doing one's part" by printing double-sided at work? How, if at all, will equipping oneself with sustainable development knowledge help career progression? The answers can be found in green-collar jobs, impact careers, CSR initiatives, the ESG movement, the forces of reporting standards, and the many narratives of people incorporating all things "susty" in various career fields.

Green collar

With the elan surrounding how the green revolution will help economies emerge successfully from global polycrises—for example, the crises of high national debt and a health pandemic—the term "green collar" continues to surface in political and career-oriented speeches. In conjunction with the green economy is a green revival of the economy, and in conjunction with this revival are green-collar jobs. The term "green collar" was coined in a paper by Professor Patrick Heffernan who presented "Jobs for the Environment: The Coming Green Collar Revolution" in a 1976 United States Congressional hearing (Girardet, 2009). The term has since been revived, especially after the 2008/2009 financial crisis that left many countries turning to "green" jobs to help revitalize their economies. The Apollo Alliance, a project in the United States organized by the Institute for America's Future and the Center on Wisconsin Strategy, provides the following definition of green-collar jobs: "well-paid, career track jobs that contribute directly to preserving or enhancing environmental quality" (Center for American Progress and Center on Wisconsin Strategy, 2008).

Green-collar jobs are in many sectors of the economy, including construction, manufacturing, and agriculture. In a report by the World Future Council, green-collar jobs are expressed as those covering many sectors, from low to high skill levels. China allocated almost 40 percent of its 2008 stimulus plans to green themes, including rail, grids, and water infrastructure, and South Korea introduced the Green New Deal that allocated more than 80 percent of stimulus to green themes (Robins et al., 2009). Author Scott Deitche describes green-collar jobs as follows: "Green collar jobs are careers that transcend the general environmental sciences, to encompass nontraditional jobs that promote sustainability, as well as jobs in old industries that are adapting to the trend of sustainability" (Deitche, 2010).

The United States Bureau of Labor Statistics defines green jobs as either "jobs in businesses that produce goods or provide services that benefit the environment or conserve natural resources" or "jobs in which workers' duties involve making their establishment's production processes more environmentally friendly or use fewer natural resources" (US Bureau of Labor Statistics, 2012). Energy-efficiency jobs, for example, include work for equipment installers, construction equipment operators, industrial truck drivers, building inspectors, civil engineers, and computer software engineers (Bell, 2012). Green-collar jobs can be found in every sector, every function, and at each level of an organization. The green economy creates direct jobs (supported directly through a shift in spending patterns resulting from an expenditure or effort), indirect jobs (generated in the supply chain and supporting industries of an industry that is directly impacted by an expenditure or effort), and induced jobs (generated by the re-spending of income resulting from newly created direct and indirect jobs) (Bell, 2012).

Impact careers

While all jobs have an impact, the term "impact" has been used in corporate and investing circles to mostly describe work that explicitly has the intention of positively impacting people and planet. The employee demand for sustainability impact has now been quantified by recent studies. A 2021 Net Impact report, which summarized a survey of 1,600+ respondents from 65 different nationalities, found that 52 percent of workers have considered leaving their job due to the poor social and environmental impact performance of their employer; in addition, poor impact employers needed to pay an 83 percent salary premium compared to impact neutral peers (Upright Project, 2021). Generation Y (also known as Millennials, those generally born from the late 1970s to the early 2000s) is especially looking for jobs and companies that allow them to impact more than the financial bottom line. The Net Impact report showed that Millennials prefer working for companies that are solving environmental challenges rather than those that are merely avoiding emissions (Upright Project, 2021).

Companies are responding to this new differentiator in the workplace; an increasing number are implementing sustainability reports and putting in place chief sustainability officers. There are a number of international, regional, and national guidelines and codes for business to act in a sustainable manner. Reporting has spurred jobs in the realm of sustainable development. There are voluntary and mandatory standards to sustainability reporting. International voluntary standards include the Global Reporting Initiative by the United Nations, the AA1000 Guidelines by AccountAbility, the ISO 14001, 9000, 26000, and 14063 by the International Organization for Standardization (ISO), the Guide to Best Practice in Environmental, Social and Sustainability Reporting on the World Wide Web by the Association of Chartered Certified Accountants, the Guidelines for Multinational Enterprises by the OECD, the standards put forth by the International Sustainability Standards Board (ISSB), the Global Compact by the United Nations, the Responsible Care Global Charter by the International Council of Chemical Associations, the World Business Council for Sustainable Development (WBCSD) Guidelines, the Sustainability Integrated Guidelines for Management (SIGMA) project, and the SA8000 by Social Accountability International based on the conventions of the International Labour Organization.

Various more localized voluntary standards include the EMAS (Eco-Management and Audit Scheme) for the European Union, and in North America, the Global Sullivan Principles of Social Responsibility, CERES (Coalition for Environmentally Responsible Economies) Principles, and the Public Environmental Reporting Initiative (PERI) (KPMG and UNEP, 2006).

One of the most encouraging recent developments has been the codification of sustainability reporting standards into national regulations—bringing the necessary weight and mechanisms for accountability to the space. Frank Bold has produced a comprehensive comparison of such rules and regulations, some of which are summarized in Table 2.2.

TABLE 2.2 Comprehensive sustainability reporting standards in select countries (Frank Bold, 2023)

Country	Sustainability Reporting Regulation
Brazil	CVM Resolution No. 59 (2021), by the Brazilian Securities Commission (CVM).
China	Guidance for Enterprise ESG Disclosure (2022) by the Chinese Enterprise Reform and Development Society (CERDS).
European Union	European Sustainability Reporting Standards (ESRS), by the European Union.
India	Circular on Business Responsibility and Sustainability Reporting (BRSR) by listed entities (2021), by Securities & Exchange Board of India (SEBI).
Indonesia	POJK51/POJK.03/2017 (2017), Otoritas Jasa Keuangan (OJK).
Nigeria	Sustainability Disclosure Guidelines (2018), by Nigerian Stock Exchange.
Philippines	Sustainability Reporting Guidelines for Publicly Listed Companies (2019), by Philippine Stock Exchange.
South Africa	JSE Sustainability and Climate Disclosure Guidance (2021), by Johannesburg Stock Exchange.
Thailand	FORM 56-1 Report for Sustainability Disclosures (2022), by the Securities and Exchange Commission of Thailand.

Corporate social responsibility

Corporate governance encompasses the way in which an organization is organized to best carry out its operations. Corporate governance includes transparency, decision-making structure, and accountability. Governance structure allows for a contribution to sustainable development or the opposite—making decisions that are detrimental to social, environmental, and intergenerational well-being. In recent history, the idea of shareholder primacy has both grown and peaked. As noted by former B Lab CEO Anthea Kelsick, "the source code error of capitalism [is] shareholder primacy" (Waite, 2020). Historically, if shareholders considered sustainability to be an outside issue and unrelated to their financial bottom line, then the company was likely to not make decisions that focus on the quadruple bottom line. Although a corporation is filled with people who may have sustainability concerns, as a collective unit, they are protected by the "firm" and may not necessarily act on these concerns through corporate policy. However, international codes of conduct, in-house risk management policies including safety, health, and environment departments, and a push from customers and other stakeholders have made sustainability not only hard to ignore but also a driver of business success in today's corporate governance structure. Investors remain important, but so do other market participants such as customers, suppliers, government, and impacted communities.

Corporate social responsibility can be defined as the idea that a business has a responsibility to the society that exists around it (Stobierski, 2021).

Corporations have taken on CSR and 95 percent of the 250 largest companies worldwide report on corporate responsibility activities (KPMG, 2011). CSR reflects the old saying of "what gets measured gets managed," and although CSR indicators are not all financial, the indicators contribute to the overall value of the company (KPMG, 2011).

Many human resources (HR) managers have not yet fully integrated sustainable development into the organization; important questions arise as to how to integrate sustainability issues into recruitment, into staff development, and into the minds of senior management (WBCSD et al., 2005). Without an adequate HR policy regarding sustainability, the subject becomes watered down to communication and public relations (PR); otherwise noted: "CSR – HR = PR" (WBCSD et al., 2005).

Environmental, social, and governance (ESG)

The concepts of CSR, sustainability, and the green economy are more commonly morphed into environmental, social, and governance (ESG) strategies today. ESG gained traction in the investing and lending domains, and is now a commonplace acronym in the business world. The coronavirus pandemic accelerated a long-standing trend of the full spectrum of sustainability investing: from merely considering how environmental, social, and governance factors may impact a company's financial performance to actively seeking positive environmental, social, and governance outcomes alongside financial returns. ESG-labeled funds have offered comparable and market-beating returns. Morningstar research indicated that in the first quarter of the pandemic year of 2020, sustainable public market investments had inflows of over US$45 billion, while the broader market experienced an outflow of over US$384 billion (Stevens, 2020). The ESG growth trend also tracks with the preferences of young(er) generations that make up the majority of the global workforce: those born after around 1981. A 2023 survey by the Society for Human Resource Management (SHRM) indicated that 46 percent of Generation Z and 55 percent of Millennials indicate that ESG is important and 75 percent of U.S. executives say ESG initiatives have a positive impact on employee engagement (Gurchiek, 2023).

Business case for sustainable development awareness

HR managers have found that individuals with a strong awareness of sustainable development "possess a powerful understanding of the challenges facing business today, and frequently command the skills to engage with a wide diversity of institutions and people" (WBCSD et al., 2005). In addition, sustainability commitments and programs can motivate employees to perform at their best. Employee motivation comes from various sources, including achievement, advancement, belonging, challenge, contribution to society, involvement, financial reward, growth and development, intellectual interest, job security, pride in organization, recognition and respect, responsibility, and work environment. In summary, sustainability commitments in any career sector can be vital for recruiting and retaining top talent, creating incentives for exceptional performance, enhancing critical competencies, and transforming organizations.

In some ways, greening the workplace initiatives are similar to greening the household initiatives. We can align our finances, including where we bank and the investment products in which we invest for retirement, with sustainability. We can make purchasing decisions for organic, fair-trade, local, and low-footprint goods. We can make our buildings energy efficient, purchase renewable energy, install rainwater harvesting systems, use waterless toilets, and build with low-footprint, durable materials. We can use public transportation, walk, and cycle. We can install devices that help us monitor our consumption. There are manuals, interactive websites, and community groups, all to help us become change agents in our physical spaces. Sustainability managers often manage the internal workplace initiatives with the help of green teams. But what happens when we enter our actual *job functions* and further our careers? In a 2023 survey of 4,000 U.K. and U.S. employees by Paul Polman, at least one-third of respondents resigned from their jobs because they felt the efforts by their company to tackle environmental and societal challenges were insufficient, also known as conscious quitting; over two-thirds want to work for a company that is trying to have a positive impact on the world (Polman, 2023).

Sustainable development in careers

The following sections will present the case for sustainability in careers grouped into various fields, including health, business, economics and financial services, education, law and policy, science and technology, entertainment and media, and agriculture. In this second edition, I have added specific sections on both climate-related careers and careers that apply a lens of justice, equity, diversity, and inclusion (JEDI). Many specific jobs and career paths, such as those in sports and theology, are outside of the scope of this work, though the general framework presented can be applied to any field and position. The majority of the examples, case studies, and anecdotes were collected during extensive in-person interviews, focus groups, and a survey. The narratives allow one to tell a fuller story that cannot be told in a company report or in a summary of survey results. What ensues is not an exhaustive treatment of each profession but a provision of useful examples that link different professions and sectors to sustainability. The emphasis is not on creating more sustainability or green officers within organizations, but on incorporating social, environmental, economic, and intergenerational equity principles into any job and career move.

The SURF Framework

After interviewing people in different roles and analyzing the requirements of sustainable development matched with professions, the author has developed a framework for ensuring that products and services, whether for a large for-profit company or for a small non-profit company, are in line with sustainable development—SURF.

SURF stands for **supply chain** considerations that address sustainability criteria; **user** considerations that address sustainability criteria; **relations** or relationships with employees, colleagues, the surrounding community, and society at large; and concern for **future** generations. Social, environmental, and economic concerns underlie each element of SURF, with future planning also receiving adequate attention. Successful implementation of the SURF Framework is dependent on planning and utilization of the most effective tools. Various tools, international standards and guidelines, and indices that were analyzed as a basis for the SURF Framework are presented in Table 2.3.

S stands for all of the things that make up the supply chain of a company's product or service. One can think of this component as focusing on the building blocks that constitute a product or help bring about a service. How do the products in the supply chain measure when it comes to governance, water, energy, land use, waste, pollutants including greenhouse gases, labor, justice, equity, diversity, and inclusion, and long-term profit? Supply chain is one of the most problematic components of transforming organizations.

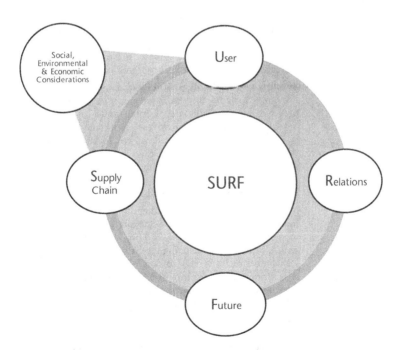

FIGURE 2.1 The SURF Framework
Source: Waite (2013)

TABLE 2.3 Specific tools, guidelines, frameworks, and indices for sustainable development decision making*

Tool/method name	Description
Backcasting	A way of planning in which a successful outcome is imagined in the future, followed by the question "What do we need to do today to reach that successful outcome?"
Carbon footprinting	Calculating the total amount of greenhouse gases that are emitted into the atmosphere each year by a person, family, building, organization, or company.
Ecological footprinting	Calculating how much area of biologically productive land and water an individual, population, or activity requires to produce all the resources it consumes and to absorb the waste it generates, using prevailing technology and resource management practices.
Lean manufacturing	The process of analyzing the flow of information and materials in a manufacturing environment and continuously improving the process to achieve enhanced value for the customer. Lean is a systematic approach to identifying and eliminating waste (non–value added activities) through continuous improvement by flowing the product at the pull of the customer.
Life-cycle analysis/ assessment	A technique to assess the environmental aspects and potential impacts associated with a product, process, or service, by compiling an inventory of relevant energy and material inputs and environmental releases, evaluating the potential environmental impacts associated with identified inputs and releases, and interpreting the results to help you make a more informed decision.
Water footprinting	Calculating the total volume of freshwater used to produce the goods and services consumed by the individual or community or produced by a business. Water use is measured in terms of water volumes consumed (evaporated or incorporated into a product) and/or polluted per unit of time.
Global Sullivan Principles	Principles for company endorsement which show support for universal human rights, equal opportunity for employees at all levels of the company, employees' voluntary freedom of association, compensation that allows employees to meet at least their basic needs and provide the opportunity to improve their skill and capability, a safe and healthy workplace, protection of human health and the environment, sustainable development, fair competition, and civil engagement.
Global Reporting Initiative	Indicators are organized into categories: economic, environmental, and social. The social category is broken down further by labor, human rights, society, and product responsibility sub-categories. Principles for defining report content include materiality, stakeholder inclusiveness, sustainability context, and completeness. Principles for ensuring report quality include balance, comparability, accuracy, timelines, clarity, and reliability.
AA1000 Guidelines	In addition to financial accountability, the AA1000 standard includes the principles of (1) inclusivity (the requirement to reflect the needs and concerns of all stakeholders in all stages of the social and ethical accounting, auditing, and reporting process), (2) completeness, materiality, regularity, and timeliness, (3) quality assurance, and (4) embeddedness and continuous improvement.

Tool/method name	Description
ISO 14000 Series, 9000 Series, 26000, and Other	The ISO 14000 family addresses various aspects of environmental management. It provides practical tools for companies and organizations looking to identify and control their environmental impact and constantly improve their environmental performance.
	The ISO 9000 family addresses various aspects of quality management and contains some of ISO's best-known standards. The standards provide guidance and tools for companies and organizations that want to ensure that their products and services consistently meet customer's requirements, and that quality is consistently improved.
	ISO 26000 provides guidance on how businesses and organizations can operate in a socially responsible way. This means acting in an ethical and transparent way that contributes to the health and welfare of society. ISO 26000:2010 provides guidance rather than requirements, so it cannot be certified to unlike some other well-known ISO standards. Instead, it helps clarify what social responsibility is, helps businesses and organizations translate principles into effective actions, and shares best practices relating to social responsibility, globally. It is aimed at all types of organizations regardless of their activity, size or location.
Guidelines for Multinational Enterprises	Recommendations addressed by governments to multinational enterprises operating in or from adhering countries. They provide voluntary principles and standards for responsible business conduct in areas such as employment and industrial relations, human rights, environment, information disclosure, combating bribery, consumer interests, science and technology, competition, and taxation.
Global Compact	Consists of ten principles: businesses should (1) support and respect the protection of internationally proclaimed human rights, (2) make sure that they are not complicit in human rights abuses, (3) uphold the freedom of association and the effective recognition of the right to collective bargaining, (4) eliminate all forms of forced and compulsory labor, (5) abolish child labor, (6) eliminate discrimination in respect of employment and occupation, (7) support a precautionary approach to environmental challenges, (8) undertake initiatives to promote greater environmental responsibility, (9) encourage the development and diffusion of environmentally friendly technologies, and (10) work against corruption in all its forms, including extortion and bribery.
Responsible Care Global Charter	Chemical industry's global initiative that drives continuous improvement in health, safety, and environmental performance, together with open and transparent communication with stakeholders. Responsible Care embraces the development and application of sustainable chemistry.
World Business Council for Sustainable Development Guidelines	The WBCSD Framework has three components: the Measuring Impact Framework Methodology, Beyond the Bottom Line (company case studies), and an Excel User Guide that helps companies carry out an assessment. The Measuring Impact Framework consists of four steps: step 1 is to set boundaries, step 2 is to measure direct and indirect impacts, step 3 is to assess contribution to development, and step 4 is to prioritize management response. The business activities are grouped into four clusters: governance and sustainability, assets, people, and financial flows.

Tool/method name	Description
Sustainability Integrated Guidelines for Management (SIGMA)	Consist of two core elements: (1) the holistic management of five different types of capital that reflect an organization's overall impact and wealth (natural capital, social capital, human capital, manufactured capital, and financial capital), and (2) the exercise of accountability by being transparent and responsive to stake-holders and complying with relevant rules and standards.
SA8000	SA8000 compliance requires adopting policies and procedures that protect the basic human rights of workers. The management system supports sustainable implementation of the elements of SA8000: child labor, forced and compulsory labor, health and safety, freedom of association and right to collective bargaining, discrimination, disciplinary practices, working hours, and remuneration.
Cleaner production	The continuous application of an integrated preventative environmental strategy to processes, products, and services to increase efficiency and reduce risks to humans and the environment.
Cradle-to-cradle	Concept that "waste" equals "food" in both biological and technical material flows.
Circular economy	A circular economy seeks to rebuild capital, whether this is financial, manufactured, human, social, or natural.
Blue economy	The blue economy is where the best for health and the environment is cheapest and the necessities for life are free thanks to a local system of production and consumption that works with what you have.
ESG Integration	The explicit and systematic inclusion of environmental, social, and governance (ESG) issues in investment analysis and investment decisions.
Green economy	The green economy results in improved human well-being and social equity, while significantly reducing environmental risks and ecological scarcities. In its simplest expression, a green economy can be thought of as one that is low carbon, resource efficient, and socially inclusive.
Sustainable Assessment Model (SAM)	Uses 22 performance indicators to measure full life cycle, environmental, economic, and resource usage impacts of a project; the impacts are then monetized and can be summed into a single measure called the Sustainability Assessment Model Indicator (SAMi).
Sustainability capital	Capital assets are divided into four categories: produced goods or human-made capital (K_M), human knowledge and skills or human capital (K_H), natural capital (K_N), and social capital (K_S).
The Framework for Strategic Sustainable Development	A generic five-level framework applied to the "society in the biosphere": (1) Systems Level: Understand, describe, and analyze the dynamic relationships between the ecological and social systems. (2) Success Level: In a sustainable society, nature is not subject to systematically increasing concentrations of substances extracted from the Earth's crust, and concentrations of substances produced by society, degradation by physical means; people are not subject to conditions that systematically undermine their capacity to meet their needs. (3) Strategic Guidelines Level: Guidelines for the process of moving global society strategically towards meeting basic principles of socio-ecological sustainability. The practice of back-casting is important to strategic planning. (4) Actions Level:

Tool/method name	Description
	All actions that will effectively help move the global socio-ecological system towards success by conforming to overall strategic principles (includes concrete actions, capacity building efforts, etc.). (5) Tools Level: Techniques, measurements, monitoring, management approaches, etc. relevant to assist in the global movement towards conformance with basic socio-ecological principles.
Better Life Index	Allows one to choose the indicators that are most important to them and then rank which location is better suited to their needs. There are 11 topics and indicators within each: housing, income, jobs, community, education, environment, governance, health, life satisfaction, safety, and work-life balance.
Environmental Performance Index	Ranks countries on 22 performance indicators spanning ten policy categories: environmental burden of disease, water, air pollution effects on human health, air pollution effects on the ecosystem, water resources, biodiversity and habitat, forestry, fisheries, agriculture, and climate change. The precursor to EPI is ESI, the Environmental Sustainability Index. ESI is a composite index tracking socio-economic, environmental, and institutional indicators that characterize and influence environmental sustainability at the national scale.
Gross National Happiness Index	Uses periodic surveys which account for demographical information. Happiness itself is not seen as a one-dimensional adjective, but rather a multidimensional state that covers nine domains: psychological well-being, time use, community vitality, cultural diversity, ecological resilience, living standard, health, education, and good governance.
Human Development Index	Composite index that measures a country's progress in health, knowledge, and income.
Gender Equity Index	A Gender Equity Index has been developed in numerous contexts, including at the sub-national, national, and sectoral levels. For example, the Gender Inequality Index (GII) by the United Nations is a composite metric of gender inequality using reproductive health, empowerment, and the labor market as the three primary markers.
Genuine Progress Indicator/Index of Sustainable Economic Welfare	The Index of Sustainable Economic Welfare (ISEW) is an analysis designed by Daly and Cobb that adjusts GDP to reflect a broader set of social and environmental criteria. ISEW was later revised and renamed the Genuine Progress Indicator (GPI). In GPI, all values are expressible in monetary units; in general, additions are made for volunteer work, non-paid household work, services of consumer durables, services of highways and streets, net capital investment, net foreign lending and borrowing, and income distribution adjustment, while subtractions are made for crime, family breakdown, automobile accidents, cost of consumer durables, cost of household pollution abatement, loss of leisure time, underemployment, commuting, water pollution, air pollution, noise pollution, loss of wetlands, loss of farmland, resource depletion, long-term environmental damage, ozone depletion, and loss of old-growth forests. The GPI is the total sum of all positive and negative values expressed in monetary units. The Sustainable Net Benefit Index (SNBI) is very similar to the ISEW and GPI, but the items are sorted into "uncancelled benefit" and "uncancelled cost" accounts; the SNBI is obtained by subtracting the total of the uncancelled cost account from the uncancelled benefit account.

Tool/method name	Description
Racial Equity Index	A Racial Equity Index has been developed in numerous contexts, including at the sub-national, national, and sectoral levels. The Racial Equity Index by the National Equity Atlas measures the state of equity based on key indicators of prosperity and inclusion by race in the United States. JUST Capital tracks corporate racial equity using 23 metrics across six specific dimensions of racial equity: antidiscrimination policies, pay equity, racial/ethnic diversity data, education and training programs, response to mass incarceration, and community investments. The Race Equality Index by the Race Equality Project measures how companies perform with respect to diversity, equity, and inclusion, and how they compare to counterparts in the tech industry.
Sustainable Society Index	The Sustainable Society Index (SSI) is a measure of sustainability at the national level. The index includes eight categories (basic needs, health, personal and social development, nature and environment, natural resources, climate and energy, transition, economy), and 21 indicators.
Social Progress Index	A measure of national progress that consists of three dimensions: Basic Human Needs (nutrition and basic medical care, air, water and sanitation, shelter, personal safety), Foundations of Well-being (access to basic knowledge, access to information and communications, health and wellness, ecosystem sustainability), and Opportunity (personal rights, access to higher education, personal freedom and choice, and equity and inclusion).

Companies often find it tedious to perform reliable life-cycle analyses of their products. They are also often uncertain about the social and environmental integrity at the most basic level of their supply chain. When organizations do consider supply chain sustainability performance, there is a tendency to focus on the supply chain of the product or service that they are selling but ignore the entirety of items required to complete the job. For example, for a consulting company, air travel used to conduct business may be considered in carbon calculations, but the office supplies that consultants use to conduct their work may not be the most "sustainability friendly" (Waite, 2013). The financial supply chain is also often overlooked; a CFA Institute and Business for Climate Finance report using data from Mercer indicated that, on average, U.S. 401(k) retirement plans have financed carbon emissions of 64 tCO2e per $1M retirement assets invested (tCO2e/$M invested); the retirement benefit correspondingly is 33 times more carbon emitting: the ratio of the median carbon intensity of retirement plans compared to the median employer's direct emissions and energy purchasing carbon intensity is 33 to 2 (CFA Institute and Business for Climate Finance, 2022).

Even companies whose core mission is socially or environmentally focused can fail to implement supply chain sustainability. Hans Wegner, the chief sustainability officer at National Geographic at the time of publication, created his CSO position after a career in purchasing and procurement. He witnessed first-hand the environmental impact of producing *Nat Geo*. "I shamed the organization into sustainability transformation," Hans admitted. "At the time, I asked a group of Nat Geo writers to raise their hand if they had changed their own habits based on what they write for an environmentally driven organization—and there were very few hands," Hans explained. Hans became a change agent and grew a bottom-up campaign for change; now there is a core team of about 50 Nat Geo staff in charge of various sustainability measures within the company.

U stands for user. One may think of the user as a consumer, customer, citizen, or client. What does the user do with the product or service? Do they throw it away immediately to pile up in a landfill? Can it be easily reused or recycled? Is it biodegradable and have the proper systems been put into place to render that biodegradability useful? Even with the best intentions, sustainability efforts can fall short if the user does not use the product or service in a sustainable manner (or if sustainability systems are unavailable to the user). A computer company can seek to ensure that the materials and labor used to assemble the computer follow sustainability criteria. However, what does the user then do with the computer? How is electronic waste dealt with in the market in which the computer is sold? Are there mechanisms to reuse or recycle the components? Are alternative ownership schemes available that would be more in line with sustainable development (Waite, 2013)? The user component of SURF revolves around managing both the consumer experience and the impacts of the product or service.

R stands for relations or relationships—both external and internal. One can approach this aspect of the framework as engaging stakeholders. Is the work environment healthy and safe for workers? Do employees feel that there is a positive, inclusive work environment? Are company operations and financing transparent? Do stakeholders participate in decisions that have an impact on them? While most organizations realize that people are important, the full range of stakeholders impacted by or somehow connected to the organization can often be neglected. Clients, employees, investors, and regulating bodies are a minimum of actors with which organizations seek to create and maintain positive relations. What can often be missing are those communities surrounding the place where the manufacturing or other levels of the product/service activity take place (Waite, 2013). In the policy-making arena, one must also ask if those making policies represent constituencies. For example, do those in the halls of the European Union in Brussels reflect the diversity of people one would find on the Brussels metro? Diversity in terms of racial and/or ethnic background, gender identity, age, LGBTQIA+ affiliation, religion, tribe and/or linguistic background, and other demographics are an important part of relationships no matter what field of work one is operating within.

F stands for future. The notion that we are responsible to future generations is one that keeps us questioning the impact of our operations. Do we have a ten-year plan? Or a 50-year plan? The consideration of future generations is what distinguishes sustainability from other concepts. The environmental movements have sought to create a natural environment whereby we live within the carrying capacity of Earth. The various social movements have sought to guarantee a more just society for all people in all places. The various economic movements, including communist, socialist, and capitalist theories, have sought to create an economy whereby the financial well-being of individuals can be assured. However, there is little intrinsic future focus in the environmental, social, and economic campaigns. Few and far between are backcasting exercises, decisions that take into account multiple generations, and a general reflection on how one's product or service will impact those not yet born (Waite, 2013). The future component of the SURF Framework can also be understood as aligned with the Seventh Generation Principle, which is an Iroquois philosophy to "think of the 7th generation coming after you in your words, work and actions, and to remember the seventh generation who came before you" (Haley, 2021).

The SURF Framework is used throughout the book to describe integrating sustainability into different fields and functions. The non-exhaustive list below provides an idea of the kind of questions that one can ask of one's work and workplace in order to increase sustainability.

Supply chain

Do the supply chain policies promote sustainability, including diversity, equity, inclusion, and justice?

Policies

- Does the financial supply chain align with sustainability?
- Does the bank used by the company and those in the supply chain indicate sustainability leadership (as measured by a national mission-driven designation, B Corporation certification, Global Alliance for Banking on Values membership, BankForGood adherence, etc.)?
- Does the bank that is used finance harmful impacts on people and planet, such as environmental injustice and fossil fuels?
- Do the retirement benefits offered by the company align with sustainability? Are the default options offered for retirement investment funds incorporating environmental, social, and governance risks, opportunities, and impacts?
- Does the employer provide information to the employee on both retirement fund financial performance (e.g., as measured by Morningstar Stars) and sustainability performance (e.g., as measured by Morningstar Globes and AsYouSow databases)?
- What policies are in place to ensure that the supply chain is antiracist, anti-ableist, ensures gender equity, and is inclusive for all?

- What efforts are made to procure products and services from under-represented communities based on the geography and sector of activity (underrepresentation could be based on women leadership, people of color or certain ethnic groups, disability, and other categories)?

Are the physical infrastructure and materials within sustainable?

Building

- If the possibility of new construction is present, have full life-cycle costs and criteria in line with the four pillars of sustainable development been considered?
- Have eco-construction labels been awarded (LEED, BREAM, ISO 14001, HQE, etc.)? Is there a certification procedure to validate sustainability initiatives?
- Does the building and large-scale infrastructure in which you conduct work activities comply with sound environmental and health criteria?

Materials

- Do the cleaning products used contain harmful toxins?
- Are plant-based products given priority (the choice of building materials and equipment will influence the choice of cleaning products)?
- Are office supplies and other support materials eco-friendly and sourced from socially responsible suppliers?

Energy

- How is energy efficiency managed? Is there a plan to reduce operational costs by implementing energy-efficiency measures?
- What are the energy metrics used in the building or for equipment? What is the energy consumption in kWh/m^2/year of the building?
- Has an energy audit been completed?
- Is natural light guaranteed to promote productivity and energy efficiency?
- What measures have been taken to save energy (such as low consumption lighting, ventilation regulators, sensors, shutdown timers on computers)?
- Is 100% renewable energy used in all parts of the supply chain and operations (rooftop solar and storage, geothermal energy, etc.)?

Air, water, landscape

- Have plants been purchased and planted to create a green roof on the building if solar panels are not viable or not installed?
- What measures are taken to improve indoor air quality?
- Does the landscaping use native plants that reduce water consumption and the use of pesticides?
- Is there a system for recycling and reusing water/wastewater? Is there a system for collecting and using rainwater?
- How are people encouraged to save energy and water?

Food

- How climate-friendly is the food procurement policy? Are local, organic, and plant-based providers and meals prioritized?
- Is the food provided to workers, clients, etc. healthy?
- Is the food made with labor that provides a livable wage to food workers?
- Is there full cost accounting used in purchasing decisions?

Is the transportation system sustainable?

- Does the local public transportation have stops at the workplace? Are there policies in place to encourage and/or incentivize the use of public transportation?
- Is the total supply chain as "short" as possible to reduce greenhouse gas emissions?
- Are there electric vehicle (EV) car-pooling programs for employees? Are EV chargers available on-site?
- How do company (including delivery, staff, and other) vehicles rate in terms of electric vehicle penetration?
- Has a cycling system been put into place (and thus necessary sanitation and shower facilities on-site)?

Is raw material use and manufacturing sustainable?

- Are recycled materials used instead of freshly mined raw materials?
- Are renewable resources used instead of fossil fuels?

- Are cradle-to-cradle and closed-loop manufacturing principles employed?
- Which air, water, and soil pollutants are produced during manufacturing and how can pollution be curtailed?

User

Are you actually doing harm to stakeholders through your work?

- Do you keep track of the toxicity of the substances used in operations and support work? Is there a detailed inventory of products used in terms of toxicity?
- Is there a program to substitute toxic or dangerous products?
- What indicators are used to measure the environmental health of the facility?
- What is done for waste reduction, waste recovery, communication and awareness building of waste sorting and processing, solid and liquid waste identification based on danger/risk to people and the environment?
- What is the consultation and communication process for creating products and services that promote sustainability for the user and during the use phase?
- Does pollution disproportionately adversely impact vulnerable communities, historically marginalized communities, or any subset of a population based on demographics?

Is the product or service sustainable for the user?

- Are there take-back programs for products to be recycled? Are these programs communicated to the end user?
- Are sustainable use methods effectively communicated to users (such as water and energy efficiency and methods to extend the useful life of a product, including care methods)?

Relations

Is the work environment healthy for all internal and external stakeholders?

- Does pollution disproportionately and adversely impact vulnerable communities, historically marginalized communities, or any subset of a population based on demographics?

- How is the workplace and the organization's stakeholder engagement antiracist, anti-ableist, and inclusive for all?
- Is there a separation of hazardous (including different types: biological, chemical, radioactive, etc.) and non-hazardous waste?
- Is there regular monitoring of the effluents emanating from the facility for hazards?
- How many sorting channels exist?
- Is sustainable development training available to personnel in your establishment? Have you undertaken such training?
- Are you a part of a sustainability network (local, international)?
- How is ergonomics reflected in your work site?
- How are the following dealt with in the facility: psychological health, health risks tied to working shifts, and absenteeism?
- What policies are in place to prevent health problems (flexible work hours, prevention training, risk reduction programs, etc.)?

Future

Is intergenerational equity given adequate attention in your work?

- Have you been through a backcasting exercise?
- How does the work facility contribute to future generational planning?
- In terms of siting, is there consideration for sustainable transportation, stormwater management, and urban redevelopment?
- Are green spaces reserved for future generations?
- Have the needs of different generations been taken into consideration in the workplace (including mobility considerations, parenting schedules, etc.)?

References

Arnold, J. (2002). Careers and Career Management. In N. Anderson, D. S. Ones, H. K. Sinangil, & C. Viswesvaran (eds.), *Handbook of Industrial, Work and Organizational Psychology. Organizational Psychology*, Volume 2, (pp. 115–132). SAGE Publications.

Bell, C. (2012). *Energy Efficiency Job Creation: Real World Experiences. American Council for an Energy-Efficient Economy*. American Council for an Energy-Efficient Economy.

British Standards Institution, Forum for the Future, and AccountAbility. (2006). SIGMA Project—Sustainability: Integrated Guidelines for Management. www.projectsigma.co.uk.

Burnett, B., & Evans, D. (2022). *Designing Your Life: How to Build a Well-Lived, Joyful Life*. Alfred A. Knopf. https://penguinrandomhousehighereducation.com/book/?isbn= 9781101875322.

Center for American Progress and Center on Wisconsin Strategy. (2008). *Green-Collar Jobs in America's Cities: Building Pathways Out of Poverty and Careers in the Clean Energy Economy.* Apollo Alliance.

CFA Institute and Business for Climate Finance. (2022). The Carbon Impact of U.S. Company-Sponsored 401k Plans. www.businessclimatefinance.org/_files/ugd/d008b0_6cd63c0a59d340338371c43f9be0af06.pdf.

Deitche, S. M. (2010). *Green Collar Jobs: Environmental Careers for the 21st Century.* Santa Barbara, CA: Praeger.

Frank Bold. (2023). Comparison of climate-related disclosure requirements. https://en.frankbold.org/sites/default/files/publikace/frank_bold_comparative_analysis_climate_reporting_standards.pdf.

Girardet, H. A. (2009). *A Renewable World: Energy, Ecology, Equality, A Report for the World Future Council.* Devon: Green Books.

Global Reporting Initiative. (2012). The global leader for impact reporting. www.globalreporting.org/Information/about-gri/Pages/default.aspx.

Gurchiek, K. (2023). Survey: ESG Strategies Rank High with Gen Z, Millennials. SHRM. www.shrm.org/hr-today/news/hr-news/pages/survey-esg-strategies-rank-high-with-gen-z-millennials.aspx.

Haley, M. (2021). Introducing The Seventh Generation Principle—to Promote True Sustainability. https://theseventhgeneration.org/blog-the-seventh-generation-principle.

JUST Capital. (2022). The 2022 Corporate Racial Equity Tracker. https://justcapital.com/reports/2022-corporate-racial-equity-tracker.

KPMG. (2011). KPMG International Survey of Corporate Responsibility Reporting 2011. www.kpmg.com/PT/pt/IssuesAndInsights/Documents/corporate-responsibility2011.pdf.

KPMG and UNEP. (2006). *Carrots and Sticks for Starters: Current Trends and Approaches in Voluntary and Mandatory Standards for Sustainability Reporting.* KPMG's Global Sustainability Services and United Nations Environment Programme.

McDonough, W., & Braungart, M. (2002). *Cradle to Cradle: Remaking the Way We Make Things.* North Point Press.

OECD (Organization for Economic Co-operation and Development). (2011). OECD Guidelines for Multinational Enterprises. https://mneguidelines.oecd.org/targeted-update-of-the-oecd-guidelines-for-multinational-enterprises.htm.

Pearce, D., & Atkinson, G. (1998). Concept of sustainable development: An evaluation of its usefulness 10 years after Brundtland. *Environmental Economics and Policy Studies* 1, 95–111. https://doi.org/10.1007/BF03353896.

Polman, P. (2023). 2023 Net Positive Employee Barometer. www.paulpolman.com/wp-content/uploads/2023/02/MC_Paul-Polman_Net-Positive-Employee-Barometer_Final_web.pdf.

PRI. (2018). What is ESG Integration? www.unpri.org/investment-tools/what-is-esg-integration/3052.article.

Robins, N., Clover, R., & Singh, C. (2009). Building a Green Recovery: Governments allocate USD470bn—and counting… HSBC Global Research. HSBC Climate Change.

Stevens, P. (2020). Sustainable investing is set to surge in the wake of the coronavirus pandemic. CNBC. www.cnbc.com/2020/06/07/sustainable-investing-is-set-to-surge-in-the-wake-of-the-coronavirus-pandemic.html.

Stobierski, T. (2021). What is corporate social responsibility? 4 Types. Harvard Business School. https://online.hbs.edu/blog/post/types-of-corporate-social-responsibility.

Sullivan Foundation. (n.d.). Global Sullivan Principles. http://thesullivanfoundation.org/about/global-sullivan-principles.

UNDP (United Nations Development Program). (2023). Gender Inequality Index (GII). https://hdr.undp.org/data-center/thematic-composite-indices/gender-inequality-index#/indicies/GII.

UNEP (United Nations Environment Programme). (2013). What is the Green Economy? Green Economy Initiative. www.unep.org/greeneconomy/AboutGEI/WhatisGEI/tabid/29784/Default.aspx.

United Nations. (2013). What is the UN Global Compact?www.unglobalcompact.org/.

Upright Project. (2021). Net Impact report 2021. Net Impact. https://netimpactreport.com/.

US Bureau of Labor Statistics. (2012). Measuring Green Jobs. www.bls.gov/green.

Waite, M. (2020). B Lab co-CEO Anthea Kelsick: "Innovate against your model" to address systemic racism. GreenBiz. www.greenbiz.com/article/b-lab-co-ceo-anthea-kelsick-innovate-against-your-model-address-systemic-racism.

Waite, M. (2013). SURF Framework for Sustainable Development and the Green Economy. *Journal of Management and Sustainability* 3(4), 25–40.

World Business Council for Sustainable Development (WBCSD); HRH The Prince of Wales's Business and the Environment Programme; University of Cambridge Programme for Industry. (2005). Driving Success Human Resources and Sustainable Development. www.cisl.cam.ac.uk/resources/archive-publications/human-resources-and-sustainable-development.

World Business Council for Sustainable Development (WBCSD). (n.d.). WBCSD Measuring Impact Framework. www.wbcsd.org/Programs/People-and-Society/Tackling-Inequality/Resources/WBCSD-Measuring-Impact.

3

PURSUING SUSTAINABILITY IN SCIENCE AND TECHNOLOGY

One can refer to the T-shaped scientist or engineer: one not only has depth in a specific scientific or engineering discipline, but also has the breadth necessary to deliver and manage sustainability in science or engineering.

Introduction

Science and technology are important economic drivers in society. It is partly for that reason that there has been an emphasis on science, technology, engineering, and math (STEM) education in many countries. It is science and math that stand as the foundation for all technological innovation. Technology is applied science and math, and it covers all areas of engineering (including agricultural, aerospace, biological, biomedical, chemical, civil, computer, electrical, environmental, materials, mechanical, and nuclear engineering). Technology is essential to everyday life and is reflected in both the construction and deconstruction of various infrastructure, including trains, bridges, shelter, electricity, and water supply. Some technologies, while not life determining in every location, are very much appreciated for well-being (including smart phones and the Internet). As the author of *Science in World History* puts it, "Science is the method that allows us to understand the universe around us, and technology is the ability to use that understanding to transform the environment to our advantage" (Trefil, 2012). This environmental transformation, be it the natural or engineered environment, is at the crux of sustainable science and technology.

Scientific decisions are rarely clear-cut; those in the science and technology fields must operate in both complicated and complex systems and understand the wider implications of their work. For every scientific application, the economic, environmental, social, and intergenerational pillars of sustainable development are always present. Engineers, for example, have a unique position

DOI: 10.4324/9781032615844-3

in sustainable development; they can design technology to last in time or design technology to break at a certain calculated moment. They can create industrial closed-loop cycles or create waste. Scientists and engineers can incorporate sustainability principles throughout their work and career—from their approach to a problem to the design of a meaningful solution.

Scientists

Scientists play an important role in discovering new knowledge and asking questions that will further our understanding of the physical and social environment. It was climate scientists who rang the bell to alert the world to changing climate patterns due to increased greenhouse gas emissions. Scientific research is at the heart of innovation and the first step to solving many problems such as diseases. Scientists often become the managers of important research laboratories and research initiatives in both the public and private sectors, where a sustainability vision can help shape objectives. By simply thinking about how a research topic fits into the objectives of sustainable development, research can become more targeted to meet society's needs of today and of the future.

The modern scientific method involves a cycle of observation, regularity, theory, and prediction. The first step in learning about the world is observing it; an experiment is one way of observing the world, often through controlled settings. The next step is finding patterns in the observations (such as the rising and setting of the sun). The third step is the formulation of theories, a deeper meaning of what we observe as predictable patterns. Theories can range from being very exact and explained in rigorous mathematical terms (such as in theories of physics), to those that describe general trends and processes (such as the original laws of natural selection) (Trefil, 2012). The final step in the scientific process involves verifying a prediction. Do the data support the hypothesis? If the data do not, then the prediction is wrong. Scientists, in their use of the scientific method, thus have a critical role to play in ensuring that our sustainability metrics are sound as we move through the development process. Will measure "x" protect the ecosystem or will it endanger a species? What will be the long-term impact on soil quality of fertilizer "y"? Scientists answer these questions and thus provide expertise for sustainability decisions.

The Science Council, a UK non-profit organization that brings together many groups to focus on the education and skills of the science community, has identified ten types of scientists as follows:

1. *The Explorer Scientist* is someone who is on a journey of discovery and will rarely focus on a specific outcome beyond scientific knowledge.
2. *The Investigator Scientist* examines the unknown by observing, mapping, understanding, and piecing together in-depth knowledge and data, setting out the landscape for others to translate and develop.

3. *The Developer/Translational Scientist* is an applied scientist whose depth of knowledge and skills of both the research environment and the potential user environment enable them to make use of the knowledge generated by others and transform it into something that society can use.

4. *The Operational/Service Provider Scientist* is one who provides scientific services in a wide range of ways (examples can be found within the health service, forensic science, food science, health and safety, materials analysis and testing).

5. *The Monitor/Regulator Scientist* is becoming increasingly important as we translate more science and technology into society and as society needs the increasing reassurance that systems and technology are reliable and safe. The monitor/regulator scientist must be able to communicate with the public and researchers and establish credibility with both.

6. *The Entrepreneur Scientist* is able to blend their science knowledge and credibility with people management skills, entrepreneurial flair, and a strong understanding of business and finance. Their scientific knowledge and connections are deep enough to be able to see opportunities for innovation.

7. *The Communicator Scientist* is able to combine science and technological know-how with an ability to communicate; they need to be credible and trusted by both the science community and the public.

8. *The Teacher Scientist* is trained in science and shares the knowledge to train the next generation. These scientists work in education and develop the tools for teaching and learning.

9. *The Business Scientist* will be found in almost all parts of the economy where a high level of science and technology knowledge and skill is playing a part. The science- and technology-based sectors employ large numbers of different types of STEM graduates working in a variety of settings from research and development (R&D) to marketing, especially in the business-to-business sectors.

10. *The Policy Scientist* combines science and technical knowledge and skills with knowledge and understanding of government and policy making, decision making, and scrutiny processes to ensure that legislation and policy have a sound evidence base.

(Science Council, 2011)

There are many variations and nuances to these ten types of scientists, but all can incorporate sustainability into their work, and all can have a meaningful impact for creating a sustainable society. Archaeologists, astronomers, biologists, chemists, ecologists, geologists, social scientists, mathematicians, physicists, and all of the specialties within, can create even more value and discovery by understanding how their role contributes to sustainable development and how to adopt a sustainability approach in their undertakings.

Most scientific discovery is the result of a multiple-year team effort. Without explicit mention of "sustainability," scientists have contributed to the various pillars of sustainable development. For example, penicillin was accidentally discovered when the bacteriologist Fleming, after a two-week vacation in 1928, noticed that one of his petri dishes contained mold. This petri dish grew mold in most corners, except for the part of the dish where a certain existing bacteria was located. Penicillin has subsequently been used as a medical treatment, extending the life years of many people.

Engineers

Like scientists, engineers of all disciplines can incorporate sustainability into their work and career paths. Civil engineers (structural, environmental, geotechnical, etc.) can ensure that infrastructure projects follow sustainability criteria such as those laid out in LEED[1] and BREEAM[2] certification systems. Software engineers can create more energy-efficient computing and processing, while hardware engineers can minimize electronic waste through cloud infrastructure. Electrical and mechanical engineers can develop sustainable energy and transportation systems such as the batteries needed to store intermittent renewable energy sources and those to run electric vehicles. Chemical engineers can design closed-loop processes and find solutions that reduce the use of scarce resources. The list goes on, but the point is that any engineer can employ sustainable engineering (which some simply call good engineering).

Engineering for sustainable development embraces the following themes: a multi-disciplinary approach that bridges the physical sciences and the humanities; a systems approach; a recognition that there are limits to what can be achieved through technology alone; an acceptance that value judgments are important; the need to engage in problem definition with all stakeholder groups; an understanding of the mechanisms for managing change in organizations; and an acknowledgment that technical innovation and business skills are vital to sustainable engineering solutions (Fenner et al., 2006). Engineers often become executive managers of technology and engineering companies, and thus can help shape the vision and action in a very concrete manner for sustainability.

An engineer must find the right balance within the quadruple bottom line of sustainable development. Some refer to the T-shaped engineer: one not only has depth in a specific engineering discipline but also has the breadth necessary to deliver and manage sustainability in engineering. "To use an engineering analogy, parts of the world have gone beyond the elastic limit and entered the plastic range" (Jowitt, 2004). The role of the engineer today is to prevent future plastic ranges and to help society function within the elastic range. As Albert Einstein said, "not everything that can be counted, counts … and not everything that counts can be counted."

Professor Paul Jowitt provides an example of how engineers have reconciled multiple concepts in the past and must do so in the present with sustainable development. It involves the equations of balance and structural equilibrium. When analyzing a determinate structure, as one often does in beginning engineering courses, only forces and loads are considered. However, when analyzing statically indeterminate systems, equilibrium considerations alone are insufficient; the concepts of displacement, the compatibility of nodal displacements and member extensions, and material strains come into play. By moving from analyzing determinate to indeterminate systems, the engineer shows their ability to move to the systems level. The challenge with sustainable development is now to extend this ability of systems analysis into systems that, though not always defined by a set of equations, are "characterized by sets of relationships between seemingly incommensurate objects" (Jowitt, 2004).

Fenner et al. present an eight-point framework for engineering for sustainable development. According to the framework, engineers must do the following:

1.   Make value judgments that are guided by a system of ethics (*Ethical Foundation*).
2.   Understand the real needs for engineering solutions by encompassing ideas of social equity, equal rights for development, democracy, public participation, and empowerment (*Justice Through Participation*).
3.   Use efficient provision and coordination of infrastructure (allows engineers to work within land use constraints and adopt approaches that link multiple goals of society; e.g., mixed use development, contaminated site regeneration, preventing construction in flood plains, etc.) (*Efficient Coordinated Infrastructure*).
4.   Maintain natural capital, or the stock of all environmental and natural resource assets (*Maintenance of Natural Capital*).
5.   Use holistic financial accounting to reflect externalities such as the cost of resource depletion and pollution (*Holistic Financial Accountability*).
6.   Take a systemic approach (no single act of development can achieve objectives in complete isolation) (*Systems Context*).
7.   Take account of linkages at different spatial and temporal levels (considerations of the impacts of a project should not stop at the site boundary) (*Interlinking Scales*).
8.   Possess the vision that improvements in the quality of the environment, social fairness, and economic prosperity can be sought through change (methods such as backcasting can be used to connect the future to the present) (*Future Vision*).

(Fenner et al, 2006)

Sustainability in science and engineering disciplines is not for scientists and engineers alone, because technological advancement and the development of both knowledge and products have implications for all of us. Some real-life scenarios are provided in the next section, which include considerations for the management of the waste that we produce and the career paths involved.

Zero waste through biosolids—Bill's story

As one rides along Interstate 295 of Washington, D.C., every once in a while, there is a whiff of sewage coming from Blue Plains. Some locals would say more than once in a while. But what is happening at the Blue Plains Advanced Wastewater Treatment Plant is transforming the idea of waste. This area in the U.S. capital is home to a robust water and wastewater plant, one of the largest advanced treatment plants in the world with a capacity of 370 million gallons per day (1.4 million cubic meters per day). That's enough to fill one large professional sports stadium per day. It is here that Bill Brower greeted me with a hard hat (one for him, one for me) and an excited demeanor to talk about what I learned to call "biosolids."

Bill studied chemical engineering as an undergraduate student in Wisconsin. He enjoyed participating in Engineers Without Borders, an organization that supports community-driven programs worldwide. In 2005, Bill flew to Rwanda to help install a gravity-fed water system that supplemented the existing piped water supply. He also led a group to analyze the potential of a solar water pasteurization system. His first job was with a polymer company. His role? Make adhesives for diapers "better" as a process engineer. Bill got bored. He decided that he wanted to do something more fulfilling, so he packed up and went to China for a year to teach English. By witnessing the deplorable state of many of the rivers and streams in central China at that time, Bill understood the importance of properly treating municipal and industrial wastewater.

While in China, Bill realized that integrating sustainability in engineering projects was one way that he could contribute to society and feel more fulfilled in his work. He therefore went to study Engineering for Sustainable Development at Cambridge in the UK. The course provided a foundation and framework for understanding the engineer's role in sustainable development, as well as a business background to implement technology solutions in the business environment. It was thus no surprise that Bill found himself in microfinance afterwards. Bill went to work for GlobalGiving, an online marketplace that connects donors with grassroots projects in the developing world. As Bill said, "It felt more substantial." After maxing out on learning, Bill went to the World Bank as a junior professional associate for sustainable development in the Africa Region. There, Bill worked on water, energy, and transportation projects. However, the work did not meet Bill's expectation for more technical and hands-on tasks.

One day, Bill attended a presentation by George Hawkins, the General Manager of DC Water. Bill was so inspired by this motivational speaker that he attended his talks on multiple occasions. He soon found a position at DC Water that matched his desire for positive impact with his desire to apply engineering skills more concretely. Bill noted:

Someone applied for the job who had 15 years of experience in this exact field—recycling nutrients, recycling energy, and recycling water. But the candidate had a mindset that this was waste to be dealt with rather than a resource to utilize. So it was my mentality towards biosolids and my understanding that this was a sustainable resource and not "gross sludge" that really won me the position.

There we were in our hard hats at DC Water's Blue Plains facility. Bill, as manager of biosolids operations, gave me a tour of each unit. With nearly US$1 billion in budget and serving a population of over 2 million in Washington, D. C., Maryland, and Virginia, the facility is immense. DC Water decided to be a leader in sustainable waste management, and Bill was happy to take part in leading the charge. The food–water–energy nexus describes how each component is interrelated and can be wisely used in a closed cycle where waste does not exist.

The plant operates 24 hours per day. Bill works during the day, where he supervises operations and solves problems as they arise. Wastewater is sent to the plant through sewage pipes; after screening to remove large, mostly inorganic material like plastic bags, the wastewater is aerated, sent to sedimentation basins, and clarified by the natural separation of solid material from lighter material. After this primary treatment, a secondary treatment follows where microbes, such as bacteria and amoebas, break down the organic material. The wastewater is then sent to tanks for nitrification, where special bugs eat away (ingest ammonia and convert nitrite to nitrate). The water is chlorinated, filtered, and de-chlorinated before being released into the Potomac River.

But what about that solid material that settled at the bottom of the sedimentation tanks?

Well, while many places either burn or landfill this nutrient-rich source, DC Water creates value from it. It takes in this solid waste and creates two valuable products—fertilizer and electricity. During the technical process, the solid undergoes thermal hydrolysis (like pressure cooking), then anaerobic digestion in order to become fertilizer. The fertilizer is divided into two classes according to quality. The majority of the fertilizer is sold to farmers as Class B, and the other class can be sold as commercial compost. During anaerobic digestion, methane is emitted and this methane gas is used to drive a turbine, which generates electricity (about one-third of the plant's energy needs). DC Water is the biggest single-point source user of electricity for Washington, D.C., at about 26 MW per year. The goal is to become energy neutral, where the biosolids on-site (combined with process improvements and solar photovoltaic power) completely power the electricity consumption.

DC Water has become a resource recovery facility, and Bill has become a champion of its sustainability transformation for biosolids. Bill was able to transform his engineering career from polymer process engineer to operational manager of a major facility. He found that by evolving his approach to be circular instead of linear, there could be self-fulfillment in his career and a great position to be achieved. His work is environmentally beneficial since it converts waste to food by creating useful soil fertilizers, socially beneficial since it has created meaningful employment during the construction and operational phases of improving the facility for the biosolids operations, economically beneficial since it creates a product to be sold where the investment pays for itself, and generationally beneficial by eliminating the amount of legacy waste that is left in landfill. There are over 400,000 centralized sewage treatment plants in the world (Pennisi, 2012); this provides plenty of opportunities for engineers to make sustainability improvements.

Bill gave me my own souvenir of the facility tour—a biodegradable paper bag filled with fresh fertilizer from a waste stream that I could use to nourish my garden and create food. All courtesy of what people put in their drains...

Making business in Greece work with the help of the sun—Thania's story

Some would argue that it's easy to be a sustainability scientist or engineer in prosperous economic conditions, but what about when times are tough? The 2010 debt crisis left many people in Greece unemployed, upset, and uninspired. Thania Christodoulou's family-owned electronic products company was performing very well in 2007 and 2008 with €3 million in revenues. The high turnover all came crashing down at the end of 2009 when the company lost its revenue.

After taking a high-speed train from Athens to Paiania–Kantza, I descended into a breathtakingly beautiful Greek countryside. The rolling valleys and surrounding mountains made for one of the most attractive industrial centers that I have seen. Thania greeted me with a big smile as we drove to Noratex SA, a company started by her father in 1975. Noratex is a wholesaler of electric industrial products. Or at least that used to be its business model.

As I entered the offices and warehouse of Noratex, I was able to see the storage of many products, and, unfortunately, empty personnel offices. Thania started to talk about the decline of the Greek economy, starting with the high debt incurred by hosting the 2004 Olympics in Athens. She explained the rise of Golden Dawn (a neo-Nazi political party), the International Monetary Fund's ever-increasing presence, and austerity measures (salary reductions of public servants, pension reductions, a sales tax of 23% on goods, and more). But while setting the tone for a rather depressing context, Thania had a plan to grow Noratex and remained convinced that sustainability would play a key role.

Thania studied electrical engineering in the United Kingdom at Bristol University and spent one year in Erlangen, Germany, as an Erasmus student. Like Bill, her passion for environmental and social issues drove her to then study for a Master's in Engineering for Sustainable Development. Armed with her new knowledge in sustainable engineering, she decided to help transform the family business and increase profits through solar products. She returned to Greece in

2008 to become the Vice President of Finance, Sales, and Marketing and co-CEO of Noratex SA.

Greece implemented a feed-in-tariff (FiT) to help spur renewable energy adoption, with particular emphasis on utilizing the abundant sunshine in the country. Noratex was able to take advantage of this policy by selling solar systems that allowed individuals to sell back electricity to the grid. Thania was able to move the company along faster in this market due to her sustainability knowledge. Noratex experienced great success. Sales and profits increased, jobs were created both within the company and outside (primarily equipment installers), and there was less pollution from fossil fuels. It seemed that Thania had made the right decision to enter the solar market and that her sustainability background gave her the impetus to be successful.

However, in 2013, with austerity measures, the government decreased the FiT and stopped accepting new applications. This had a negative impact on Noratex's business, and the company had to lay off numerous workers. Thania had the tough job of letting workers go, and sales plummeted. Even green tech is not immune to the general woes of a struggling economy.

"We in Greece are living more sustainable lives because of the crisis. We use less lighting; we waste less; we drive smaller and more fuel-efficient cars. Saving money is what is really motivating us, and this has positive spillover effects on the environment," Thania explained. Thania's experience in austere Greece caused her to rethink her ideas about sustainable development. "I now have a problem with the 'development' piece," Thania added. "In Greece, GDP decreased 6–7 percent in 2012; development for me means there is new construction, new buildings. Now, nothing like that is happening here. But we need to be sustainable regardless if we are growing or not." For Thania, sustainability in the context of her technology company is about "thinking more completely." She believes that one should "do the things you would do at home at your job, such as saving energy, reducing water use, and recycling." As co-CEO, Thania applies sustainability concepts freely, both in deciding what technologies to sell and how to run day-to-day operations.

How did the drop in the solar market impact Thania and Noratex in the long term? Thanks to a sustainability approach, Thania did not get bogged down in one product and market, but rather saw opportunities in other areas like net metering, waste management, and recycling PV panels at the end of their life. Thania is shifting Noratex's business model to be aligned with the functional economy, where they lease some products. Noratex now sells *off-grid* solar solutions, which are really attractive in an environment where government incentives are severely strained. People like the idea of being self-sufficient with energy. Noratex recently won a tender for solar lighting poles in the Athenian suburbs. One of their next goals is to sell LED street lights that save the local municipal budget because of energy savings.

As an engineer and business manager, Thania has had to make tough choices regarding both technology and business direction. Understanding that a sustainable, or long-lasting, business must be able to adapt to different economic situations is something that has helped her keep Noratex alive. By focusing on how energy savings and off-grid solutions fit into the new reality of the Greek economy, Thania was able to capitalize on green solutions for the benefit of her family-owned company.

SURF Framework for careers in science and technology

The SURF Framework of *Supply Chain, User, Relations, and Future* is a practical framework that can be used to structure the sustainable transformation of not only scientific and technological endeavors, but also the careers within.

Science and tech careers involving supply chain

Supply chains mostly involve tangible goods, from raw materials to final products, where design and innovation are incorporated at each step. There are therefore pertinent roles for scientists and engineers within supply chains. Many trained engineers now work in supply chain management (SCM), which seeks to optimize the delivery of goods to customers. Engineers can seek to decrease the carbon emissions of a certain supply chain by creating regional centers that limit long-distance transportation. Life-cycle analysis can be performed for the product in order to make better decisions regarding materials, location, and design. There are numerous certifications in greening supply chains and sustainable SCM.

Roles in supply chain that solicit science and math backgrounds include supply chain managers, procurement managers, green product designers, manufacturing managers, environmental managers of mining operations, green building certification professionals, architects, urban planners, green chemists, and more. If one's role is to create new or optimize existing components that make up a product supply chain, then one will likely use scientific and/or technological principles at some point. For instance, a hardware supply chain manager may be in charge of overseeing an international sustainability certification for IT products, such as the TCO (Telecommunications Certification Organization) Certification. They may have to alter how a certain metal is used and may have to find technically sound alternatives for materials.

Science and tech careers involving the user

Designing for the end user is a part of product innovation. Companies are constantly trying to understand what customers want and what will improve their living experience. However, design for "end of use" for the end user is often neglected. Sometimes a great product that incorporates sustainable features will be rendered less sustainable when the user throws it away to pile up in landfill. In other words, the end user needs products designed for sustainability post-use. Scientists and engineers who incorporate both the use and end-of-use stages into their design and business model are more fully adhering to sustainability principles.

Engineers that design for programmed obsolescence have followed a short-term business model that is based on a linear economy of "buy and throw away." And although programmed obsolescence is still widespread, alternative models in a circular and collaborative economy are making headway. Printers and coffee machines are good examples, where many companies are designing and building robust products since they have "take-back" programs at the end of product life. These products are then prepared to be resold on the market.

Science and engineering careers that involve the user include customer-facing and partnership roles. For example, external relations for a technology company may involve forming partnerships with local authorities to provide recycling or return policy infrastructure. Product designers may work with end-user-focused programs, such as those provided by TerraCycle, to create products that can be upcycled into other valuable materials.

Science and tech careers involving relations

Scientists and engineers are also project managers for new endeavors. The Project Management Institute (PMI) has recently added stakeholder engagement as a key knowledge area for any project manager. A stakeholder, according to PMI, is "An individual, group or organization who may affect, be affected by, or perceive itself to be affected by a decision, activity or outcome of the project" (PMI, 2013). Those working in the science and technology fields have to be especially mindful of their stakeholders. The public does not always understand scientific activities and concepts, and so science communication has arisen as a vital role and career path in this field.

Roles in science and tech involving stakeholder engagement and relations include science communication, external and government affairs, science and technology policy, and general managers of science and technology laboratories and establishments. Public perceptions of science and technology vary across nations, generations, and other socio-economic categories. However, there will always be a need for scientists and engineers to engage with the public on new methods, discoveries, processes, and products that emerge from the field. There will therefore always be career opportunities specific to stakeholder relations, as well as a need for all scientists and engineers to effectively communicate their work.

Alfred Nobel, a chemist and engineer, invented dynamite. He understood that this product could be used for good and for harm. His understanding of the wider implications and stakeholders of his invention motivated him to create the Nobel Prize for outstanding achievements in physics, chemistry, medicine, and literature, and for work in peace. Wangari Maathai, a biologist, later received the Nobel Peace Prize. She applied her scientific knowledge to benefit a large group of stakeholders through her work founding the Green Belt Movement.

Science and tech careers involving the future

The future is something at the heart of science and technology. When those in this field look back, it is normally to understand something that will help with the future. The field of prospective analysis, or foresight analysis, has risen as a way of creating different scenarios for the future. Professionals can then create solutions for different possible futures. The foundation of the various industrial revolutions was technological advances such as the cotton gin and steam engine, the Internet and digital communication. It has been shown in many economies that as the number of scientists and engineers increase, the number of economic transactions also increase.

It would be difficult to list a role, job description, or career trajectory in science and engineering that did not focus on the future. There are particular roles that enable one to concentrate on medium- and long-term advances. These roles include institutional research and development, innovation management, knowledge management, technology entrepreneurship, and prospective studies.

Author and professor Susan Krumdieck proposes that we think of "transition engineers" as the key to a more sustainable world; transition engineers respond to risks and not disasters. Krumdieck defines transition engineering as "the research, modeling, development, and application of state-of-the-art knowledge to bring about changes in existing engineered systems in order to improve the odds of survival by reducing risks to safety, security, and sustainability" (Krumdieck, 2013). By focusing on mitigating risks and creating opportunities, instead of post-disaster solutions, these engineers are future oriented.

Conclusion

The U.S. Society of Mechanical Engineers (ASME) Code of Ethics states, "Engineers shall consider environmental impact and sustainable development in the performance of their professional duties" (Sprouse et al., 2021). This chapter provided frameworks and examples of how engineers and those with a scientific background have specifically incorporated sustainability into their careers. The professionals have found useful problem-solving tools, financial and emotional fulfillment, and positive impact. Authors Seager, Selinger, and Wiek have consolidated various science and technology orientations towards sustainability, from business as usual (BAU) to sustainable engineering science. They define attitudes towards technology, focus, expert and ethical culture, approach to complexity, and approach to conflicting views, as illustrated in Table 3.1 (Seager et al., 2012).

The goal in incorporating sustainability into the science and tech fields is to move away from BAU towards more sustainable engineering and science. Some practical tips for professionals in the science and tech sector include:

- Use frameworks to gauge sustainability progress, such as:
    - The SURF Framework for the science or engineering laboratory, office, or other establishment, as well as for the job and career trajectory

TABLE 3.1 Science and technology orientations towards sustainability (Seager et al., 2012)

	Attitude towards technology	Focus	Expert and ethical culture	Approach to complexity	Approach to conflicting views
Business as usual (BAU)	Optimism	Creating new things, resources. Ignores scale and efficiency	Depth in a single sub-discipline. Professional ethics	Simplification and reduction	Defense of techno-industrial ethos. Denial of opposing perspectives
Systems engineering:					
Engineering within ecological constraints	Pragmatism	Cost optimization of maturing technology. Ignores scale	Compartmentalized, multi-disciplinary teams. Social ethics	Cost-benefit optimization and efficiency	Litigation and regulation
Sustainable engineering		Optimization for triple bottom line. Ignores scale		Risk minimization	Structured participation
Sustainable engineering science	Skepticism	Sustainability as a wicked problem[3]	Interactional expertise. Macro ethics	Anticipation, adaptation, and resilience	Cooperation and deliberation

- The Eight-Point Framework for Engineering for Sustainable Development by Fenner et al. (2006).
- Use best practices, reference guides, and certification schemes, such as:
  - Various international and national green building standards (see sustainable building certification list by World Green Building Council)
  - Life-cycle analysis and assessment.
- Join professional networks that address sustainable science and technology, such as:
  - Engineers for a Sustainable World
  - Engineers without Borders
  - International Society for Sustainability Science
  - Various social media and online groups that are focused on sustainability and science & engineering.
- Attend conferences that address sustainable science and technology.

Notes

1 Leadership in Energy and Environmental Design (LEED) is a green building certification program that recognizes best-in-class building strategies and practices.
2 The Building Research Establishment Environmental Assessment Method (BREEAM) is a standard for best practice in sustainable design for buildings and large-scale developments.
3 A wicked problem denotes resistance to resolution; it is a problem that is difficult or impossible to solve because of incomplete, contradictory, and changing requirements.

References

Fenner, R. A., Ainger, C. M., Cruickshank, H. J., & Guthrie, P. M. (2006). Widening Engineering Horizons: Addressing the Complexity of Sustainable Development. *Engineering Sustainability* 159(4), 145–154. Proceedings of the Institution of Civil Engineers.

Jowitt, P. W. (2004). Systems and Sustainability: Sustainable Development, Civil Engineering and the Formation of the Civil Engineer. *Proceedings of the Institution of Civil Engineers: Engineering Sustainability*. 157, 78–88.

Krumdieck, S. (2013). Transition Engineering: Planning and Building the Sustainable World. *The Futurist*, 47(4), 35–41.

Pennisi, E. (2012). Water Reclamation Going Green. *Science*, 674–675.

PMI (Project Management Institute). (2013). *A Guide to the Project Management Body of Knowledge*. Project Management Institute.

Science Council. (2011). 10 Types of Scientist. https://sciencecouncil.org/about-science/10-types-of-scientist.

Seager, T., Selinger, E., & Wiek, A. (2012). Sustainable Engineering Science for Resolving Wicked Problems. *Journal of Agricultural and Environmental Ethics* 25(4), 1–18.

Sprouse, C. E., III, Davy, M., Doyle, A., & Rembold, G. (2021). A Critical Survey of Environmental Content in United States Undergraduate Mechanical Engineering Curricula. *Sustainability* 13(12), 6961. https://doi.org/10.3390/su13126961.

Trefil, J. (2012). *Science in World History*. New York, NY: Routledge.

4

PURSUING SUSTAINABILITY IN HEALTH CARE

It is not possible to have healthy people on an unhealthy planet.

Introduction

Few would argue that good health forms an essential foundation of a successful career. A healthy population underpins economic productivity and well-being. Fit workers can carry out the tasks required for their jobs, not to mention professional development activities that are indispensable for a fulfilling career. Those working in the health care sector have a special connection to sustainable development. Doctors, nurses, administrators, and those working all along the health care supply chain have a mandate to provide care without causing harm. This mandate requires that health care professionals consider the impact of their job on future generations: the consequences of the products, equipment, and materials that they use; their role in the social fabric of society; and their role in economic health. In order to diagnose, cure, research, and find solutions to various health problems, different forms of products are required that, if not properly managed, can have a negative impact on the environment (and subsequently the health of the populace).

The health care profession has rapidly adopted sustainability guidelines and practices. For example, the Global Green and Healthy Hospitals network has over 1,750 members in more than 80 countries, while the Health Care Climate Challenge signatories represent the interests of over 26,000 health care facilities in 46 countries (GGHH, 2023). More than 2,000 CEOs and presidents, including those in the health care sector, have signed the CEO Action for Diversity & Inclusion[TM] pledge (Bettencourt, 2021). Most of the world's largest pharmaceutical companies have programs to increase access to medication in low- and middle-income countries; pharmaceutical job postings that mention social

DOI: 10.4324/9781032615844-4

responsibility increased by 161 percent in 2022 compared to the previous year (Pharmaceutical Technology, 2023). In this chapter we explore the many facets of the link between careers in health care and sustainable development through three impressive professionals: Arthur in Brazil, and Ingrid and Pia in Sweden.

From dentistry to inclusive health tech startup—Arthur Lima's story

In the capital of Brazil's northeastern Bahia region, Salvador, there emerges an example of how even the most precise and specialized of professions can give way to sustainability innovation and action.

Arthur Igor Cruz Lima is a dentist. His formal education includes dentistry and family health diplomas from the Bahiana School of Medicine and Public Health and the Federal University of Bahia. He has published in many scientific journals and is a recognized leader in public health. Yet his path to professional success was anything but smooth sailing.

Brazil has the largest Black population outside of the African continent, with Afro-descendent people making up over 56 percent of the general population and over 80 percent of Salvador. Unfortunately, centuries of systemic racism and discrimination in Brazil have translated into an underrepresentation of Black Brazilians in well-paid professions and leadership positions, from business to politics. It thus was not a surprise to Arthur that his patients would ask him, "Are you really a dentist?" His dentistry class counted around 60 students but only a handful were Black.

If the problem for Afro-Brazilians were only a matter of adequate representation, Arthur may have been content in simply encouraging the community to take advantage of Brazil's relatively new racial justice system in education. This system, created by the government in 2012, reserves seats in universities for students of Black African descent, Indigenous descent, and low-income backgrounds. The policy is not race-blind—it's rather race-forward. According to research scholars and policy experts, one best practice in anti-racist policy is specificity. Universalist policies have their role, yet if there were historical *exclusionary* policies based on specific criteria such as race and ethnicity, then there need to be specific *inclusionary* policies based on those same criteria. The racial quota policy, though limited to public universities, has been enormously successful and in just one decade has led to a 400 percent increase in Black student enrollment in Brazilian higher education (Meyerfeld, 2023).

Nevertheless, Afro-Brazilians face multi-faceted difficulties that access to education alone cannot solve. For example, there is a lack of adequate public health policies and health care professionals addressing the issues disproportionately facing the community, such as sickle cell disease, folliculitis (common among Black men but often mistaken for acne for those unfamiliar with melanated skin), and mental health challenges linked to racialized trauma. Arthur witnessed first-hand how Afro-Brazilian patients needed the cultural competence of Afro-Brazilian health professionals. He co-founded AfroSaúde in 2019 as a result of his observations.

AfroSaúde is a health care application and platform that centers racial diversity and cultural competence. The platform specializes in showcasing racialized Brazilian health care providers and offers appointment scheduling, online payment ease, and telemedicine. One can find dentists, doctors, and therapists on the app. During the COVID-19 pandemic, AfroSaúde accelerated mental health support given the increased demand and is now a go-to resource with over 600 Afro-Brazilian mental health therapists registered to provide care for users. AfroSaúde has helped tens of thousands of patients, of any racial background, connect with caregivers that have been previously "hidden" from Brazil's mainstream sight. The team is growing quickly and constantly improving the app for inclusion; for example, the video consultations can now function well with low bandwidths for remote parts of the country without access to optical fiber. AfroSaúde also works with organizations to implement mental health programs in the workplace, focusing on the Black population that is present in corporate environments.

As a telehealth platform, AfroSaúde is playing a role in reducing transport-related greenhouse gas emissions, as well as providing inclusive health care access to individuals with low mobility. Despite the success of AfroSaúde, Arthur does not plan on resting on his laurels. He is pursuing a PhD part-time that focuses on sickle cell disease and public health. He would like to support more entrepreneurship in Salvador, which has markedly less access to capital for startups than São Paulo.

When thinking about advice to give to his 16-year-old self, Arthur reflected, "Trust more in yourself." He remembers his mom, who is a nurse, urging him to be an engineer. "I wasted a lot of time studying engineering in the beginning. I was interested in public health."

Arthur turned the laser-sharp skill of dentistry into a tool for broader societal impact.

From general practitioner to public health specialist—Ingrid's story

> Sustainability and health care today is a bit like smoking and health care many years ago. Health care practitioners used to say, "Do you mean we are expected to talk to our patients about smoking?" Well, Ingrid asked, aren't you supposed to talk to your patients about health?
>
> *(Ingrid Eckerman)*

Fever. Vaccines. Trouble sleeping. Bird flu. Ingrid has dealt with it all as a family doctor turned public health practitioner. Ingrid, also the president of Swedish Doctors for the Environment (Läkare för Miljön), came to the Karrtorp train station to pick me up by bicycle (filled with organic produce in the bike basket). She resides in a sustainability-conscious living community in Sweden. Kollektivhuset Sockenstugan is a unique living situation for those aged 40 and over, where people pledge to take care of each other and the environment as much as possible. The "co-house," as Ingrid calls it, is a place where all forms of waste are sorted. On one hand, co-house residents can sort what some might consider the publicly recognizable: glass and newspaper. But the list goes much further: tins, electronic waste, toxic materials (such as those from cleaning products, sprays, and aerosols), light bulbs, batteries, and textiles. Although this level of sorting could be expected from every Swede, this particular house is very careful about the sorting and thus earns the title of an environmental advocate's haven.

Ingrid and I sat down for dinner, where baked fish and vegetable stew were served. Just as we began to eat, Ingrid shook her head, "You know, it's a real tragedy. The fish in the Baltic Sea are so polluted that the European Union has essentially banned their consumption."

Ingrid warns women not to eat the herring from the Baltic "until after one has finished breastfeeding their last child." I later learned that dioxins, persistent and bio-accumulative, are spread all over the Baltic Sea area; their presence is mostly due to several industrial pollution sources such as emissions from the chemical, paper and pulp, and metal industries, low-temperature incineration of municipal and hazardous waste, and fossil fuel energy production (Helsinki Commission, 2004). Because the fat-soluble properties of dioxins cause them to accumulate in fatty tissues, fatty fish such as herring and salmon are especially at risk for contamination. The current recommended maximum consumption rate of Baltic Sea herring and salmon for children up to 18 and women of childbearing age is two to three times per year (Swedish National Food Agency, 2023). It became resoundingly clear to me that health begins before the plate, and as the common saying goes, "We are what we eat." Food and nutrition are an important element of a healthy society, and those working in the health care sector have a special role to play. Food menus in health care settings can be adapted to various pathologies, and one of the main challenges of hospitals today is making sure patients with lost appetites are able to eat.

After eating, Ingrid and I went to her living quarters to discuss her career path. Ingrid welcomed me into her apartment, simple yet inviting, with bits and bobs of clutter from over a half-century of work. An elephant ornament swings attentively over our heads as we sit down. "In 1962 in Sweden, you had two choices as a baccalaureate graduate with high marks: medicine or engineering." Ingrid reminisced about the beginnings of her career path and explained, "I chose medicine, probably because my mother wanted to do so but never had the opportunity and partly because I spent a lot of time in hospital for a hip operation when I was eight." Ideas poured into my head as she spoke: the hospital can indeed be a place of trepidation for many people, especially young children. In many hospitals worldwide, *green sheets* help describe a child's environmental history and children who are in contact with risk factors such as pollution and toxic substances.

Ingrid did not brood over what to do next after high school. Medical school it was, and she followed the classic pathway of her time: she went into medicine, got married, and had children. She abstained from the "hippie movement" that was surrounding her, but she certainly kept her eyes and ears open when it came to environmental concerns.

Ingrid became a general practitioner (GP) and believed that doctors could have an impact on the environmental, economic, and social fabric of society if they really wanted. As a GP, with much less resources than a hospital doctor, Ingrid noted "You can use your ears, nose, eyes, and more; you can produce less waste, use less energy, and prescribe less harmful drugs." Pharmaceutical drugs can negatively impact the environment by, for example, polluting waterways and interfering with the hormonal and reproductive systems of animals. Solutions include reducing the stock and wastage in pharmaceuticals, replacing polluting substances in pharmaceuticals with alternatives better for the environment and equally effective for the patient, and creating and enabling appropriate waste handling of drugs. Sweden, like many countries, has a policy where individuals are instructed to return unused or expired drugs to the pharmacy as opposed to disposing of the drugs themselves. Non-pharmaceutical methods, such as counseling, physical activity, music, and physiotherapy, are important components that de-materialize health care and add to the sustainability of care.

Ingrid sighed:

> The problem is that doctors belong to a privileged elite. They are well paid and can work very few hours. It is much easier to tell patients that they shouldn't do this and that than to, say, cut down your own energy use.
>
> But Ingrid didn't fall into the disassociation trap. She enjoyed, most of all, learning from her patients: "If you listen … you can learn a lot about the plethora of different lives out there," she acknowledged.

There was one patient that Ingrid especially remembered. The patient (we'll call him David to protect his privacy) was someone of Jewish descent from Austria. He married a Swedish woman late in his life and would often visit Ingrid's office for non-serious health problems, like a stomach ache. Although his health issues were not life-threatening, the problems were multiple and reoccurring. As the consultations increased, David began to open up to Ingrid. He described how he did not feel recognized at work and how he was not only physically sick but emotionally discontent. Eventually, he described his life story—fleeing to the Soviet Union during World War II, somehow losing his mother and siblings along the way, and managing alone. He went back to Austria after the war. Austria had changed, and so had he. Ingrid determined that David was suffering from survivor's guilt. The continuous check-ups and support by the family doctor allowed David eventually to talk about his experience and begin a healing process. Ingrid said, "Politicians in the past few decades have pumped a lot of money into big hospitals, but you need sustainable primary care for a truly healthy population." Ingrid's experience as a GP highlights the role that health care professionals play not only in caring for a specific illness but in providing a nurturing environment where many health issues can be healed.

Ingrid went to the Nordic School of Public Health and continued a career in the health sector by focusing on public health problems. Sadly, about 25 percent of all human disease and death in the world can be attributed to what the World Health Organization considers to be environmental factors. This includes unsafe drinking water, poor sanitation and hygiene, indoor and outdoor air pollution, industrial hazards and accidents, automobile accidents, climate change, poor land use practices, and poor natural resource management (HCWH, 2013).

In 1991, Ingrid joined the new organization Swedish Doctors for the Environment (LfM). She became very active, participating in "green health care" exhibitions. In 1998, LfM received funding from the Stockholm County Council and published an impactful report on pharmaceuticals and the environment. LfM subjects range from nano-safety to climate change and health.

"I was 52 when my teacher encouraged me to apply for a stipend from the Swedish International Development Cooperation Agency in order to go to Bhopal, Madhya Pradesh, India." Ingrid's fervor ascended as she discussed her unique experience as a population doctor where she advised colleagues and other professionals on public health issues related to a serious environmental disaster in Bhopal that occurred in 1984.

This disaster, a gas leak at the Union Carbide India Limited pesticide plant, led to thousands of immediate deaths and hundreds of thousands of injuries; Ingrid's work culminated in a book released in 2004 entitled *The Bhopal Saga* (Eckerman, 2013). Ingrid watched her career change from GP to public health doctor, to chemical accident researcher, to author. Her experience examining the Bhopal incident further motivated her to help reduce chemical pollution in the health care sector.

Ingrid was president of LfM, with a membership of 200 and growing. Ingrid has retired as president but is still active. Since 2012, she is the editor in chief of *AllmanMedicin*, a scientific journal for GPs; she tries to add something about the environment and sustainable development in each issue. Ingrid's career evolved in unexpected yet exciting ways because she applied the outlook of sustainable development to the health care profession. She found fulfillment, impact, meaning, and a great compensation package in return.

Emergency pediatrics at Karolinska Hospital—Pia's story

> You can't just shut your eyes on sustainability.
>
> *(Doctor Pia Malmquist)*

Anaphylaxis. Head Trauma. Seizures. Laryngo-tracheo-bronchitis. Pia has seen it all working as an emergency room pediatrician at Stockholm's Karolinska University Hospital. After completing her medical training in Germany, Pia became a surgeon specializing in vascular and endocrine surgery. She worked as a military physician in Bosnia and Rwanda, as a physician caring for leprosy patients in Ethiopia, and then became a pioneer in the field of emergency medicine.

As I entered the children's emergency room at Karolinska, it looked as if I could have been in many parts of the world. The exterior Red Cross symbol assured visitors that they were in the right place for medical treatment. There was a feeling that this is a place where serious things happen: serious life-threatening conditions, serious treatment, and serious staff. *Who really likes visiting a hospital?* Either you are there to take part in some shape or form for the care of patients (so you would probably like it), or you are a patient (generally, you would rather not be there), or you are accompanying or visiting a patient (also, no fun). I turned to the left to find a reception desk where I was greeted with a bright smile and a "Hej," the Swedish word for "Hello." After introducing myself, I was told that Doctor Pia was dealing with a trauma patient, and a kind receptionist escorted me into the medical staff kitchen lounge. To my delight, there were reusable ceramic mugs for use and a cookie jar. Suddenly, the aura of being in a pediatric emergency facility did not seem so somber. The doctors and nurses ate cookies and spoke around a table, just like any other employees in any other sector.

In came Pia and out came some interesting historical perspectives:

> In 2013, you can't just shut your eyes on sustainability. As a nation, we have thought that the environment required special attention for some time. In the 1970s and 80s, there was a slogan that amounted to something like "Keep Sweden Clean." We have unique legislation that brings people closer to nature ... for example, you can go tent anywhere.

Sweden's Right of Public Access gives one the freedom to roam the countryside and camp freely, all under the premise of "do not disturb—do not destroy" (Visit Sweden, 2023). This national context has brought sustainability awareness to many professions in Sweden, including those in medicine.

As a doctor, Pia has a main role to care for patients—not necessarily to transform the hospital to become environmentally friendly, socially aware, economically viable, or lasting for future generations. Yet her job task does touch on all these elements. She sites saving energy (shutting down equipment, lights, and computers) when not in use, not prescribing a lot of antibiotics unnecessarily, and sorting and recycling waste as all being an important part of the job. "We all have to look for ways of saving money," Pia insists. In 2013, a visit to the emergency room costs SEK120 (less than US$20) to see a doctor. Doctors and nurses working in the hospital can contribute to sustainable development by providing excellent care to the patients and thus helping to maintain the very thing that underpins well-being and economic activity—health. According to Pia, those in the medical profession also contribute to sustainable development by wasting as little as possible and using resources as efficiently as possible, saving money for the taxpayers. At Karolinska Hospital, each new staff member must follow an online educational course in medical waste that teaches things such as the harmful impact of certain medicines if they are placed in the wastewater stream. Karolinska in general abides by sustainable practices, many of which follow the criteria recommended by *The Green Guide*.[1]

Due to a large inventory of toxic substances at Karolinska Hospital, about 100 chemicals are being abolished on-site (C2DS, 2012). Of particular concern are mercury, bisphenol A (BPA), brominated flame retardants, and di (2-ethylhexyl) phthalates. Mercury can be present in Cantor tubes, esophageal dilators, feeding tubes, dental amalgam, thermometers, vaccines (as a preservative), laboratory reagents, and more (Shanks, 2009). Contamination by physical contact, ingestion, or inhalation of mercury can cause problems to the brain, spinal cord, liver, kidney, and reproductive system (Quinna et al., 2006). BPA is a chemical, an endocrine disruptor, used to make lightweight, hard plastics and epoxy resins; it can be found in food and drink packaging, water bottles, infant and baby bottles, infant feeding cups, reusable cups, impact-resistant safety equipment, plastic dinnerware, eyeglass lenses, and medical devices (U.S. National Library of Medicine, 2010). Flame retardants, which can be inhaled, ingested via dust particles, or consumed through contaminated food and liquids such as breast milk, can be found in items such as IV pumps, curtains, refrigerators, ventilators, monitors, furniture, hospital beds, and packaging; brominated flame retardants are endocrine disrupters that affect thyroid and sex hormone functioning (Shanks, 2009). There is a specific project underway that seeks to produce blood bags without phthalates at Karolinska. Phthalates, used in consumer products such as soap, shampoo, shower curtains, and food packaging, are chemicals used to soften and increase the flexibility of plastic and vinyl; di (2-ethylhexyl) phthalate is a carcinogen, and high levels of exposure may adversely affect human reproduction or development (Casale & Rice, 2023).

There is a long list of sustainability transformation at Karolinska Hospital, in Stockholm, and in Sweden at large. In Sweden, the ambulances went from "yellow" to "green" by eliminating toxic oils (polycyclic aromatic hydrocarbons) from tires, using seats that do not contain PVC, and implementing VOC-free glues for the cables (C2DS, 2012). Recent plans for the sustainable renovation of the entire infrastructure at Karolinska University Hospital will benefit the people of Stockholm and their visitors for many generations. The specifications include an energy footprint of 110 kWh per square meter, ISO 14001 certification, LEED certification, disposal and recycling of products sorted and transported using a vacuum/pneumatic tube, and renewable energy.

The area of emergency pediatrics is especially connected to future generations since care is geared towards the young (up to 15 years of age for surgery in Sweden). The status of emergency medicine varies from country to country, but as a specialty, it was virtually unheard of in Sweden in the 1990s. Pia credits her passion for emergency care from a year she spent in Australia working in a hospital, where emergency medicine was quite developed. Today, doctors can take courses on advanced cardiac life support; "there were no courses like this 50 years ago," Pia affirmed. "Knowledge has increased on how we organize ourselves for trauma care."

What's a typical day like for Pia? She normally checks in at 7:30 am, then secures a briefing with doctors and various groups who have been on overnight duty. By 8:30 am the entire team meets to lay out formally "who works with whom" and spends 30 minutes going over one of the 45 most common themes in sustainable health care with the aid of an alphabetical checklist. "We believe in repetition," Pia stated convincingly. Repetition is a key part of medical training in the first place, but it also helps in driving home sustainable practices in the hospital environment.

The Health Care Without Harm (HCWH) international coalition has issued a comprehensive environmental health agenda for hospitals and health systems worldwide. According to HCWH, a green hospital is:

> One that promotes public health by continuously reducing its environmental impact and ultimately eliminating its contribution to the burden of disease. A green and healthy hospital recognizes the connection between human health and the environment and demonstrates that understanding through its governance, strategy and operations. It connects local needs with environmental action and practices primary prevention by actively engaging in efforts to foster community environmental health, health equity and a green economy.
>
> *(HCWH, 2019)*

Although Pia is a senior doctor in the unit and is more in a supervisory role to junior doctors, she still sees five to ten patients daily. She has spent more than 14 years trying to improve emergency care in Sweden, which she refers to as "almost accepted" now as a specialty. I was surprised to learn that only about 80 doctors were now specialized in emergency care ("not enough for all of Sweden," Pia lamented). "My job is very stimulating; every week there is something that stands out," Pia added. Emergency rooms are a place where people survive and die. That slight melancholic feeling I had when I entered the hospital (before seeing the cookie jar) was slowly coming back to me as Pia described how it is always difficult when a child patient dies. Pia helps to ensure that doctors have team support and that they attend to their emotions whenever they lose a patient. "There is no one story that sticks with you; rather, it is a multiple of stories—real people and their relatives. It is the grandmother of a child that was hit by a car ... parents who take care of a disabled child 24/7 ... the sister of someone chronically ill." As Pia explained, I knew that the list could go on and on.

Medical advances have helped to make medicine more sustainable for the environment, the patient, the economy, and future generations. Pia reported, "The way we give low-molecular heparin for patients with thrombosis has completely changed, for instance. Fifty years ago, the patients were on a drip for many days, but now with advances in pharmacy and medical care, outpatient treatment will suffice." Outpatient care, now more developed than ever, has also helped the health sector in its role as the backbone of the economy and individual health. Pia confirmed that "outpatient care has helped working people; they can go to work instead of being on sick leave. We save on materials. Patients may have to go to an outpatient clinic to have an injection or they can be taught to inject on their own."

Pia cited a specific example of how a nurse's passion for improving sustainability in health care helped land the nurse the job. After passing the basic criteria of nursing diplomas and certification and the ability to deliver excellent care to patients, Pia was impressed by the candidate's leadership in environmental issues. She knew this person would also be able to safeguard the health care investment by saving money through numerous sustainability practices and by searching for healthier alternatives for patients, such as food, materials, and care methods.

Separate lives, separate roles, same vision for sustainability

Pia's and Ingrid's roles and career path are both in the health care sector as doctors, but there are differences in their relationship to the patient and their everyday work. Pia will often never see a patient again as an emergency care physician, whereas a family doctor like Ingrid can monitor someone's health for a long period of time—an entire lifespan in some cases. Ingrid began her career treating individual patients as a GP, and then shifted to public health. A highlight of her public health career was monitoring the health implications of the Bhopal disaster. Pia started out as a highly specialized surgeon who then further specialized in emergency care. Pia moved up an established hierarchy in a hospital setting, becoming a supervising doctor.

Both Pia and Ingrid are pioneers in their fields for different sub-categories of the health sector. And they both recognize the importance of sustainable development in their careers—both how individuals contribute to sustainable development through their work and how sustainable development is a useful framework for individuals to better do their work. Careers in the health care field can be linear and nonlinear, involving specialization, lateral moves, geographical changes, and unexpected shifts. Sustainability can be a valuable skill set as one builds their own way in this care-centered sector.

SURF Framework for careers in health care

The SURF Framework of *Supply Chain, User, Relations, and Future* can be used to structure sustainable transformation of the health care system and all the careers that it encompasses. The supply chain of health care involves multiple exchanges in the global economy. Needles, radioisotopes, textiles for operating rooms, plastics, ceramics, metal, organic materials, blood—these are all complex supply chains that involve numerous professions. The end users of health care are patients of all ages, backgrounds, and professions. The patient is generally where doctors and nurses concentrate their attention to provide care. At the user stage, various social, intergenerational, environmental, and economic questions come into play, including patient confidentiality, religious and cultural contexts, workplace health risks, accessibility of after-care and medicine, and the environmental impacts of medicines prescribed. There are numerous relationships and stakeholders involved in the health care sector, from patients to employers, including those intimately involved in the sector such as researchers, pharmacists, doctors, nurses, hospital staff, primary care assistants, dentists, laboratory technicians, and more. Lastly, future generations are at the heart of health care professions. Every cavity filled, heart transplanted, cancer cured, or vaccine administered is directed towards guaranteeing a future. This "future" is both that of the patient and that of the people in the patient's life.

New jobs and career paths are being created because of the greening of the health care sector, with sustainable healthcare being expanded to include careers in medical waste management, energy, water and land conservation management, pollution prevention (chemicals, waste), sustainable purchasing for the health care sector, sustainable pharmaceutical products and business models, sustainable infrastructure (buildings, equipment), spatial considerations for a nurturing environment, and sustainable food for health (including plant-based diets).

In addition to spurring the emergence of new professions such as sustainability officers and green architects, applying sustainability to the health care sector involves every employee working together under the same framework. According to Luc Montagnier, Nobel Prize winner for medicine for the discovery of HIV in 1983, "we are gradually going from curative medicine in the last century, towards 4P medicine—preventive, predictive, personalized, participative" (C2DS, 2012). The 4P framework ties nicely with a four-pronged or quadruple bottom line framework of sustainable development. It is not possible to have healthy people on an ill planet. Prevention recognizes the relationship between the "would be" patient and the environment, and we all eventually become a patient of some sort, although the duration of that status may vary from person to person. Being able to predict future illness helps in individual and social planning. Personalized and participative medicine empowers the end user to take a leading role in their health care. This new paradigm for health care also creates new economic models and revenue-generating activities, aligning with the economic well-being pillar of sustainable development.

Health care careers involving supply chain

Purchasing is a profession that cuts across all sectors and industries. Worldwide, hospital purchases alone represent over €450 billion per year (C2DS, 2012). In health care, there is an emerging specialty of green purchasing that relies on health care professionals including pharmacists, logistics managers, and administrative staff. The health care sector produces masses of liquid and solid waste and uses a variety of products that have an impact on the environment. The wastewater from medical facilities can contain antibiotics and mutagenic substances that can cause harm to the environment (and thus, to people) if not properly eliminated. Systems such as bioreactor membranes and dry macrophyte plant basins can help treat the water to protect the public from the dangers of certain health care substances.

There are "thirsty" activities in the health care environment such as laundry, autoclave use, and hemodialysis. Just as in the home, basic gestures such as avoiding running half-loaded washing machines and dishwashers can also apply in the workplace. The USP Hospital La Colina in Spain, for example, uses the hemodialysis water rejected by osmosis to flush toilets; at the Sarrus Teinturiers Clinic in France, the autoclaves operate in a closed loop (C2DS, 2012). An ophthalmologist by the name of Dr. Zaluski at the Saint-Roch Clinic in France calculated the CO_2 emissions from performing one cataract operation—an operation that involves a two-centimeter-long organ. It takes an astonishing 3,903 tons of CO_2 equivalent—equal to emissions from circling a plane around the Earth 400 times (C2DS, 2012). These various examples show that the production of waste in the health care industry has some very ironic implications for our own health.

Needless to say, there are many career opportunities for logistics and purchasing personnel who can master the challenges of rendering the health care supply chain sustainable.[2]

Health care careers involving the user

Focusing on the patient may seem obvious for health care professionals, but the patient's needs are evolving with aging populations, eco-conscious users, and preferences for holistic medicine and healing. Patients can now choose, in many locations, their hospital preference in accordance with sustainability criteria, but they too need to know what these criteria are. For example, consider the ranking of green hospitals in the U.S. according to 12 criteria: siting, water efficiency, energy and air pollution, materials and resources, indoor environmental quality, healthy hospital food, green education, procurement, contaminants, green cleaning, waste reduction, and healing garden (Rabin, 2006). Information like this, if available to patients, can enable them to make health care decisions that further protect their health and that of society at large.

According to Ingrid, "the bottom line is this: a doctor feels good about their job when their patient heals." That value corresponds to thinking about the user—how will the user, or patient in this case, respond to the treatment? How can we best support the patient's post-treatment? How often should the patient receive check-ups and evaluations? However, as Ingrid pointed out, there is much room for improvement in medicine for thinking about the *quality* of the user's life after treatment: "If this person is saved (or extended life years), what kind of life will this person have? At what cost? Is this the wish of the person?"

Doctors and health care practitioners trying to address sustainable development are starting to have a dialogue about these questions. For those in the profession, it is useful to think about how one's role helps achieve sustainability by focusing on the end user.[3]

Health care careers involving relations

The patient or end user is one part of an entire ecosystem of stakeholders in the health care sector. Co-workers, employees, employers, parents, children, community organizers, and all of the professionals involved in the health care supply chain are critical for furthering sustainability.

The Hippocratic Oath is often compromised in health care settings that overuse chemicals to clean, sanitize, and disinfect. Biocides, when rejected into the effluent of the hospital, have a detrimental effect on the atmosphere and air quality and can reinforce the resistance of future bacteria (C2DS, 2012). Health care professionals should not have to put themselves at risk for respiratory illness because of intense formalin cleaning. Health sector workers have the highest rate of adult asthma among all major occupational groups and are at greater risk of developing chronic respiratory illnesses (HCWH, 2013). It is possible to use steam cleaning, microfiber mopping cloths, and limited odoriferous disinfectants for only patient rooms with infectious diseases. At the Fletcher Allen Hospital in the U.S., environmental managers equipped the hospital with microfiber mopping cloths to adequately eliminate nosocomial infections. According to the managers, the microfibers

> absorb the entire contents of a bucket of water at once and reduce the use of disinfectants and water consumption; the microfiber mopping cloths have also helped to decrease use of disinfectants by 33%, representing savings of $21,000 on the purchase of a single product.
>
> (C2DS, 2012)

Included in the relations pillar of the SURF Framework is the relationship between a person and the road. Cars, vans, and trucks play a critical role in transporting health care materials and people in need. Boats, trains, and airplanes also play a role, but here we focus on driving. The social, intergenerational, economic, and environmental implications of driving include accidents and fatal injuries, air pollution, pollution associated with automobile manufacturing, and the economic consequences of the aforementioned. For caregivers who go to individual homes, equipment delivery personnel, and the hospital or clinic shuttle, eco-driving, including choosing electric vehicles, is an important part of helping to transform practices.

Health care careers involving the future

Health systems are based on generational interdependency. Childcare and pediatrics, for example, are directly concerned with maintaining healthy young generations who will become the breadwinners and caregivers of tomorrow. Family health is also focused on providing adequate care to multiple generations. Childbirth, whether with the help of a childbirth assistant or obstetrician, has direct responsibility for ushering in new generations.

In Sweden, the most common painkiller to ease childbirth is nitrous oxide (N_2O). However, nitrous oxide has a climate change impact 265 times higher than carbon dioxide (Canadell et al., 2019). To ensure that childbirth was considerate of future generations both in terms of the quality of the care and quality of the climate in which the child would be born, a N_2O-reprocessing solution was implemented at the New Karolinska University Hospital. The nitrous oxide is isolated, split into tetroxide and dioxygen, and destroyed by electrolysis (90% is eliminated); energy is produced in the process that is then used to heat the building (C2DS, 2012).

Conclusion

The quadruple bottom line of sustainability is visibly present in careers in the health care sector. The questions within each component of the SURF Framework serve as guides for transforming current roles, responsibilities, job descriptions, and career paths to ones that are contributing to sustainable development. Without addressing social, environmental, economic, and equitable intergenerational considerations, career climbers may find it difficult to succeed. Those that do actively transform these aspects will likely stand out and be rewarded. Employers that wish to retain their best talent, especially those of Generation Y and after, would do well to ensure that their employees understand how their role helps sustainable development. A sustainability focus does not mean distraction from the real ability to perform a technical duty such as draw blood or perform a root canal; sustainability provides greater meaning to those jobs and helps the professional think about the wider implications of the tasks (e.g., materials used, waste created, and patient healing). Some professionals may even find specific jobs at some point in their career for leading sustainability transformation of a hospital or lab, bringing a sustainability prospective to a board, or keeping their part of the Hippocratic Oath, "Do No Harm."[4]

Some practical tips for professionals in the health sector include:

- Use pertinent frameworks and concepts:
    - Apply the SURF Framework to the establishment, to the job, and to the career trajectory.
    - Apply the 4P framework of prevention, prediction, personalization, and participation.

- Use reference guides, such as:

  - Ethical Trading Initiative
  - Fair Medical Trade by the British Medical Association
  - Green Guide to Health Care
  - Global Green and Healthy Hospitals Agenda
  - Practice Greenhealth's Sustainability Procurement in Health Care Guide
  - Sustainability Roadmap for Hospitals.

- Eliminate toxic substances, using resources such as:

  - HCWH's Guide to Choosing Safer Products and Chemicals
  - Environmental Working Group's databases (including Skin Deep for cosmetics and the Tap Water database)
  - Registration, Evaluation, and Authorization of Chemicals: REACH
  - Sustainable Chemistry Hierarchy (USEPA).

- Refer to existing best practices, such as:

  - GREEN and CLEAN hospitals program in Thailand
  - PROPER in Indonesia
  - WHO's Health in the Green Economy Initiative
  - Greenhealth NGO
  - Health Care Without Harm
  - Health and Environment Alliance (HEAL).

- Join professional networks that address sustainable health care:

  - Global Green and Healthy Hospitals network
  - Practice Greenhealth/Teleosis Institute
  - Care2 Social Network
  - Physicians for Social Responsibility
  - Healthy Building Network.

- Adopt sustainable health care pledges:

  - Charter for Environmentally Sustainable Self-Care
  - CEO Action for Diversity & Inclusion™
  - Equity of Care Pledge
  - Health Care Climate Challenge.

Notes

1 The Green Guide criteria includes water efficiency, air pollution reduction (chlorofluorocarbon reduction, ozone reduction, etc.), sustainable materials and resources, indoor environmental quality (low-VOC paints and adhesives, enhancing day lighting, etc.), providing healthy hospital food (pathology sensitive, local, organic, etc.), staff training in waste reduction, environmental, and social responsibility focused procurement, toxic contamination reduction (mercury and PVC in

IV drip bags and tubing, etc.), using non-hazardous cleaning products, composting, and reducing, reusing, and recycling waste (using air dryers instead of paper towels, cloth diapers, reusable water pitchers, bed pans, and linens, reusable medical instruments, washable gowns, graduated measuring containers, and food utensils and silverware) (Rabin, 2006).

2 Here are sample sustainability-related questions for the health care supply chain:

- Are the physical infrastructure and materials within healthy?
- If the possibility of new construction is present, have full life-cycle costs and criteria in line with the four pillars of sustainable development been considered?
- Have eco-construction labels been awarded (LEED, BREAM, ISO 14001, HQE, etc.)?
- Have any specific health care sustainability certifications been awarded (such as Gütesiegel in Germany, administered by the BUND association for best hospital energy performance)? Are systems in your location designed to award health care sustainability certifications?
- Is there a certification procedure to validate sustainability initiatives?
- Is there a policy to avoid toxic material use?
- Have PVC and phthalates been eliminated from medical equipment (tubes for infusion, transfusion and enteral nutrition, hospital gloves)?
- Does the building and large-scale infrastructure in which you conduct health care activities comply with sound environmental and health criteria (materials)?
- Do the cleaning products used contain harmful toxins?
- Are plant-based products given priority (the choice of building materials and equipment will influence the choice of cleaning products)?
- How is energy efficiency managed? Is there a plan to reduce operational costs by implementing energy efficiency measures?
- What are the energy metrics used in the building or for equipment? What is the energy consumption in kWh/m2/year of the building?
- Has an energy audit been completed?
- Is there a system for recycling and reusing water/wastewater? Is there a system for collecting and using rainwater?
- What measures have been taken to save energy (such as low-consumption lighting, ventilation regulators, sensors, shut-down timers on televisions and computers, etc.)?
- How is low-carbon energy incorporated?
- How are people encouraged to save energy and water?
- Have plants been purchased and planted to create a green roof on the building?
- Have you made the shift to digital radiology to decrease the use of chemicals?
- Is the food provided to patients healthy and specific to their pathology?
- Is the food provided to patients organic, fair-trade, local?
- Is there full cost accounting used in purchasing decisions?
- Is the transportation system healthy?
- Does the local public transportation have stops at the health care facility (clinics, hospitals, pharmacies, etc.)?
- Is the total supply chain as "short" as possible to reduce greenhouse gas emissions?
- Patients share rooms—why not transportation? Are there car-sharing programs?
- Is there a carpooling policy for staff?
- How do medical vehicles rate in terms of fuel efficiency, electric vehicles (and charging stations), hybrid vehicles, etc.?
- Do personnel use eco-driving principles for transportation?
- Has a cycling system been put into place (and thus necessary sanitation and shower facilities on site)?

3 Here are sample sustainability-related questions for the health care end user, or patient:

- Is the health care environment healthy for the end user?
- What measures are taken to improve indoor air quality?
- Does the hospital have healing gardens where patients, staff, and visitors can reflect, relieve stress, and reconnect with nature?
- Are there green roofs?
- When plants are used (e.g., green roofs), have allergenic properties and water requirements been taken into account?
- Does the landscaping use native plants, which reduce water consumption and the use of pesticides?
- Is natural light guaranteed for the user (examples: outpatient room, hospital room)?
- How will the patients and other stakeholders react to the colors in the building?
- How are the acoustics in the workplace (do the acoustics protect confidentiality)?
- Is the facility designed to optimize the flow of patient movement?
- Is entertainment provided to patients? As stated by Nuria Vidal, a technician at Palamos Hospital in Spain, "patients often fall asleep in front of the television" (C2DS, 2012). Are televisions automated to save energy?
- Are you actually doing harm to the patient through administering care?
- Do you keep track of the toxicity of the substances used? Is there a detailed inventory of call products used in terms of toxicity?
- Is there a program to substitute toxic or dangerous products?
- What indicators are used to measure the environmental health of the facility?
- What is done for waste reduction, waste recovery, communication, and awareness building of waste sorting and processing, solid and liquid waste identification based on danger/risk to people and the environment?
- Do you prescribe exercise and cultural events as part of treatment?
- Do you reduce use of antibiotics as much as possible?

4 The Hippocratic Oath originates from Greek medical texts. It requires a new physician to swear upon a number of healing gods that he/she will abide by professional ethical standards. It has been rewritten and adapted to many cultures and serves as a common ground for many in the medical and health professions.

References

Bettencourt, E. (2021). Hospital CEOs Signing Action Pledge for Diversity and Inclusion. DiversityNursing.com. https://blog.diversitynursing.com/blog/hospital-ceos-signing-action-pledge-for-diversity-and-inclusion.

Canadell, P., Tian, H., Patra, P., & Thompson, R.Nitrogen fertilisers are incredibly efficient, but they make climate change a lot worse. The Conversation. (2019). https://theconversation.com/nitrogen-fertilisers-are-incredibly-efficient-but-they-make-climate-change-a-lot-worse-127103.

Casale, J., & Rice, A. R. (2023). Phthalates Toxicity. *StatPearls* [Internet]. www.ncbi.nlm.nih.gov/books/NBK587442.

C2DS. (2012). *Guide des practiques vertueses* [Guide to virtuous practices]. www.c2ds.eu/guide-des-pratiques-vertueuses-2012.

Eckerman, I. (2013). About Me. http://eckerman.nu.

Global Green and Healthy Hospitals (GGHH). (2023). Acting together for environmental health. https://greenhospitals.org.

HCWH, (2019), Why Asian Hospitals Need to Shrink Their Carbon Footprint. Health Care Without Harm. https://noharm-global.org/articles/news/asia/news-why-asian-hospitals-need-shrink-their-carbon-footprint.

HCWH. (2013). Global Green and Healthy Hospitals Agenda: A Comprehensive Environmental Health Agenda for Hospitals and Health Systems Around the World. Health Care Without Harm. https://noharm-europe.org/documents/global-green-and-healthy-hospitals-agenda-english.

Helsinki Commission. (2004). Dioxins in the Baltic Sea. https://helcom.fi/wp-content/uploads/2019/08/Dioxins-in-the-Baltic-Sea.pdf.

Meyerfeld, B. (2023). Brazil's racial quotas have given rise to a new generation of Black graduates. Le Monde. www.lemonde.fr/en/international/article/2023/08/15/brazil-s-racial-quotas-have-given-rise-to-a-new-generation-of-black-graduates_6094394_4.html.

Pharmaceutical Technology. (2023). The rise and rise of ESG in the pharmaceutical sector—is a zero-waste supply chain possible?www.pharmaceutical-technology.com/sponsored/the-rise-and-rise-of-esg-in-the-pharmaceutical-sector-is-a-zero-waste-supply-chain-possible.

Quinna, M. M., Fullerb, T. P., Belloa, A., & Galligana, C. J. (2006). Pollution prevention—Occupational safety and health in hospitals: Alternatives and interventions. *Journal of Occupational and Environmental Hygiene* 3(4), 182–193.

Rabin, E. (2006). America's Top 10 Green Hospitals. GreenBiz. www.greenbiz.com/article/americas-top-10-green-hospitals.

Shanks, D. (2009). *Ecological Sustainable Healthcare at the Hospital of the University of Pennsylvania*. Master's Thesis, Drexel University, School of Public Health. https://doi.org/10.17918/etd-3088.

Swedish National Food Agency. (2023). Dioxins and PCBs in Swedish food. www.livsmedelsverket.se/en/food-and-content/oonskade-amnen/miljogifter/dioxiner-och-pcb.

U.S. National Library of Medicine. (2010). Bisphenol A. Tox Town. www.nlm.nih.gov/pubs/techbull/ma10/ma10_sis_reprint_bisphenol.html.

Visit Sweden. (2023). The Right of Public Access. https://visitsweden.com/what-to-do/nature-outdoors/nature/sustainable-and-rural-tourism/the-right-of-public-access.

5

PURSUING SUSTAINABILITY IN LAW AND POLICY

Incorporating sustainability into one's law or policy career is increasingly necessary and continually fulfilling.

Introduction

The legal- and policy-oriented career trajectories are engrained in nearly every sector. In-house lawyers can be found in large corporations, no matter what product or service the company sells. The complexity of the legal system at the local, national, and international levels leaves much to be interpreted—by policy analysts and legal practitioners. Even in jurisdictions where contracts matter much less than relationships, there are career opportunities for people who understand the existing written and unwritten laws, and who influence the making of future laws. But how does sustainable development translate into actual legal prose? How do lawmakers and policy officials use, in their everyday professional work, the concepts of a flourishing society, a healthy environment, and a vibrant economy that safeguards future generations?

This chapter highlights the stories of people driving legal change in Nigeria, policy change at the state level in the U.S., and policy change at the regional level in Europe. Some are trained as legal professionals, others as economists. The reoccurring theme is the same—incorporating sustainability into one's law or policy career is increasingly necessary and continually fulfilling.

The policy arena

The role of government in the green economy includes leveling the playing field for more sustainable products. This involves eliminating old subsidies, creating new incentives, strengthening market-based mechanisms, and ensuring that

DOI: 10.4324/9781032615844-5

public investment and public procurement favors more sustainable products and services (UNEP, 2011). Many governments have internalized a sustainability outlook through procurement norms. Malaysia, Brazil, India, the Philippines, Nigeria, Thailand, South Africa, Singapore, Costa Rica, and Indonesia are but a few examples of countries that have issued mandatory corporate sustainability standards by public authorities or stock exchanges, mostly based on a company's impact on people and the planet; Nigeria's Stock Exchange, for instance, published its Sustainability Disclosure Guidelines in 2018 and explicitly recommends companies use the Global Reporting Initiative (GRI) standards (Frank Bold, 2023).

From the 1980s until recently, more capital was dedicated to property, fossil fuel, and structured financial assets than investment in renewable energy, energy efficiency, public transportation, sustainable agriculture, ecosystem and biodiversity protection, and land and water conservation (UNEP, 2011). In 2022, fossil fuel subsidies reached US$7 trillion (Black et al., 2023) while global investment in climate solutions was a mere US$1 trillion (Bocca & Ellerbeck, 2023). The United Nations Environment Programme (UNEP) outlines the following enabling conditions for national governments and policy makers: establishing sound regulatory frameworks; prioritizing government investment and spending in areas that stimulate the greening of economic sectors; limiting spending in areas that deplete natural capital; employing taxes and market-based instruments to shift consumer preference and promote green investment and innovation; investing in capacity building and training; and strengthening international governance (UNEP, 2011).

One step that governments can take to drive corporate sustainability accountability is to establish a unit similar to the Canadian Ombudsperson for Responsible Enterprise (CORE). This position was created to hold Canadian firms accountable for misconduct in overseas operations; the ombudsperson is tasked with reviewing human rights issues, making recommendations, including trade measures, and publicly disclosing key elements of the process (Sandhu, 2022). While CORE has been criticized for not having the independence, investigative powers, and power to issue the full range of needed remedies, if these elements were remedied, CORE could be a policy and legal model for reducing corporate action that seeks to take advantage of economies with less capacity to enforce sustainability standards.

The legal field

When thinking about the legal field and sustainable development, the work of environmental lawyers immediately comes to mind. Environmental law encompasses the variety of laws and statutes that pertain to the natural environment and ecosystem. Lawyers in this field often have backgrounds in environmental science and other environmental studies, and represent a diverse array of clients including corporations, governments, individual citizens, and non-governmental organizations. But there are other categories of law that directly pertain to sustainable development, including human rights law and commercial law. One of the most publicized cases of environmental justice is *Erin Brockovich, Anderson et al v. Pacific Gas & Electric Company*. Erin Brockovich, with formal education in applied arts, taught herself enough law to lead and win a lawsuit against a company accused of contaminating the drinking water in California. One of the most notable cases in the U.S. Supreme Court recent case history is *Massachusetts v. Environmental Protection Agency (EPA)*, where the Court held that the U.S. Clean Air Act gives the EPA the authority to regulate greenhouse gas emissions. This case spurred many initiatives with the legal weight required to induce change. In 2023, a court in the U.S. state of Montana recognized that the constitutional right to a clean and healthy environment includes the right to a safe climate; in the landmark youth-led case of *Held v. Montana*, the judge Kathy Seeley noted, "Because of their unique vulnerabilities, their stages of development as youth, and their average longevity on the planet in the future, plaintiffs [16 young people] face lifelong hardships resulting from climate change" (Clark, 2023).

Any social, economic, environmental, and future-oriented issue that impacts business in a contractual and legal way can potentially be a sustainability concern. This includes real estate, infrastructure, energy, water, waste management, corporate governance, employment, greenwashing, intellectual property (green trademark and intellectual property), and supply chain issues. Lawyers need to understand the meaning and legal implications of sustainability in order to best advise their clients. In addition, corporations, the clients of many legal institutions, increasingly want to know what their law firms are doing for sustainability. Requests for proposals are now including pro-bono, diversity, and sustainability components (Tripoli, 2012). Some law firms, such as Boston-based Nixon Peabody, have hired their own in-house chief sustainability officers (CSOs). Therefore, there are sustainability initiatives within the firms in the legal field, and there are legal initiatives within firms in the sustainability fields.

According to French in *International Law and Policy of Sustainable Development*, the role of law is to provide the mechanisms for the elaboration of the sustainable development objective (French, 2005). There have been numerous environmental, social, and economic laws written at the local level throughout history. Sustainable development calls for the *integration* of these rules and regulations. There are a number of norms, from "soft law" instruments such as international declarations to strict embedded laws and policies, which integrate economic, social, and environmental criteria. The 2002 New Delhi Declaration on the Principles of International Law Related to Sustainable Development identified seven principles as follows:

1. The duty of States to ensure sustainable use of natural resources,
2. The principle of equity and the eradication of poverty,
3. The principle of common but differentiated responsibilities,

4. The principle of the precautionary approach to human health, natural resources and ecosystems,
5. The principle of public participation and access to information and justice,
6. The principle of good governance, and
7. The principle of integration and interrelationship, in particular in relation to human rights and social, economic, and environmental objectives (refers to both inter-generational equity and intra-generational equity).

(Cordonier Segger & Khalfan, 2004)

International sustainability laws have roots in a number of treaties and conventions. The 1946 International Convention for the Regulation of Whaling, the 1958 Convention on Fishing and Conservation of the Living Resources on the High Seas, and the 1982 UN Convention on the Law of the Sea, for example, all call for exploitive marine operations to be done in a sustainable manner (French, 2005). Today, there are more than ten international texts that use sustainable development with the meaning it has in this book. Chief justices and senior judges from over 60 countries adopted the 2002 Johannesburg Principles on the Role of Law and Sustainable Development at the 2002 Global Judges Symposium in South Africa (Cordonier Segger , 2010). The legal professionals agreed on the following four principles in their resolution:

1. A full commitment to contributing towards the realization of the goals of sustainable development through the judicial mandate to implement, develop and enforce the law, and to uphold the Rule of Law and the democratic process,
2. To realise the goals of the Millenium Declaration of the United Nations General Assembly which depend upon the implementation of national and international legal regimes that have been established for achieving the goals of sustainable development,
3. In the field of environmental law there is an urgent need for a concerted and sustained programme of work focused on education, training and dissemination of information, including regional and sub-regional judicial colloquia, and
4. That collaboration among members of the Judiciary and others engaged in the judicial process within and across regions is essential to achieve a significant improvement in compliance with, implementation, development and enforcement of environmental law.

(UNEP, 2002)

As Thomas Bourne, a member of Bond Pearce LLP's sustainable law steering group noted:

> Lawyers that do not put sustainability in a box marked "someone else's problem," but understand how it connects with the bigger picture, have a

genuine opportunity to help unlock sustainable business opportunities for organisations with an ambition to lead change.

(Bourne, 2012)

Those with legal training need sustainability training to be effective in today's legal environment. The worldwide trend is for more sustainability in every aspect of the law. More sustainability reporting for corporations. More pressure to comply with societal, environmental, and beyond-bottom-line economics. Lawyers may find opportunities working for rating bodies and governmental entities such as the Securities and Exchange Commission in the U.S., which are increasingly requiring disclosure in sustainability themes (Tripoli, 2012).

Small is beautiful: pursuing sustainability wins in the backdrop of an oil extractive economy—Peace Nsoko-Nkwor's story

"I hate to think I would need to relocate to the Global North to have a global voice in sustainability. Why can't I have influence from Lagos?" Peace Nsoko-Nkwor asked rhetorically as she took our call on the way to work in Nigeria's most populous city.

Peace makes an excellent point as Nigeria is Africa's largest economy by gross domestic product, boasting a population of 225 million people. Part of Nigeria's wealth emanates from oil and gas resources, and the nation consistently ranks as one of the top-ten oil-exporting countries. Nigeria's black gold is the source of Peace's sustainability story, for she is from the Niger Delta region—the hub of the economy's extractive oil industry.

"Hailing from Delta State, I realized that there was nothing cute about oil. The oil pollution affected the health, well-being, and means of livelihood of many people. I recognized this as an injustice," Peace explained.

Peace obtained her first degree in law from Benson Idahosa University in Benin City. She credits her choice of study to both nature and nurture. She was a highly inquisitive kid, needing to be convinced of the "why" before believing. Peace was able to witness first-hand the legal field as a viable career path since her father was a lawyer. She worked in litigation after graduating with her Bachelor of Law degree but very soon became bored with litigation. In addition, she felt the need to use her skills to address environmental and social injustice. Peace flew across the pond to another hub for oil and gas and attended the University of Houston in the U.S. There, she pursued a Master of Law in energy, environment, and natural resources.

After finishing her master's degree, Peace returned to Nigeria and started to work for her family's law firm, Nkem Law Firm. Most of the legal cases in the law firm were focused on property contracts and commercial issues. There was nothing explicitly environmental or sustainability-focused about the law firm until Peace expanded the practice to include sustainability, ESG, and environmental justice.

Initially, Peace was a bit skeptical about working for the family business as she did not want to be perceived as favored. Ultimately, she realized the law firm provided a nurturing environment for her to expand possibilities. While working at Nkem Law Firm, she pursued certifications in corporate governance and was recruited as a compliance officer for a pharmaceutical company.

Eventually, Peace returned to the family-owned law firm determined to incorporate sustainability knowledge and help slowly build up a practice that would also serve the sustainability-related needs of corporate clients. Her most memorable experience applying the "R" element of the SURF Framework—that is, understanding and managing stakeholder relationships—emerged in a property case. A client sought to purchase land to store shipping containers, given the lack of available space at the seaports in Lagos. However, the community living near the land protested such an acquisition and use case, citing the risk of increased traffic and congestion. While some at the law firm wanted to bypass community input and apply the legal codes strictly, insisting that their client had a legal permit, Peace put on her stakeholder engagement hat and decided to consult with the community. "It turned out that the community just wanted the basics: employment, help maintaining the roads, and access to clean water. All these things are less costly than hiring security to deal with a potentially hostile surrounding," Peace expressed. The buyer, Peace's client, was able to meet the needs of the community while achieving their commercial goal. Peace ensured that this project adopted a just transition pathway by ensuring access to decent job opportunities and by fostering inclusion for community members.

Peace believes examples like this illustrate how one does not need to bend over backwards to find a role with sustainability keywords, but rather can apply sustainability frameworks to achieve better outcomes for whatever the task at hand requires. She wants to see voices like hers in the Global South, otherwise known as the Global Majority, elevated when it comes to driving sustainable development. It is indeed professionals working in these economies that are reflective of the masses and have the lived experience and solutions most pertinent for the masses. Peace is now an Associate Partner at Nkem Law Firm and serves as a sustainability consultant in addition to performing her legal duties.

"Sustainability is a beautiful space," Peace stated. She wants others who are interested in pursuing sustainability in their careers to know that doing so can be very rewarding and gratifying. She explained, "It is important for people to not put themselves down if they are not radically changing the world overnight." In thinking about the practicing professional, Peace concluded, "Do not think the small wins for people and planet are not a big deal—they are a big deal. One does not have to build a solar plant to be engaged in sustainability."

From shipbuilding and oil and gas barrister to environmental activist lawyer—Elspeth Owens' story

In the heart of Hackney, London's iconic eastern district, one finds 274 Richmond Road. Only when I walked in front of the address, a series of tin barriers, arrows, and otherwise modern artistic designs pointed me to an entrance around a footpath. Finally, I arrived at The Hothouse, a shared office space built on a formerly polluted site near the London Fields park. As I entered the offices of ClientEarth, I was directed towards the kitchen corner where I could find a full supply of fairtrade and organic coffee and tea. As I waited for my interviewee, I indulged in reading environmental magazines that were freely available on the table—including ClientEarth's own publication, *People Law Planet*.

ClientEarth is an environmental law organization with offices in London, Brussels, and Warsaw. Made up of activist lawyers, ClientEarth tackles various sustainability issues such as conservation, deforestation, toxic chemicals, and climate change. The main topical areas include oceans, energy, forests, health, and environmental justice. The legal advice provided includes how new legislation should be written, how new laws should be implemented, and how laws should be enforced.

Elspeth studied law at the University of Oxford and then qualified as a barrister in London. There are two main paths in the legal profession in the United Kingdom—becoming a solicitor and becoming a barrister. Solicitors work in law firms and can either work on non-contentious or contentious cases. In the latter case, the solicitors are sometimes referred to as litigators. Barristers, by contrast, are only litigators and can defend or present cases in court. They are often self-employed and work in "chambers." As I listened to Elspeth explain the British legal system, I couldn't help but wonder how on earth one would begin to incorporate sustainability in what sounded like a stringent "old boys club" of a structure. "After studying law," Elspeth explained, "a solicitor will go to law school and a barrister will go to bar school." During her law degree program, Elspeth interned in a firm that focused on debt and equity markets, and she found the subject impenetrable; nevertheless, she also liked the idea of standing up on her feet in a court. So she decided to go for the barrister route. One has to secure a pupilage to become a barrister, and every barrister must join one of four Inns of Court: Middle Temple, Inner Temple, Gray's Inn, or Lincoln's Inn. "It goes back to Medieval times and is very old-fashioned." Elspeth read my mind. Dinner 12 times a year at the Temple can be a part of one's duties. Elspeth was accepted into Middle Temple and she joined the Chambers of 4 Pump Court, named after the address of the building.

Elspeth spent six years working as a barrister. She started by working on small claim disputes for automobile insurance companies, as well as for a local council dealing with problematic housing cases. "So you began your career defending insurance companies and evicting people?" I asked sarcastically. We both laughed. Elspeth then progressed to work on bigger commercial cases, first in shipping and then in oil and gas. Shipping is a multi-trillion-dollar industry, and there are all sorts of disputes. Ships turn up late. Ships break down. Eventually, Elspeth became known as an expert on legal shipping and oilrig matters. "Commercial cases are full of adrenaline, and I enjoyed it; when you win a big case, you are thrilled that you have satisfied your client," Elspeth explained. "But then I took a step back. Is this something that I want to do for the rest of my life?" Elspeth asked herself. She was torn between wanting to be a great barrister and not seeing the professional lifestyle as sustainable (long hours, little work and life balance, and not always able to work for the "good guys").

In a panicky moment of job searching, Elspeth stumbled on ClientEarth. Before then, it had never occurred to her that she could combine her legal and environmental passions. A keen diver, Elspeth is at ease in nature. She grew up in North Wales—the countryside—surrounded by mountains, ponds, and wild flowers. Elspeth was an example of someone who did much for sustainability in her private life but did not manage to apply sustainability values to her profession. But that all changed. Elspeth took the risk and resigned from 4 Pump Court without any solid job prospects. She applied for a job at ClientEarth in the biodiversity team a year before leaving her barrister job, but she was not accepted. A year later, once she quit, she applied again as an intern. Within one week of interning, a job opened up in the climate and energy team at ClientEarth. This time, Elspeth was selected.

Elspeth's story is particularly compelling because she did not start off a career incorporating environmental and social principles. But she found a position that allowed her to do just that while still thriving in a career in the field of law. She did not have to abandon her sound legal acumen and experience of winning cases on behalf of clients. She just put the skills to use for environmental justice issues. Elspeth had spent the last year setting up a new litigation program for ClientEarth. The new team of 12 lawyers makes innovative legal interventions designed to reduce carbon emissions and to support the transition to a low-carbon world. In recruiting the new team Elspeth looked for lawyers who were passionate about environmental and social issues, but not necessarily experienced in an environmental area. Lawyers are mainly trained to structure their thinking from a client perspective. But what if the client has not been identified? At ClientEarth, the lawyer must be able to start with an objective, and then build the case and find the clients.

When asked what she values most in her work, Elspeth's response included working towards an objective that she really believes in, accelerating a transition to a low-carbon economy, and being inspired each day. In Elspeth's case, incorporating sustainability into her career path translated to a pay cut (non-profit salaries in the U.K. are generally lower than for-profit salaries). But this trade-off doesn't have to occur if salary ranks higher on what one values in work. Elspeth gave numerous examples of paths in the legal profession that involve private sector pay and sustainability knowledge. In the barrister world, there are chambers specialized in human rights and environmental issues.

Structurally, however, there are some barriers in the English system. There is what is known as the cab rank rule where a barrister has to take on the first client that comes into the door; one cannot pick and choose the client. "Companies normally contact lawyers when something has gone wrong, so it's easy to find yourself on the 'wrong' side as a lawyer," Elspeth admitted. It seems that if the barrister system in the U.K. does not reform, it may well lose out on the amazing talent of younger generations and those who wish to maintain their sustainability values in their professional life.

In the solicitor world, there are in-house counsel roles for many companies working in clean technologies or that otherwise drive a sustainability mission of their product or service. There are also niche law firms or large law firms that have niche departments where one can work on public interest cases or environmental cases. In addition, those with legal training can also work for government departments such as the European Union Commission. The offices at ClientEarth illustrate that the organization practices what it preaches. Recycling bins. Plants on almost every desk. Open space to encourage interaction. Even the trophies like "Business Green Leaders Awards' NGO of the Year" indicate that the place means business. When I complimented Elspeth on the office space, she kindly replied, "It's the perfect setting. We look out of the window at our clients." Outside of the windows, there is a children's playground.

Environmental policy work in the European Union—Dr. Camilla Bausch's story

Dr. Camilla Bausch grew up in the 1980s in Berlin during the time of the "going green" political movement. The Green Party in Germany was established in 1980. The Chernobyl accident happened in 1986, triggering the establishment of the German Ministry of the Environment in the same year. The Berlin Wall fell in 1989.

Camilla founded her first environmental organization at the age of seven: she and her best friend started to pick up trash in the neighborhood and wrote letters to their neighbors encouraging them to not pollute. Needless to say, Camilla cared about the environment and human rights from an early age. She followed the traditional German educational system and studied law in Berlin and Cologne. She then pursued a PhD—writing a comparative study on electricity grid access rules in Europe.

During that time and quite unexpectedly, the Boston Consulting Group (BCG) offered her a job and she went to work for them for a few years. "I never thought I would work for a management consulting firm," Camilla admitted, "but I did learn a lot." While at BCG, she did not attempt to revolutionize the consulting world, but she did start to think about how she could steer her career more towards the environment.

A friend of hers had told her about the work of the environmental policy think tank Ecologic Institute, so Camilla sent an open inquiry to the Ecologic

Institute to explore opportunities. She later joined as a fellow, quickly became a senior fellow, then head of the energy and climate unit, and then senior manager. "I consider the environment as a basis for who we are and how we live," Camilla explained.

Camilla went to work in the U.S. Congress for a yearlong fellowship from 2008 to 2009. There, she helped draft the Waxman-Markey cap and trade bill in the House of Representatives and organized hearings for the Select Committee on Energy Independence and Global Warming.

Her daily tasks at the various stages of her career at the Ecologic Institute involved research, policy analysis, drafting legal text at the national, European, and international levels, teaching, and management.

Camilla attributes her success to being passionate about her work, creating alliances with others, having an inner drive, and working diligently on projects. "The environment is a crosscutting issue in any country, as it impacts health, security and the economy," Camilla emphasized. "Environmental protection has to be achieved by policy makers' determination as well as public engagement of different actors—at the sub-national, national, and international levels."

She became the director of the Ecologic Institute in 2015.

Moving beyond GDP to the GPI—Sean McGuire's story

"No one said, 'Here do this.' I had to make my own path," Sean McGuire said just before we agreed to speak again when we were both at least on the same continent. Sean is a pioneer in implementing the Genuine Progress Indicator (GPI) at the state level in the United States. Although he grew up in Southern California, he went to the East Coast to study environmental policy. But after about a year, Sean got frustrated. There was a mismatch between the academic theory and the skills needed to drive change in a policy environment. Sean was able to land a job with the State of Maryland in 1998, where he experienced on the ground the challenges of environmental work. He worked on Chesapeake Bay restoration efforts, which involved multiple states and multiple stakeholders. "I was able to delve into a variety of subjects, such as agriculture, forestry, and nutrient pollution," Sean described.

While working, Sean returned to university for a Master of Public Policy with a focus on environmental policy and ecological economics. But it wasn't the classical economics literature that inspired Sean to pursue a career path in policy metrics for sustainability. It was the work of many of his professors, including Herman Daly. Daly, along with Cobb, created the GPI's precursor, the Index of Sustainable Economic Welfare (ISEW). This index adjusts gross domestic product (GDP) to illustrate a broader set of social and environmental criteria. Sean was in the right place at the right time and was able to receive cutting-edge research data and analysis in ecological economics.

What sparked Sean's interest in the environment in the first place? "My mom was both an avid outdoorswoman and a realtor. So she instilled in me that there was no 'either/or' when it comes to the economy and the environment. You can make money without ravaging our natural resources," Sean reflected on his upbringing.

In his 15-year career in the State of Maryland, Sean led numerous projects, from Chesapeake Bay restoration to green buildings. Maryland was one of the first states to make buildings with a certain square footage owned or leased by the state government to have LEED certification. In 2006, with the election of a new governor, Sean went to the department's secretary to ask if they could create a new Sustainability Office. "Frighteningly, the secretary said yes," Sean remembered.

In the newly formed office, Sean focused on the green economy and alternative metrics, with the GPI being a major focus. Officially calculated and released in 2010, Sean led the GPI initiative and was able to implement the GPI metric in a concrete manner for the state government. During this time, he worked with other states to help implementation.

When I asked Sean about the metrics that governments currently use to measure progress, he told me that there are three words that dominate current policy: jobs, jobs, and jobs. "Behind the scenes, GDP is still pulling the strings, and its importance is inflated." Sean asserted:

> GDP is still useful; for example, it has shown that the United States is moving to a service-based economy; however, the challenge with GDP is that it is like having only one dial in your car. Sure, you may know the speed, but you also need to know the level of charge in the battery. GPI complements GDP by placing a value on the things that were not calculated before. For example, we need to know more about the quality of jobs being created (some people work two and three jobs and still cannot make ends meet), the level of pollution in a community, and whether local businesses are losing ground.

Sean's day-to-day work is quite varied. He works with the budget office on spreadsheets in order to calculate the GPI. He compares notes with other states and works on messaging for communication and outreach. He also interprets the GPI data for helping to make policy decisions, most recently in education and transportation. For Sean, sustainability is about recognizing that we have limits, and the key question is whether we can carry on an activity forever without an ecological or societal deficit. Early in his career, Sean was able to see a field on the horizon while working on green buildings. Sean stated that integrating sustainability into his career in policy definitely helped his career. He sees that sustainability is moving into the mainstream, so it will be here to stay and important for future generations thinking about career choices. "It is important to remember that most people are hired for a specific job," Sean explained. "And the systems thinking component of sustainability will be very relevant to any job. You can do 'your job,' but don't ignore everything else; sustainability thinking will give you one leg up in understanding the bigger picture since each job does not exist in complete isolation."

SURF Framework for careers in law and policy

The SURF Framework of *Supply Chain, User, Relations, and Future* is a practical framework within which lawyers, judges, politicians, mediators, consultants, policy makers, law clerks, legal writers, paralegal professionals, and more can lead a fruitful career with impact. SURF can be used to structure sustainable transformation in the legal and policy arenas and all of the careers that they encompass. The professional may ask: "How does my role help to bring about a sustainable supply chain? What are the consequences of my professional actions on the end user (clients, companies, individuals, etc.)? How does my work improve community or stakeholder relationships? How do my daily tasks guarantee the social, environmental, and economic viability of future generations?"

Law and policy careers involving supply chain

Policy and legal careers in the supply chain involve creating and interpreting laws about the policies that govern logistics, inventory, and transportation. As stringent regulations for the carbon, water, and ecological footprint of goods grow, professionals that understand the various relevant legal texts will have an important role to play in both proactive measures and compliance. The Poseidon Principles, for example, provide an agreement among the world's largest shipping financers to assess and disclose the climate alignment of ship finance portfolios; this is coherent with the International Maritime Organization's goal to reduce shipping's total annual GHG emissions by at least 50 percent by 2050 (Global Maritime Forum, 2020). Legal and policy advisors must also be knowledgeable on the environmental and social requirements throughout a supply chain in order to provide adequate advice. It is common for lawyers to look at a chain of contracts, and this often follows a particular supply chain. In drafting contracts, legal professionals can add clauses that require the contracting parties to adhere to sustainability measures. This is one way to manage reputational and operational risk for their clients.

Government procurement guidelines are increasingly requiring sustainability elements. This means that both suppliers to the government and government personnel overseeing purchasing must be sustainability savvy. Green procurement laws exist in many locations for printing toner, paper products, energy-efficient equipment, and more. Sustainability purchasing policies open up career opportunities for professionals in this domain. These career prospects include purchasers, contract managers, and law enforcers who are knowledgeable in sustainability criteria.

Government can also legislate and regulate compliance with sustainability criteria throughout corporate supply chains. In some ways, the upward trend of sustainability reporting being required by national governments and financial institutions illustrates that organizations must comply or face legal repercussions. Law firms are also increasingly implementing sustainability initiatives, in-house, to attract and retain clients. There are, therefore, opportunities for non-legal professionals to work in the legal environment by "greening" a law firm's supply chain and operations.

Law and policy career roles in supply chain include contract lawyers, policy makers, and legal advisers (in the shipping, maritime, and general transportation space), environmental, human rights, and corporate lawyers who deal with sustainability in the supply chain legal issues, and procurement professionals working for legal or governmental entities.

Law and policy careers involving the user

The user in the case of public policy is essentially everyone. Some policies may only pertain to certain people at a time (e.g., parking spaces for disabled people and tax breaks for families with children). But everyone must be aware of the laws and regulations in order to function and fully participate in a society. In many legal jurisdictions worldwide, ignorance of the law is not an excuse to not abide by the law. It is therefore important that each member of society be aware of the social, environmental, economic, and generational legal framework of the society. This is increasingly complex as people migrate to different jurisdictions for short and long periods of time. Due to climate change, migration is only increasing; there will be an expected 1.2 billion climate refugees by 2050 according to the Institute for Economics & Peace (IEP, 2020). One example of a public policy that directly affects the user is sustainable construction policy. Some governments have required that government-owned or -leased buildings become sustainability certified. A sustainable or green building provides numerous benefits to the user, including better health (e.g., not breathing in harmful chemicals) and increased productivity (natural lighting, comfortable temperature, etc.).

Activist lawyers—those who pursue an agenda with their cases—can play many roles on behalf of the "user." The work of activist lawyers has led to many triumphs for the end consumer. A few examples include, in some jurisdictions, company mandatory reporting on gender equity to help end discrimination and mandatory reporting on carbon emissions to help end climate change. Reducing plastic waste has been another victory of legal and policy officials. Bangladesh was the first country to ban single-use plastic bags, and most countries, including sub-national governments, have followed suit (UNEP, 2021). Plastic is no longer an option. In Germany, grocery store customers can literally leave all of their packaging inside of the store. Cereal boxes. Plastic covering for fruit and vegetables. You name it. By instituting laws that allow customers to leave their packaging "waste" in-store, German grocery stores are more motivated to not procure overly packaged goods. Purchasing packaged goods only increases the grocery store's waste disposal bill. Berlin's Unverpackt, which opened its doors in 2014, is Germany's first zero-waste, zero-packaging supermarket.

Law and policy career roles involving the user include social and environmental justice legal and policy professionals, contract lawyers involved in creating public–private partnerships, and any policy professional, whether elected, appointed, or hired as a bureaucrat, that works for their constituency.

Law and policy careers involving relations

It is rare that a legal case, contract, or transaction only impacts the two contracting or disputing parties. Even in the case of family law, such as a divorce, there can be other stakeholders involved (such as children, extended family, and a community). Nature does not understand boundaries, so trans-boundary environmental issues widen the stakeholders that policy makers and legal professionals must address. The Rights of Nature (RoN) doctrine, whereby nature itself is recognized as having inalienable rights and is entitled to legal personhood status so that nature can defend itself in courts, has gained traction. Ecuador is the first country to formally adopt RoN, and such rights exist in some form in over 39 countries (Putzer et al., 2022). Law and policy necessarily involve a large range of stakeholders; legal and policy professionals thus must be acutely aware of who their stakeholders are and how their job impacts those stakeholders.

Activist lawyers need what in legal jargon is known as "standing" to bring a case against another entity. This means that they cannot bring a case in their own name; the case must be brought to court by a person who is directly impacted by the problem. Therefore, activist lawyers must go out and engage a community to encourage them to stand up for their rights. There is therefore a great deal of community engagement in this part of legal work. Halfway House lawyers work with the neighbors of the correctional and transitional facility in order to understand concerns and deal with the concerns adequately. In 2021, China's Zhejiang Province launched a new era in China for public interest litigation. The courts held a company responsible for illegally using the ozone-depleting substance freon. The company was sentenced to pay over 600,000 RMB as compensation for ecological and climate damage (ClientEarth, 2021).

Law and policy career roles involving stakeholders include activist lawyers, public interest law firms, corporate lawyers that must understand the wider implications of a case in order to adequately represent their client, judges at all levels, and elected and unelected policy officials whose job description is to represent and act on behalf of their constituents.

Law and policy careers involving the future

In some ways, law and policy are all about future generations, as rarely do new regulations refer to something that must be changed in the past. Sustainability metrics such as the GPI provide a better lens for the future, and professionals who are knowledgeable in metrics such as this will have growing opportunities. Politicians often evoke the past, but it is almost always in order to portray their plan for the future. Common political slogans include "vote for tomorrow," "hope for tomorrow," "vote for the future now," "our children deserve better," and "building a brighter tomorrow." While politicians come and go, and political term limits and re-election cycles can drive short-term thinking, institutional knowledge and those who have a long-term career in law and policy can have a lasting impact on future generations. As Sean McGuire mentioned, "Elections are important as they tell us what is most important to the populace at a given moment; policy institutions allow us to explore non-traditional and more long-term options to create solutions for what will be best for future generations."

Policy and law have a critical role to play to ensure intergenerational equity and the well-being of future generations. One noteworthy development in the legal profession is the application of the Public Trust Doctrine to sustainable development. The doctrine states that certain resources, such as land, air, and water, are preserved for public use and that the government's duty is to maintain those resources for future generations. The term "trust" in this case is the idea that the government can hold the legal title on a resource—and the people trust the government to protect it. The government acts as a trustee and must determine how the resources should be used and who the beneficiaries are. Trust is a legal concept used worldwide. It has been used in a few cases in the U.S. regarding the atmospheric air. In an article by climatologist James Hansen and environmental attorney Dan Galpern, they note that:

> the U.S. Supreme Court has also recognized the public trust doctrine, both as a limitation on government action and a source of its affirmative duty. In 1892 it held, for example, that government may not fully sell off public resources and so deprive future legislatures of their authority to provide for the people. Neither may government mismanage resources that it holds in trust for the people as part of the public domain.
>
> *(Hansen & Galpern, 2014)*

The Public Trust Doctrine in this case is an example of how people can use the law in an attempt to meet the needs of future generations.

Law and policy career roles involving future generations include activist lawyers, politicians, public policy analysts that deal with trends, outlooks, and foresight studies, public servants, and lawyers, including judges, who work on cases that have long-term implications.

Conclusion

There are many ways that lawyers, those trained in the legal and policy professions, and those that pursue careers in the public servant space can incorporate sustainability into their everyday tasks, strategic thinking, and a career trajectory. If law firms do not incorporate sustainability knowledge and legal expertie in this arena, they may lose ground as the trusted adviser to their clients, as other professional advisers and consultants make headway. Some practical tips for professionals in this sector include:

- Use frameworks to gauge sustainability progress:

  - Employ the ABA SEE Sustainability Framework for Law Organizations.
  - Apply the SURF Framework to the legal establishment, to the job, and to the career trajectory.

- Use reference guides, such as:

  - Tools provided by Lawyers for a Sustainable Future (LSF)
  - The American Legal Industry Sustainability Standards (ALISS).

- Join professional networks that address sustainable law and policy, such as:

  - The Law Firm Sustainability Network
  - The Legal Sector Alliance (LSA).

- Familiarize oneself with sustainability-related conventions, declarations, and treaties, such as:

  - African Convention/Commission on Human and People Rights
  - Advisory Committee on Pollution of the Sea
  - International Environmental Law: Multilateral Treaties
  - Clean Development Mechanism
  - Commission for Environmental Co-operation
  - Committee on Trade and Environment
  - Convention on Biological Diversity
  - Convention for the Conservation of Antarctic Marine Living Resources
  - Convention on the Elimination of all forms of Discrimination against Women
  - Convention on International Trade in Endangered Species
  - Convention on the Rights of a Child
  - Declaration on the Right to Development
  - European Convention/Court of Human Rights
  - Exclusive Fishery Zone
  - Goa Guidelines on Intergenerational Equity
  - Global Environmental Facility
  - High Seas Treaty
  - International Covenant on Civil and Political Rights
  - International Council on Exploration of the Seas
  - International Covenant on Economic, Social and Cultural Rights
  - International Convention for the Regulation of Whaling
  - International North Sea Conference
  - International Oil Pollution Compensation Fund

- International Seabed Authority
- International Tropical Timber Agreement
- Johannesburg Principles on the Role of Law and Sustainable Development
- Kunming-Montreal Global Biodiversity Framework
- New Delhi Declaration on the Principles of International Law Related to Sustainable Development
- Universal Declaration on Human Rights
- United Nations Convention on the Law of the Sea, 1982.

- Read and contribute to sustainable law and policy literature, such as:

  - *Annual Review of Ecological Systems*
  - *Annual Review of Energy and Environment*
  - *Asia Pacific Journal of Environmental Law*
  - *Chinese Journal of Environmental Law*
  - *Colorado Journal of Environmental Law*
  - *Columbia Human Rights Law Review*
  - *European Human Rights Reports*
  - *Environmental Lawyer*
  - *European Environmental Law Reviews*
  - *Fishing News International*
  - *Fordham Environmental Law Journal*
  - *Georgetown International Environmental Law Review*
  - *Harvard Environmental Law Review*
  - *Harvard Human Rights Yearbook*
  - *Human and Ecological Risk Assessment*
  - *International Journal of Estuarine and Coastal Law*
  - *International Journal of Marine and Coastal Law*
  - *International Environmental Law Reports*
  - *Journal of Environmental Law*
  - *Journal of Environment and Development*
  - *Journal of European Environmental and Planning Law*
  - *Journal of International Economic Law*
  - *Journal of International Wildlife Law and Policy*
  - *Journal of International Environmental Law and Policy*
  - *Journal of Law and Sustainable Development*
  - *Journal of Planning and Environmental Law*
  - *Journal of Sustainable Development Law and Policy*
  - *Law of Sea Bulletin*
  - *Marine Pollution Bulletin*
  - *Natural Resources Journal*
  - *New York University Environmental Law Journal*
  - *Ocean and Coastal Management*
  - *Ocean Yearbook*
  - *Ocean Development and International Law*

- *Pace Environmental Law Review*
- *South African Journal of Environmental Law and Policy*
- *Stanford Environmental Law Journal*
- *The Carbon and Climate Law Review*
- *The Sustainable Development Law & Policy Journal from the American University, Washington College of Law*
- *Tulane Environmental Journal*
- *University of California at Los Angeles Journal of Environmental Law and Policy*
- *Virginia Environmental Law Journal*
- *William and Mary Environmental Law and Policy Review*
- *Yearbook of International Environmental Law.*

- Participate in continuing education, workshops, and conferences that address sustainable law and policy, such as training provided by the Centre for International Sustainable Development Law (CISDL).

References

Black, S., Liu, A., Parry, I., & Vernon, N. (2023). IMF Fossil Fuel Subsidies Data: 2023 Update. International Monetary Fund. www.imf.org/en/Publications/WP/Issues/2023/08/22/IMF-Fossil-Fuel-Subsidies-Data-2023-Update-537281.

Bocca, R., & Ellerbeck, S. (2023). Over $1 trillion invested in green energy in 2022. Here's what you need to know about how the energy transition is powering up despite the crisis. World Economic Forum. www.weforum.org/agenda/2023/02/energy-transition-investment-record-global-energy-crisis-3-february.

Bourne, T. (2012). Why lawyers have a part to play in sustainable development. *The Guardian*, February 16. www.theguardian.com/sustainable-business/blog/sustainable-business-development-law.

Clark, L. (2023). Kids Sued Montana over Climate Change and Won. Scientific American. www.scientificamerican.com/article/kids-sued-montana-over-climate-change-and-won.

ClientEarth. (2021). China's first climate change public interest case could herald new era. www.clientearth.org/latest/latest-updates/opinions/china-s-first-climate-change-public-interest-case-could-herald-new-era.

Cordonier Segger, M.-C. (2010). Sustainability, global justice, and the law: Contributions of the Hon. Justice Charles Doherty Gonthier. *McGill Law Journal*, 337–355.

Cordonier Segger, M.-C., & Khalfan, A. (2004). *Sustainable Development Law: Principles, Practices, and Prospects*. Oxford: Oxford University Press.

Frank Bold. (2023). Comparison of climate-related disclosure requirements. https://en.frankbold.org/sites/default/files/publikace/frank_bold_comparative_analysis_climate_reporting_standards.pdf.

French, D. (2005). *International Law and Policy of Sustainable Development*. Manchester: Manchester University Press.

Global Maritime Forum. (2020). Poseidon Principles. www.globalmaritimeforum.org/poseidon-principles.

Hansen, J., & Galpern, D. (2014). Earning Our Children's Trust. The Huffington Post. www.huffpost.com/entry/earning-our-childrens-tru_b_6154426.

IEP. (2020). Over one billion people at threat of being displaced by 2050 due to environmental change, conflict and civil unrest. www.economicsandpeace.org/wp-content/uploads/2020/09/Ecological-Threat-Register-Press-Release-27.08-FINAL.pdf.

Putzer, A., Lambooy, T., Jeurissen, R., & Kim, E. (2022). Putting the rights of nature on the map. A quantitative analysis of rights of nature initiatives across the world. *Journal of Maps* 18(1), 89–96. https://doi.org/10.1080/17445647.2022.2079432.

Sandhu, E. (2022). Closing the Accountability Gap? Early Lessons from the Canadian Ombudsperson for Responsible Enterprises. In C. Liao (ed.), *Corporate Law and Sustainability from the Next Generation of Lawyers* (pp. 242–262). McGill-Queen's University Press. https://doi.org/10.2307/j.ctv307fhn2.

Tripoli, L. (2012, May). Sustainability: What law firms have at stake. *Of Counsel*, 19–22.

UNEP. (2011). Towards a Green Economy: Pathways to Sustainable Development and Poverty Eradication—A Synthesis for Policy Makers. www.unep.org/resources/report/towards-green-economy-pathways-sustainable-development-and-poverty-eradication.

UNEP. (2002). WSSD: Johannesburg Principles on the Role of Law and Sustainable Development Adopted at the Global Judges Symposium held in Johannesburg, South Africa, on 18–20 August 2002. www.jstor.org/stable/44248411.

UNEP. (2021). From birth to ban: A history of the plastic shopping bag. www.unep.org/news-and-stories/story/birth-ban-history-plastic-shopping-bag.

6

PURSUING SUSTAINABILITY IN BUSINESS, ECONOMICS, AND FINANCIAL SERVICES

Sustainability metrics, when robustly measured, are the only means to really make wise investment decisions.

Introduction

The business, economic, and financial services community is taking sustainable development seriously. Some companies are implementing sustainability policies due to regulation, while other companies view sustainability as critical for risk management and long-term viability. Professionals involved in marketing, sales, business consulting, economic analysis, and financial services fall under the umbrella of the business and finance sector. The goal of this chapter is to explore the sustainability considerations for tasks tied directly to financing, improving the bottom line, and distributing monetary resources. This chapter will cover sustainability from various business perspectives—corporate sustainability policy, consumer demand for sustainable products, public relations and communications, sustainability reporting, and sustainability algorithms in financial services. The stories of professionals working in public relations, financial analysis, and sustainability reporting are shared.

The corporate world

The for-profit corporate world has witnessed the rise of sustainability in the last decade, as companies, small and large, understand the sustainability business case. There are three main reasons why businesses become sustainable: *revenue and cost optimization*, *risk management*, and *brand and reputation management*. There is one prevailing equation that dominates business: profit is equal to revenue minus costs. For some types of capital, such as venture capital,

DOI: 10.4324/9781032615844-6

profit is not essential: growth is. Nevertheless, at some point in the future, risk-seeking investors expect even their loss-bearing bets to become profitable. For-profit organizations are continually aiming for lower costs and higher revenues, and it has become more apparent for businesses to achieve both through critical approaches in sustainability. For example, when a company reduces its water, energy, and waste, it also reduces its water, energy, and waste bills. When a company recycles the solvents used in a chemical process, the company not only prevents pollution, but they also decrease the costs associated with purchasing new solvent. In addition, when a company asks critical questions such as "How can we transform this product to last for future generations, create social cohesion, protect the environment, and create economic well-being?" companies spur innovative solutions. Sustainability drives new product innovation and new business models; it is an approach that benefits both the business and society.

Before the word "sustainability" came into widespread use, the word "risk" encompassed many sustainability considerations. Ensuring social, environmental, and future orientations helps reduce litigation, compliance costs, and the need for pollution cleanup. Companies can avoid the expensive costs associated with lawsuits by following ethical standards in the labor supply chain, using cradle-to-cradle principles in manufacturing, and more. Corporations can eliminate the need to be "compliant" by employing practices that are ahead of stricter environmental, social, and governance (ESG) regulations. If companies install on-site, off-grid renewable energy, then they are also reducing the risk of being without power to their operations.

The jury is in concerning consumer concern for sustainability. A good image goes a long way. Sustainable companies are better able to maintain brand loyalty. Not only have customers shown a concern for people and the planet, but employees have as well. Companies can attract and retain talent by showing that sustainability is integral to their business model, by attaching bonuses and financial rewards to sustainability results, and by creating opportunities for employees to engage in the issues.

There are numerous leaders in sustainable business with corresponding rankings from entities such as ESG rating agencies and non-profit leaders. In 2011, Patagonia launched a "Don't Buy This Jacket" campaign; for nine months, they told their customers to buy less to help the environment and Patagonia's sales subsequently increased almost one-third, as the company opened 14 more stores (Stock, 2013). Patagonia also helped to found the Sustainable Apparel Coalition, made fleece jackets out of recycled bottles, and used organic cotton. In 2022, founder of Patagonia, Yvon Chouinard, announced that instead of going public, Patagonia was "going purpose," meaning that Patagonia's wealth would be completely dedicated to climate and the environment (Patagonia, 2022). Practically speaking, 100 percent of the company's voting stock is transferred to the Patagonia Purpose Trust and 100 percent of the nonvoting stock is transferred to the Holdfast Collective, a non-profit dedicated to fighting the environmental crisis and defending nature (Patagonia, 2022). Some companies use an Environmental Profit and Loss Statement (the EP&L). The EP&L places a monetary value on the environmental impacts along the entire supply chain of a given business, and defines environmental impact as a change in the make-up, functioning, or appearance of the environment. For example, greenhouse gases contribute to climate change, which is associated with a range of environmental impacts such as reduced crop yields, changes in water availability, and increases in extreme weather.

Pavin Sukhdev, who served as the head of the United Nations Environment Programme's Green Economy Initiative from 2008 to 2011, outlined four solutions to move the corporate world to the green economy: (1) disclose externalities in statutory annual reports; (2) provide more information value in advertising; (3) limit leverage (the proportion of borrowed funds as opposed to the owner's capital); and (4) increase taxation at the point of resource extraction (Sukhdev, 2012). Many guidelines and tools are available to for-profit businesses to partake fully in the green economy. The *Benefit Corporation* status has taken root in the United States. Businesses can now incorporate under a decision-making structure that is reflective of considerations regarding their impact on their employees, the environment, and society at large; this goes beyond the traditional shareholder-only perspective of the incorporated status in the U.S. (Institute on the Environment, 2012). Legally, in some countries, corporations must consider shareholder financial interests first—shareholder bottom line trumps all other considerations. Now, with the Benefit Corporation, companies are legally free to make quadruple bottom line decisions—they can choose to pay a premium on more environmentally friendly products, for example. More than 40 states and the District of Columbia have adopted the Benefit Corporation status. Various companies have incorporated under this status, such as Patagonia, Method Products, and Kickstarter Inc. In addition to the Benefit Corporation, the *B Corporation* certified status from non-profit B Lab is available to every business regardless of corporate structure, state, or country of incorporation. B Corp certification mirrors the idea of the Benefit Corporation, and requires organizations to achieve a minimum verified score based on the B Impact Assessment. As more and more companies begin to see the mutual values of sustainability and financial success, they too will consider a change in perspectives towards more sustainable approaches to business conduct.

The consumer

Greendex, a research survey project by National Geographic and GlobeScan, measures and monitors consumer progress towards environmentally sustainable consumption. Sustainable consumption is defined as consumption that demands less of the ecosystem services than the Earth provides and is less likely to impair the ability of future generations to meet their own needs as a result. Four broad areas are covered: housing, transportation, food consumption, and goods.

Consumer behavior and material lifestyle are tracked across 18 countries with a pool of 1,000 people per country.[1] The 2014 survey found stark differences and similarities among various countries: 51 percent of consumers in the 18 countries believed that climate change would negatively affect their own lives; in Brazil, 78 percent of consumers believed this to be the case (National Geographic and GlobeScan, 2014). The survey indicated that while the majority of people say they are very concerned about environmental problems, the concern is not translating into substantive behavior (National Geographic and GlobeScan, 2014). In order to close this action gap, careers are increasing in the fields of behaviorial economics and behavioral change.

Industries

Ray Anderson founded Interface Inc., the world leader in carpet tile production, in 1973. In 1994, after more than two decades of company financial success, Anderson received a note from a sales associate from the west coast of the U.S. The note said, "Some customers want to know what Interface is doing for the environment. How should we answer?" (Anderson, 2009). Anderson decided to set up an environmental task force. The only problem was that he did not have an environmental vision. He picked up the book *The Ecology of Commerce* by Paul Hawken, was inspired to change, and the rest is history. Interface has since "walked the talk" of sustainable development. Interface has cut its greenhouse gas emissions by 82 percent, fossil fuel consumption by 60 percent, waste by 66 percent, and water use by 75 percent, while it increased sales by 66 percent, doubled earnings, raised profit margins, and invented and patented new machines, materials, and manufacturing processes in the past 15 years (Anderson, 2009). Anderson, in his book *Confessions of a Radical Industrialist*, states that:

> Sustainability has given my company a competitive edge in more ways than one. It has proven to be the most powerful marketplace differentiator I have known in my long career. Our costs are down, our profits are up, and our products are the best they've ever been … And a strong environmental ethic has no equal for attracting and motivating good people, galvanizing them around a shared higher purpose, and giving them a powerful reason to join and to stay.

Financial services

The financial services industry uses debt, equity, and revenue-share instruments to enable sustainable industries. On the debt side, commercial loans now routinely require environmental and social credit risk assessments in some form. Bank lenders are concerned that they may face direct and indirect liabilities due to sustainability criteria. For example, lenders may be held directly liable for contaminated land taken as security for a debt; there may be credit default if the borrower's environmental costs adversely impact their ability to repay a loan (Smith, 1994). Retail loans are also subject to sustainability assessment. For example, if a property is no longer insurable due to physical risk caused by climate change, the lender may decide against providing a loan. On the positive side, a whole movement of retail lenders, such as the Clean Energy Federal Credit Union in the United States, are actively providing climate-friendly loans such as home-scale geothermal energy, solar panels and battery storage, and electric vehicles.

On the equity side, investors are increasingly participating in socially responsible investment, impact investment, or sustainability investment. They use negative or positive screening processes. Negative screening entails avoiding investment in companies perceived to have a negative impact on the environment and society, whereas positive screening entails actively seeking investment in companies with a positive impact on the environment and society (Coulson, 2007). Investment exists on a spectrum as illustrated in Figure 6.1, ranging from investments that strictly seek a societal return (philanthropy) to those investments that strictly seek a financial return (traditional investing with shareholder primacy).

There are numerous initiatives to render the financial services industry more sustainable. Long-term institutional investors such as pension funds and insurance companies are increasingly seeing the potential for minimizing ESG risks by building green and socially responsible portfolios. Similarly, commercial and retail banks are increasingly bringing ESG considerations into lending policies and in designing sustainable financial products. In the renewable energy sector, for example, around $627 billion of private capital was already invested between 2007 and mid-2010 (UNEP, 2011). There are even sustainability aims for stock exchanges. For example, the Sustainable Stock Exchanges (SSE) is an initiative aimed at exploring how exchanges can work together with investors, regulators, and companies to enhance corporate transparency (and ultimately performance) on ESG issues and encourage responsible long-term approaches to

Financial-only	Responsible	Sustainable	Impact				Impact-only
Delivering competitive financial returns							
	Mitigating Environmental, Social, and Governance (ESG) risks						
		Pursuing ESG opportunities					
			Focusing on measurable high-impact solutions				
Limited or no regard for environmental, social or governance (ESG) practices	Mitigate risky ESG practices in order to protect value	Adopt progressive ESG practices that may enhance value	Address societal challenges that generate competitive financial returns for investors	Address societal challenges where returns are as yet unproven	Address societal challenges that require a below-market financial return for investors	Address societal challenges that cannot generate a financial return for investors

FIGURE 6.1 Spectrum of capital
Source: Adapted from Bridges Fund Management (2015).

investment. SSE is co-organized by the United Nations Conference on Trade and Development, the United Nations Global Compact Office, the United Nations-supported Principles for Responsible Investment and the United Nations Environment Programme Finance Initiative.

In 2003, BankTrack, a global network of civil society groups tracking the operations and investments of commercial banks and their effect on people and the planet, brought to fruition the *Collevecchio Declaration*. This Declaration calls on financial institutions (FIs) to embrace six commitments that reflect civil society's expectations of the role and responsibilities of the financial services sector in fostering sustainability. More than 200 civil society organizations have endorsed the Collevecchio Declaration with six commitments to sustainability: do no harm, be responsible, be accountable, be transparent, promote sustainable markets, and promote governance.[2]

A coalition of banks have developed and adopted the *Equator Principles*, a risk management framework for determining, assessing, and managing environmental and social risk in projects. It is primarily intended to provide a minimum standard, to ensure due diligence, and to support responsible risk decision making (Equator Principles Association, 2015). There are 80 Equator Principles Financial Institutions in 34 countries; the principles apply to all industry sectors and to four financial products: (1) project finance advisory services; (2) project finance; (3) project-related corporate loans; and (4) bridge loans (Equator Principles Association, 2015). The ten principles cover: review and categorization; environmental and social assessment; applicable environmental and social standards; environmental and social management system and Equator Principles action plan; stakeholder engagement; grievance mechanism; independent review; covenants; independent monitoring and reporting; and reporting and transparency (Equator Principles Association, 2015).

The United Nation's *Principles for Responsible Investment (PRI)* initiative is a worldwide network of investors working together to put the six Principles for Responsible Investment into practice. The Principles were launched in 2006 at the New York Stock Exchange after an investor group made up of institutions and experts from the investment industry, intergovernmental organizations, and civil society developed the codes. There are over 5,300 signatories to the principles,[3] representing over US$120 trillion of assets under management; signatories pay an annual fee to PRI and there are no legal or regulatory sanctions associated with the Principles (PRI Association, 2023).

The United Nation's *Principles for Responsible Banking (PRB)* is also a global initiative that focuses on the bank lending community. Over 300 banks representing roughly US$90 trillion of assets have signed on to the principles. The six principles include aligning business strategy with the Sustainable Development Goals and the Paris Climate Agreement; continuously increasing positive impacts and reducing the negative impacts on people and planet resulting from banking activities, products, and services; encouraging sustainable practices among customers; consulting and partnering with relevant stakeholders to achieve the SDGs; implementing the Principles through effective governance and a culture of responsible banking; and periodically reviewing the implementation of the Principles (UNEP FI, 2023).

The economist

Economists can be found in numerous settings, including in corporations, universities, and policy circles. While their roles can be segmented by macro- or microeconomics, sectors such as fisheries or manufacturing, and other delineations, economists are increasingly incorporating social and environmental metrics in their calculations and modeling. There are a number of economic and accounting models that move beyond strict financial considerations, such as the System of Integrated Environmental and Economic Accounting (SEEA), the Genuine Progress Indicator (GPI), Genuine Savings (GS), Green Net National Product (GNNP), the Index of Sustainable Economic Welfare (ISEW), the Sustainable Net Benefit Index (SNBI), and the Sustainability Assessment Model (SAM).

In 1993, the United Nations published the UN's System of Integrated Environmental and Economic Accounting (SEEA), which was revised in 2003 and 2012. The accounts have four components: natural resource asset accounts; pollutant, energy, and resource flow accounts; environmental protection and resource management expenditures; and environmentally adjusted macroeconomic aggregates. The environment is said to provide three functions for the economy that contribute both indirectly and directly to human well-being: (1) resource functions, (2) waste absorption functions, and (3) environmental service functions (United Nations, 2000). The SEEA is not without its critics, with some pointing to the great difference of economic and ecologic spatial and time scales, the lack of empirical data, and the challenges of placing monetary value on environmental components (Holub et al., 1999).

Full cost accounting is a system that allows current accounting and economic numbers to produce the right prices by incorporating all potential and actual costs and benefits into the equation (including environmental and social externalities) (Bebbington, 2001). There are two approaches: bottom up (emissions and inputs from a given site, service, or product are first inventoried using such tools as life-cycle analysis or eco-balances) and top down (a given external effect is evaluated at a very global level, such as at a country or continent level). An example of the bottom-up approach is listing the physical damage of inputs and outputs and assigning market values for the damage (such as to human health or crops). An example of a top-down approach is to calculate the cost of damages due to climate change on a global basis, divide the costs by total world greenhouse gas emissions, and obtain an average cost per unit of emission that is not site specific. In addition to full cost accounting, there is sustainability accounting. Using the Sustainable Assessment Model (SAM),[4] one can move towards sustainability full cost accounting. The SAM uses 22 performance indicators to measure full life cycle, environmental, economic, and resource usage impacts of a project; the impacts are then monetized and can be summed into a single measure called the Sustainability Assessment Model Indicator (SAMi) (Antheaume, 2007).

The Genuine Progress Indicator (GPI), Green Net National Product (gNNP), and Genuine Savings (GS) (also known as Adjusted Net Savings) were introduced to overcome the shortfalls of using gross domestic product (GDP) as a national indicator of economic welfare. GDP is the monetary value of goods and services produced in a country irrespective of how much is retained in the country; gross national income (GNI) expresses the income accrued to residents of a country, including some international flows, and excluding income generated in the country but repatriated abroad (UNDP, 2011). GDP was not intended to indicate general economic progress; it was introduced as a monetary measure of wartime production capacity during World War II (Wen et al., 2007). Simon Kuznets, the architect of GDP/GNP warned against using it as an overall indicator of welfare, arguing that it did not include any criteria for social productivity (Wilson & Tyedmers, 2013).

GDP measures progress only in terms of what is being bought and sold, but it does not distinguish between what is desired and undesired by a society (Wilson & Tyedmers, 2013). GDP is far from being a measure of economic sustainability, especially when analyzing social, environmental, and economic indicators. GDP treats car accidents, security systems, insurance, crime, legal fees, and other activities linked to social issues as economic gains; it ignores the environmental costs of activities that lead to the depletion of natural resources; and it does not benefit *all* people economically (while GDP in the U.S. rose by 55% between 1973 and 1993, real wages declined by 3.4%) (Wen et al., 2007). The need to have an index that debunks the use of GDP as an indicator of economic welfare and well-being can be illustrated by the broken window parable summarized as follows by Natoli and Zuhair:

> The parable tells the story of incomplete accounting for unintended consequences. In the story, a little boy breaks a shopkeeper's window. After initially sympathizing with the shopkeeper the onlookers conclude that the little boy is a public benefactor due to the economic benefits created for everyone. For instance, the broken window makes work for the glazier who can buy bread benefiting the baker, who will then buy shoes benefiting the cobbler, etc. However, the onlookers ignore the hidden costs. For example, the money the shopkeeper is forced to spend on the glazier cannot be spent elsewhere, for instance on a suit. Thus, the glazier's gain is the tailor's loss. Hence, instead of a window and suit, he has only a window.
>
> *(Natoli & Zuhair, 2011)*

Genuine savings (GS) is an adjustment to conventional GDP-based national accounting. The term "genuine" was coined by Kirk Hamilton of the World

Bank to reflect the fact that GS includes all forms of utility generating capital, including natural capital, human capital, and social capital. (Dietz & Neumayer, 2004). The goal of GS is to maximize the present value of social welfare over time, solving which produces a measure of green net national product (gNNP).

The Index of Sustainable Economic Welfare (ISEW), designed by Daly and Cobb, adjusts GDP to reflect a broader set of social and environmental criteria. ISEW was later revised and renamed the Genuine Progress Indicator (GPI). In GPI, all values are expressible in monetary units; in general, additions are made for volunteer work, non-paid household work, services of consumer durables, services of highways and streets, net capital investment, net foreign lending and borrowing, and income distribution adjustment, while subtractions are made for crime, family breakdown, automobile accidents, cost of consumer durables, cost of household pollution abatement, loss of leisure time, underemployment, commuting, water pollution, air pollution, noise pollution, loss of wetlands, loss of farmland, resource depletion, long-term environmental damage, ozone depletion, and loss of old-growth forests (Wilson & Tyedmers, 2013). The GPI is the total sum of all positive and negative values expressed in monetary units. The Sustainable Net Benefit Index (SNBI) is very similar to the ISEW and GPI, but the items are sorted into "uncancelled benefit" and "uncancelled cost" accounts; the SNBI is obtained by subtracting the total of the uncancelled cost account from the uncancelled benefit account (Lawn, 2005).

In the U.S. alone, GPI has been used for many local contexts including the San Francisco Bay area, Vermont, Utah, northeast Ohio, Minnesota, and Maryland, where it is now a government requirement (Bagstad & Shammin, 2012).

The IESW, GPI, GNNI, and GS are not without their critics. They are indicators of weak sustainability as opposed to strong sustainability (Mota et al., 2010; Wen et al., 2007). They require the analyst to make value judgments and thus reflect arbitrary values, choices, and preferences in what costs and benefits are included or excluded and in what methodologies are used to estimate costs and benefits (Clarke & Lawn, 2008). The aforementioned economic frameworks and tools are being used by policy makers and business professionals alike. Let's learn more from those who have incorporated sustainability into their work in the financial bottom line.

From securities analyst to founder of financial sustainability indices—Michael Muyot's story

There's a certain charm to the Hudson River Valley. Although the river has been victim to numerous chemical and industrial waste-dumping episodes, it is a vibrant and vital part of the ecosystem of eastern New York. As I rode the Amtrak train from New York City to Poughkeepsie, the meandering river surrounded by thick greenery provided a peaceful prelude to my encounter at Marist College.

I tend to envision financial services in the bustling centers of Hong Kong, London, or New York. I imagine frantic traders and people constantly selling and buying financial securities with the help of computers and telephones. So Marist College was a bit unexpected. But it is here that I met the founder and president of CRD Analytics, a financial analytics firm that creates mostly sustainability index-based products.

Michael Muyot has a rather traditional Wall Street banking background. He grew up in the Hudson Valley and saw the original 1987 movie *Wall Street*. Motivated primarily by financial gain, he moved to the city to attend university and find work in financial services. After studying economics at the undergraduate level and econometrics at the postgraduate level, he served as a securities analyst at Citibank. After a few years, he went over to Technovations, a marketing communications company where he was director of Information Management Systems. At Technovations, Michael built a financial model to track 12 healthcare sectors and regularly presented to C-level Pfizer executives. It was, therefore, a natural progression to start his own company, Tracer Technologies, which focused on analytics in the health care industry. By 2003, Michael established Tracer Analytics, developing the Tracer LSI 100 Index (the premier financial index of the life science industry) and the ProForma analytical modeling for the acquisitions of Warner-Lambert and Pharmacia by Pfizer.

Throughout Michael's career as an analyst and financial modeler, he was always answering the question "Which company is better to buy?" "And that's sustainability in a nutshell," Michael explained. Sustainability metrics, when robustly measured, are the only means to really make wise investment decisions. Michael stumbled upon the world of sustainability by needing to provide clients with the best metrics for measuring value. Michael began to expand to clients outside of the pharmaceutical industry. He was amazed by the amount of savings lurking in social, environmental, and governance indicators. For example, when working with a utility, he found that the company could save millions of dollars per day eliminating the evaporation (and thus, loss) of water.

Michael partnered with CRD and formed CRD Analytical with about $100 million in angel investment. When Michael started his career in finance, there were about 50 sustainability reports per year in the U.S. Now, there are over 5,000.

CRD Analytics does algorithms, analytics, and advisory work. It is known for its SmartView® 360 Platform, which powers indexes, rankings, and research reports, including the NASDAQ CRD Global Sustainability Index, the Sustainability Leadership Report, and regional sustainability rankings. Using SmartView®360, a company can gauge their performance through clear visuals and transparent metrics. The NASDAQ CRD Global Sustainability Index has reached its five-year milestone, a time frame that is important for reputation in the financial community. It covers large publicly listed companies with a minimum market capitalization of $8 billion. The index uses 200 metrics to analyze the ESG operational and financial performance of more than 2,000 companies.

The index picks the top 100; the scoring algorithm is based on a best of class universe. "This makes the index highly competitive, which drives sustainability change," Michael noted. The CRD Index is not a black box; it is mapped using the Global Reporting Initiative (GRI) guidelines and other standards, such as the Carbon Disclosure Project. It is a transparent, rules-based methodology. The index includes common stocks, ordinary shares, American Depository Receipts (ADRs), shares of beneficial interest or limited partnership interests, and tracking stocks.

Michael found there was a need in the labor market for people with both financial and sustainability knowledge. He needed workers who understood sustainability reports and the different metrics of sustainability, while he also needed the same people to understand financial filings (like the SEC form 10K) and use quantitative means to calculate performance. He, thus, started to train students at numerous universities and is developing an asynchronous blended curriculum at Marist College. It will be a formalized online platform for turning data into sustainability rankings and investment products.

"The large financial institutions like Morgan Stanley and UBS all have ESG researchers and analysts," Michael affirmed. There is ESG across the board, from long-term investors like endowments and pension funds to the portfolio builders like Bloomberg. Insurance companies, which lose billions yearly due to increasingly common extreme weather events, now need to quantify climate change risk. "The industry needs professionals who have studied an environment-related subject, with specific courses in sustainability or environment, health, and safety, coupled with financial accounting and analysis." There is currently more demand than supply for sustainability finance skills. "Since these jobs require both financial and sustainability competencies, one could expect to be paid more at the analyst, portfolio manager, and business development levels."

Michael sees the world differently since he began to incorporate sustainability into his career. His daily habits have changed to eating less meat, conducting more virtual meetings, and passing on a sustainability value system to his children. For Michael, sustainability means "doing more with less to have a net positive impact on the environment and society." He added that financial services in the U.S. have to evolve their business models: "the credit cards, student loans, and 30-year mortgages are all unsustainable in their present state, and will eventually implode."

"Five years ago, there was a rather negative perception of sustainability in the U.S. finance community," Michael stated. "It was perceived as more polar bear saving and tree hugging than finance; but now, funds are signatories to the PRI, make public statements of the importance of sustainability, and view it as an alpha generator."

Michael is an Advisory Board member of the Sustainability Accounting Standards Boards (SASB) and is widely recognized as a thought leader in his field. His data show that ESG matters for financial results. The global companies that improved on ESG performance from 2006 to 2008, for example, outperformed the MSCI World Index by over 11 percent from 2008 to 2009. Michael would like to continue to build CRD Analytics as president and perform less data crunching and more teaching and managing. The company has been asked to build out algorithms in other sectors. For example, it recently analyzed social media data as a predictor of political elections. Michael would like CRD Analytics to perform industry-wide analysis, such as for the banking sector. Tony DiMarco, director of Strategic Initiatives at Marist College, is one of his mentors. The work on curriculum development at Marist fulfills a dual need of skills development and possible recruitment. "I would also like to implement more online courses to reach people across the globe," Michael affirmed. Michael told me about the numerous times throughout his career that he had been faced with sustainability and ethical dilemmas. "It's disheartening when a pharmaceutical executive tells you that there is no money in cures," Michael sighed. "I started my career focusing on earnings but not fulfillment; now I have both—the intellectual challenge of sustainable finance indicators and algorithms and the emotional fulfillment of fully valuing companies and industries through a sustainability lens."

Changing the PR and communications consultancy model—Kathryn Sheridan and Bárbara Mendes-Jorge's stories

As I walked down the Boulevard du Général Leclerc in Reims (pronounced "Rance," which almost rhymes with France in U.S. English), I couldn't help but notice how easy it was to get around without carbon emissions—by foot. The Reims Congress Center is surrounded by a continuous strip of green space—the perfect setting for a conference about the bio-based economy.

I met Kathryn Sheridan, founder and CEO of Sustainability Consult, at the European Forum for Industrial Biotechnology and the Biobased Economy in Reims, where she was exhibiting her firm and presenting on behalf of clients.

In her childhood years, Kathryn did a lot of camping as a Scout and describes herself as "outdoorsy." It is common for people who spend their leisure time outdoors to want to protect the natural environment. Kathryn moved from the United Kingdom to Belgium in 1999 for a position in journalism. Although she started off working on financial topics, her passion for nature led her to work on environmental issues. She soon became deputy editor for an environmental publication, as she understood the inner workings of the Brussels policy environment.

The shift from journalism to public relations (PR) emerged informally. Kathryn had a friend who owned a PR firm and was recruited to work there on the chemical industry. She learned how to do crisis communication and work with many clients. "There are a lot of ex-journalists in PR," Kathryn affirmed. It's a natural progression since one needs to have a journalistic fiber, or a skill for telling stories, in order to be good in PR. She enjoyed the work, she but found that sometimes she was not working for the "good companies." That is to say, she had worked more on "defensive" PR instead of PR that sought to explain how companies were taking concrete action to improve for sustainability. So in 2008, Kathryn took a leap and founded her own media and communications firm, Sustainability Consult. "The company was a one-woman band for the first year; I worked both Western European and eastern North American time zones," Kathryn explained. The hard work paid off. Today, Sustainability Consult has a full team of consultants, designers, and other staff; business is growing.

From the outset, Kathryn wanted to start a different kind of consultancy. A consultancy that chooses its clients (as opposed to a pure billing factory). A consultancy that pays its interns (a fair wage is a part of sustainability, right?). A consultancy that contributes profit to help environmental projects. As Kathryn stated, "Even if you are small, 1 percent is a real number and by contributing 1 percent of our profits to the One Percent for the Planet organization, we illustrate our values and build credibility." Sustainability Consult has turned down clients, from oil companies to certain forestry companies. "If the company's intention is to greenwash, then our answer is a definite no," Kathryn emphasized; "But if a company is ready to make a change and would like to be more transparent, then we can represent them."

Kathryn's day-to-day work is high energy and varied. She meets with the team, potential clients, and current clients, reviews the work progress, provides crisis support, and participates in conferences and trade shows, and more. Her clients include both startups, where Sustainability Consult plays the role of an in-house communications department, and very large companies, where Sustainability Consult works with CEOs and business development staff. She values being challenged, developing her team, and feeling that her work has value. She also strongly believes in learning by doing. "I'm looking for people who are naturally curious," Kathryn affirmed. Kathryn also established professional opportunities for those working in the sustainability space. She hosts a sustainability communications lunch once per month. She also established Green Drinks Brussels, a networking organization that gives people who are passionate about the environment the opportunity to meet and share ideas.

Kathryn has implemented a number of in-house sustainability initiatives, including reimbursing staff for cycling to work, maintaining a library full of sustainability literature, and ensuring the trade show stands are made out of recycled cardboard. (I did double-check while at the conference.) For Kathryn, the key question is "Are we going to be able to mainstream sustainability?" There will be more and more job opportunities that require sustainability knowledge if the answer to this question is "yes." Kathryn has never had to advertise a job. All of her hires have *found her*, including on social media. She has recruited people of various academic backgrounds, and her next hire will likely be someone with a science (chemistry or biology) background with a passion for science communication. Kathryn admits that she likes to "date her colleagues before hiring them." She does not care about diplomas in a small team; she hires for fit.

I met one such "fit," Bárbara Mendes-Jorge. Bárbara studied psychology and went into human resources as a default option. She did an internship after her studies within the learning and development team in a construction management company. "It was OK, but not inspiring," Bárbara told me. Bárbara did not grow up in a particularly green household, but her partner at university did. He awakened her to the dire issues at the interface between humankind and the ecosystem as a whole. While interning in human resources, Bárbara discovered the CSR department. And then it clicked—she could have a green career within industry. But by the time things clicked, she was already on her way to do a Master's in Social and Cultural Psychology in London.

While at the London School of Economics, she attended an event by Amy Fetzer, author of *Climb the Green Ladder: Make Your Company and Career More Sustainable*, Ed Gillespie, co-founder of the sustainability creativity and strategy firm Futerra, and Jo Confino, then executive editor of *The Guardian*. Inspired by the talk, she went to intern within the CSR department of the European Investment Bank in Luxembourg. There, she worked on CSR reporting, auditing, and strategy. She went on to another internship at Carbon Brief and learned how to write better under intense time constraints.

Afterwards, things were not so good. Bárbara went through a period of unemployment for five months in 2012. She began to question herself, "Can I keep this green career?" But by intelligently using social media and sticking to her passion for CSR, she was able to land an internship at Sustainability Consult that evolved into a full-time position. "I finally got off of the intern wagon," Bárbara explained. Bárbara became a consultant, with a typical day at work involving social media management for clients, media relations, press releases, proofreading, marketing materials, communication audits, and client liaising. She noted that the skills for doing green or sustainability PR are not the same as general media and PR. "You need more skills for sustainability media because you cannot just presume that green is good or bad. Sustainability has many associations, and they can be positive or negative," Bárbara clarified. For example, there was a discount store in Belgium that invested heavily in renewable energy; however, the company did not want to communicate on this because they felt that sustainability might be interpreted as costly among consumers.

Bárbara wanted a job where she could be challenged, be appreciated for what she did, and have an overall positive working environment. She found that in Sustainability Consult and credits the push for mainstreaming sustainability with the positive future outlook of careers in this arena. She was recently headhunted to become a sustainability communications manager in a retail position, but turned it down because she is enjoying her current work so much. "A job is not everything, but I need to have a job to be a useful member of society," Bárbara added.

Eventually, Bárbara decided to become an entrepreneur herself, first by testing freelancing for one day a week. As there is no exact playbook for "How does one obtain clients as a sustainability communications freelancer?" she decided to take trips to a few European cities and use what has always been her source for progress: social media. Bárbara admitted that the social media scene is in great flux today for the sustainability-conscious community, with the most consistent resource being LinkedIn. Interestingly, her main question when reaching out for business development was not who has the biggest or most connected network, nor who was able to afford her services. It was simply this: "Who is nice?" Bárbara tried to ascertain who would be willing to meet with her over coffee. And Bárbara reflected, "It turns out it was often the nice people who had opportunities for me or were more than happy to connect me with those that did."

Bárbara's first client—an insurance startup that she met through a friend—gave her the confidence she needed to pursue her freelance work full-time. Yet, when the coronavirus pandemic hit, Bárbara questioned whether she made the right choice at a time of global upheaval. She enjoyed working out of cafés and from clients' offices, and now she was stuck at home. Bárbara was diagnosed with attention deficit hyperactivity disorder (ADHD) during the COVID period, which came as a huge relief to her; from then on, she had a framework for understanding and managing what can be a superpower. "I can see quickly what will keep someone's attention in the communications world," Bárbara explained. At Sustainability Consult, Bárbara would handle a lot more events and media outreach. On her own, she finds that she is supporting clients more with their sustainability reporting, websites, and social media. She covers a wide variety of topics, including oceans and the blue economy, anti-greenwashing, and sustainable construction.

When asked about her observations on corporate sustainability progress over the past decade, Bárbara mentioned that she is surprised by how much companies are lagging. She agrees with Professor of Strategic Design and Management Raz Godelnik's assessment that we've moved from business as usual to sustainability as usual. "We should be centering climate and social justice"; and "if a company's Scope 3 emissions are still high, they are not engaging enough with their suppliers," Bárbara added. In recent years, there has been a #GreenBrusselsSoWhite campaign to elevate the lack of diversity in the European Union's (EU) green movement. Bárbara also lamented that there also has not been progress on embedding justice, equity, diversity, and inclusion into the EU work, but she sees rays of hope due to the sustainability reporting standards. For now, she maintains her adage of speaking with nice people and helping her clients become sustainability champions and communicate sustainability leadership.

For-profit, membership-based sustainability—Michael Spanos' story

Michael Spanos found his way in sustainable finance by sheer naming and shaming. As we sat in his office in the city center of Athens, he recounted his journey from production to financial engineering. Despite the financial crisis in Greece, Michael was able to build Global Sustain, a membership-based organization offering "online and off-line services related to sustainability, corporate responsibility, responsible investing, green economy, business ethics and excellence, transparency, human rights, and accountability."

Michael worked as a production engineer, helping factories and supply chains in the manufacturing sector. He then obtained an MBA with a focus on financial engineering, which led him to work in credit risk management for a consulting firm. In the financial world, there are three types of risk: market risk, credit risk, and operational risk. It turns out that operational risk includes all "other" risks like legal, reputational, climate change, IT, etc. And this operational risk was often difficult to quantify. Michael pitched the idea to measure operational risk for clients as a part of his consulting firm's services. But his firm was not buying it. They found it a bit "vague," and they did not see how it would bring immediate financial results.

So when a company does not let you spread your wings, what do you do? You quit. Michael left his job and, using the IT skills of his brother, set up a website to offer the same services to clients that his former company declined. His approach was simple: upload everything a company was doing for CSR (volunteering, sponsorships, and more). He used sustainability reporting, capital market indexes like Dow Jones and FTSE4Good, various frameworks, and benchmarking tools. He built a large database. "In the beginning, the focus was more on philanthropy and charity, but then things became more widespread to look at sustainability in the company's business model," Michael stated. "Things started to get more serious. Companies started to call us and said, 'Hey what do you think you're doing?' So I said, 'Well, become a member and we can work together.' Many of them did and Global Sustain took off." Now, sustainability is not only a measure of operational risk but also a measure of overall financial viability.

Today, Global Sustain has more than 100 members in the corporate and non-profit space. They offer a space for members to dialogue and learn from each other, as well as a place to receive concrete resources for transforming for sustainability. Michael laid out the sustainability universe in Greece. "There are about 150 companies active in sustainability; about 45 produce annual sustainability reports, and 20–25 have a CSR department." The CSO role is not yet popular in Greece, but it is gaining traction, and studies show that the consumer base is more likely to purchase goods that are produced sustainably. "Consumption is falling in Greece, but companies feel that having sustainable products gives them a better bottom line," Michael explained. "There are two types of businesses: one that perceives CSR as a marketing tool (and these businesses cut their public relations budget in crisis) and one that perceives sustainability as the driver of business opportunity."

Michael sees that sustainability is here to stay and would like to continue to grow Global Sustain as its founder and managing partner. "We're getting ready for the SRI [socially responsible investor]," Michael added. The traditional investor is interested in three things: return, liquidity, and risk. The responsible investor adds three more things: environment, social, and governance (ESG) issues. Michael notes that his former consulting firm would probably embrace sustainability measurement in finance now. Risk managers today must incorporate more than classical market risk, such as supply chain risk and climate change risk. Global Sustain is for-profit, a signatory of the UN Global Compact and the UN Principles for Responsible Investing, and is growing. Global Sustain is incorporated in London with offices in Brussels, Berlin, and Dubai. Now that's a success story that shows the power that a sustainability mission can have when combined with good old-fashioned quitting, naming, and shaming, and perseverance.

SURF Framework for careers in business, economics, and financial services

The SURF Framework of *Supply Chain, User, Relations, and Future* can help companies transform for sustainability by serving as a tool to benchmark their efforts. SURF can also be used to group and understand the various positions that lie within sustainable business, finance, and economics.

Business, economics, and financial services careers involving supply chain

Supply chain management is a subset of business management, and it is now taught in business programs worldwide. Increasingly, the business community understands that Company A does not compete with Company B, but rather the supply chain of Company A competes with the supply chain of Company B. The supply chain is a critical component of business operations. Unsustainable practices can damage brand reputation and sales. In August 2014, a sub-supplier for McDonald's in Asia delivered stale meat to its customers. Subsequently, sales for McDonald's products declined, and McDonald's announced that it would have difficulty meeting its sales target for the year. Events such as these point to the need to have supply chain positions that ensure health, safety, and other sustainability criteria throughout the vertical and horizontal chains.

There are numerous career opportunities in integrating sustainability into business supply chains and in economics and analytical financial work. Economists analyze supply chain dynamics as a means to understand both the macroeconomic trends in the labor market and the microeconomic trends in supply and demand. Financial services companies analyze risk in the supply chain when valuing companies and when making equity and debt investment decisions. Positions include vice president of supply chain that oversees greening the supply chain and ensuring that it is socially responsible; operational supply chain managers who, through just in time (JIT) delivery, lean manufacturing, or other methods, ensure that waste is minimized; environmental economists who calculate the impacts of environmental degradation on the economy (including supply chain risks); socially responsible investors and fund managers who analyze supply chain risk; and financial analysts who help calculate sustainability indexes such as the NASDAQ OMX CRD Global Sustainability Index.

Business, economics, and financial services careers involving the user

The end user in the finance and economics fields ranges from a customer buying a product to society at large. Even people who do not invest or take part in debt or equity transactions are impacted by those who do. The user in this sector includes the investor who receives financial advice, the pension fund participants who receive a pension based on decisions made by fund managers, the citizen who is impacted by economic incentives implemented by governments (due to the advice of economists), and the end user of a product or service from any business. Careers involving the user are numerous and far-reaching.

Marketing managers, community managers (including social media managers), PR managers, and CEOs are all performing roles closely linked to the end user. One of the most notable positions in the business world that integrates sustainability, the user, and business is the chief sustainability officer. A study by PwC of 650 companies found that 42 percent of companies had a CSO or other senior executive with a similar title, such as *Corporate Responsibility Officer, Director of Citizenship, Chief Responsibility Officer, Vice President of Sustainability*, and *Director of Sustainability* (Longsworth et al., 2012). The study found that there are four main roles of the CSO: (1) *strategy* (developing the business case, developing the sustainability strategy, analyzing and identifying issues), (2) *internal engagement* (engaging employees and business units, measuring progress and reporting internally, supporting senior executives and the board, communicating and socializing the case for change), (3) *external engagement* (developing partnerships with external groups, reporting externally to stakeholders), and (4) *core business and operations* (supporting products and service sustainability efforts, working on operational improvement, engaging suppliers/sourcing) (Longsworth et al., 2012).

Someone in a business, whether it's the CSO or CEO, must think critically about the users of the business's products and/or services. What happens after product x is sold? How can the company recuperate those materials after its useful life? Is the company really providing a socially and environmentally responsible service to the end user? All roles in a company are somehow linked to the commercial goal of the company. And to achieve that commercial goal, professionals must be knowledgeable about the end user (their needs, their preferences, and the implications for sustainability).

Business, economics, and financial services careers involving relations

Open up any sustainability report or head to any investment firm. Stakeholder relations will be present. Although companies have historically placed greater emphasis on shareholder or investor relationships, the current trend is to engage a broader range of individuals and groups that perceive themselves to be impacted by business decisions. Stakeholders are internal and external to the business, and the careers closely related to building and maintaining positive stakeholder relations include those in customer relationship management, human resources, communications, finance (especially those in contact with banks and financial reporting officials), executive management, public affairs, and outreach.

Human resources managers are tasked with recruiting and retaining top talent, creating incentives for exceptional performance, enhancing critical competencies, and transforming organizations. Sustainability is now a critical component of all of these tasks, especially for Generation Y workers. One of the most effective tools to drive sustainability transformation is to link social and environmental performance with managerial and executive bonuses. It is, therefore, important that HR managers understand how each individual in the company addresses sustainability through their work.

The trend is to move towards more mandatory sustainability reporting, which will formalize the incorporation of sustainability competencies in many positions. South Africa, Brazil, and many countries in the European Union have mandated sustainability reports for companies of a certain size. Many of the GRI criteria are required through SEC 10k filings. Firms will increasingly need workers to collect, analyze, and interpret data for reporting. Firms will also need communication and PR managers to manage the stakeholder relations.

Business, economics, and financial services careers involving the future

There is a future orientation to the corporate and finance worlds. There are financial analysts who work on forward markets, economists who work on market outlooks, and foresight managers in the research and development departments of large companies. Green funds in private equity and venture capital are examples of investment tools that particularly cater to future sustainable companies; these firms in general do not invest in long-established business models but in new, disruptive technologies, products, and services. The CEO is also charged with setting a vision for the company. Although the business ecosystem has incorporated the future, this future is still dominated by short-term profits and quarterly financial results unless a sustainability approach is adopted. Many people[5] have said it throughout ancient and modern history, and many of us know this to be true: there is a difference between price and value. Organizations that have historically focused on price or cost are now moving towards value using sustainability. It is the value and not the monetary amount that transcends generations. The careers catering to a sustainable future in the business world are, thus, boundless.

Conclusion

In 2014, at least \$21.4 trillion worth of professionally managed assets incorporated ESG concerns in investment decisions; this represents about 30 percent of the total assets managed professionally (GSIA, 2015). This indicates that the investment community has more assets to cover, opening up opportunities for finance and investment professionals to incorporate sustainability metrics in their work. Not only is sustainability information needed in the business, economics, and financial sectors, but that information must also be reliable. Bringing reliability to sustainability data is one of the challenges facing professionals in this sector. There are numerous career paths for incorporating sustainability in the business, economics, and finance sectors. Whether you are or become a vice president of supply chain, a vice president of HR, a CSO, or a CEO, there is a role for you to bring about change that will positively impact the company financially, socially, environmentally, and generationally. Some practical tips for professionals in this sector include:

- Use frameworks to gauge sustainability progress, including the SURF Framework.
- Join professional networks that address sustainable business.
- Attend conferences that address sustainable finance and business.
- Read and contribute to sustainability publications.
- Adhere to sustainable finance, investing, and accounting standards, frameworks, and guidelines, such as:
  - Due Diligence 2.0 Commitment
  - The Principles for Responsible Banking
  - The Principles for Responsible Investment
  - The Greenhouse Gas Protocol (GHGP)
  - The Partnership for Carbon Accounting Financials (PCAF)
  - The Equator Principles
  - The Private Equity Council's Guidelines for Responsible Investment
  - Taskforce on Inequality-related Financial Disclosures (TIFD)
  - Taskforce on Climate-related Financial Disclosures (TCFD)
  - Taskforce on Nature-related Financial Disclosures (TNFD).

Notes

1 The 2014 survey countries include India, Brazil, China, Australia, the U.S., Mexico, Argentina, Canada, France, United Kingdom, Russia, South Africa, South Korea, Spain, Sweden, Germany, Hungary, and Japan.

2 The six commitments of the Collevecchio Declaration are as follows:
  1. *Commitment to Sustainability*: FIs must expand their missions from ones that prioritize profit maximization to a vision of social and environmental sustainability.

A commitment to sustainability would require FIs to fully integrate the consideration of ecological limits, social equity, and economic justice into corporate strategies and core business areas (including credit, investing, underwriting, advising), to put sustainability objectives on an equal footing to shareholder maximization and client satisfaction, and to actively strive to finance transactions that promote sustainability.

2. *Commitment to "Do No Harm"*: FIs should commit to do no harm by preventing and minimizing the environmentally and/or socially detrimental impacts of their portfolios and their operations. FIs should create policies, procedures, and standards based on the Precautionary Principle to minimize environmental and social harm, improve social and environmental conditions where they and their clients operate, and avoid involvement in transactions that undermine sustainability.

3. *Commitment to Responsibility*: FIs should bear full responsibility for the environmental and social impacts of their transactions. FIs must also pay their full and fair share of the risks they accept and create. This includes financial risks, as well as social and environmental costs that are borne by communities.

4. *Commitment to Accountability*: FIs must be accountable to their stakeholders, particularly those that are affected by the companies and activities they finance. Accountability means that stakeholders must have an influential voice in financial decisions that affect the quality of their environments and their lives—both through ensuring that stakeholders rights are protected by law, and through practices and procedures adopted by FIs themselves.

5. *Commitment to Transparency*: FIs must be transparent to stakeholders, not only through robust, regular, and standardized disclosure, but also by being responsive to stakeholder needs for specialized information on FIs' policies, procedures, and transactions. Commercial confidentiality should not be used as an excuse to deny stakeholders information.

6. *Commitment to Sustainable Markets and Governance*: FIs should ensure that markets are more capable of fostering sustainability by actively supporting public policy, regulatory and/or market mechanisms which facilitate sustainability and that foster the full cost accounting of social and environmental externalities (BankTrack, 2006).

3   The signatories of the Principles for Responsible Investment sign the following:

As institutional investors, we have a duty to act in the best long-term interests of our beneficiaries. In this fiduciary role, we believe that environmental, social, and corporate governance (ESG) issues can affect the performance of investment portfolios (to varying degrees across companies, sectors, regions, asset classes, and through time). We also recognize that applying these Principles may better align investors with broader objectives of society. Therefore, where consistent with our fiduciary responsibilities, we commit to the following:

- *Principle 1*: We will incorporate ESG issues into investment analysis and decision making processes.
- *Principle 2*: We will be active owners and incorporate ESG issues into our ownership policies and practices.
- *Principle 3*: We will seek appropriate disclosure on ESG issues by the entities in which we invest.
- *Principle 4*: We will promote acceptance and implementation of the Principles within the investment industry.
- *Principle 5*: We will work together to enhance our effectiveness in implementing the Principles.
- *Principle 6*: We will each report on our activities and progress towards implementing the Principles. (PRI Association, 2016)

4   The SAM is a four-step approach:

1. Define cost objective;
2. Specify the scope of the analysis (the boundaries of the SAM evaluation are widely defined to track the impacts of a project over its full life cycle, extending beyond those impacts directly controllable by the project team);
3. Identify impacts of the cost objective (these are considered under four headings: economic, resource use, environmental, and social);
4. Monetize the impacts (a variety of monetization approaches may be adopted, with current prices of the open literature being used as far as possible, for identifying a monetization mechanism).

5 One such person was author and poet Oscar Wilde, who said, "Nowadays people know the price of everything and the value of nothing."

References

Anderson, R. C. (2009). *Confessions of a Radical Industrialist*. New York: St. Martin's Press.

Antheaume, N. (2007). Full cost accounting: Adam Smith meets Rachel Carson? In J. Unerman, J. Bebbington, & B. O'Dwyer (eds.), *Sustainability Accounting and Accountability* (Chapter 11). New York: Routledge.

Bagstad, K. J., & Shammin, M. R. (2012). Can the genuine progress indicator better inform sustainable regional progress? A case study for Northeast Ohio. *Ecological Indicators* 18, 330–341.

BankTrack. (2006). The Dos and Donts of Sustainable Banking. www.banktrack.org/news/the_dos_and_donts_of_sustainable_banking.

Bebbington, J. G. (2001). *Full Cost Accounting: An Agenda for Action*. London: ACCA.

Bridges Fund Management. (2015). The Bridges Spectrum of Capital: How we define the sustainable and impact investment market. www.bridgesfundmanagement.com/wp-content/uploads/2017/08/Bridges-Spectrum-of-Capital-screen.pdf.

Clarke, M., & Lawn, P. (2008). Is measuring genuine progress at the sub-national level useful? *Ecological Indicators* 8, 573–581.

Coulson, A. (2007). Sustainability considerations in finance. In J. Unerman & J. Bebbington (eds.), *Sustainability Accounting and Accountability* (Chapter 18). New York: Routledge.

Dietz, S., & Neumayer, E. (2004). Genuine savings: A critical analysis of its policy-guiding value. *International Journal of Environment and Sustainable Development* 3 (3/4), 276–292.

Equator Principles Association. (2015). Equator Principles. https://equator-principles.com.

GSIA. (2015). 2014 Global Sustainable Investment Review. Global Sustainable Investment Alliance. www.gsi-alliance.org/wp-content/uploads/2015/02/GSIA_Review_download.pdf.

Holub, H. W., Tappeiner, G., & Tappeiner, U. (1999). Some remarks on the "System of Integrated Environmental and Economic Accounting" of the United Nations. *Ecological Economics* 29, 329–336.

Institute on the Environment. (2012). *Big Challenges Promising Solutions*. St. Paul: University of Minnesota.

Lawn, P. (2005). An assessment of the valuation methods used to calculate the Index of Sustainable Economic Welfare (ISEW), Genuine Progress Indicator (GPI), and Sustainable Net Benefit Index (SNBI). *Environment, Development and Sustainability* 7(2), 185–208.

Longsworth, A., Doran, H., & Webber, J. (2012, September). The Sustainability Executive: Profile and Progress. PwC. https://growthorientedsustainableentrepreneurship.files.wordpress.com/2016/07/od-chief-sustainability-officer.pdf.

Mota, R. P., Domingos, T., & Martins, V. (2010). Analysis of genuine saving and potential green net national income: Portugal, 1995–2005. *Ecological Economics* 69, 1934–1942.

National Geographic and GlobeScan. (2014). Greendex 2014: Consumer Choice and the Environment: A Worldwide Tracking Survey. https://globescan.com/wp-content/uploads/2017/07/Greendex_2014_Highlights_Report_NationalGeographic_GlobeScan.pdf.

Natoli, R., & Zuhair, S. (2011). Measuring progress: A comparison of the GDP, HDI, GS and the RIE. *Social Indicators Research* 10, 33–56.

Patagonia. (2022). Earth is now our only shareholder. www.patagonia.com/ownership.

PRI Association. (2023). What is the PRI?www.unpri.org/about-us/about-the-pri.

Smith, D. (1994). Environmental Risk: Credit approaches and opportunities, an interim report. UNEP Roundtable on Commercial Banks and the Environment.

Stock, K. (2013). Patagonia's "Buy Less" Plea Spurs More Buying. Bloomberg. www.bloomberg.com/news/articles/2013-08-28/patagonias-buy-less-plea-spurs-more-buying#xj4y7vzkg.

Sukhdev, P. (2012). Sustainability: The corporate climate overhaul. *Nature* 486, 27–28. www.nature.com/articles/486027a.

UNDP. (2011). Frequently Asked Questions (FAQs) about the Human Development Index (HDI). https://data.un.org/_Docs/FAQs_2011_HDI.pdf.

UNEP. (2011). *Towards a Green Economy: Pathways to Sustainable Development and Poverty Eradication.* www.unep.org/resources/report/towards-green-economy-pathways-sustainable-development-and-poverty-eradication-10.

UNEP FI. (2023). Principles for Responsible Banking. United Nations Environment Programme Finance Initiative. www.unepfi.org/banking/bankingprinciples.

United Nations. (2000). *Integrated Environmental and Economic Accounting. An Operational Manual.* New York: United Nations.

Wen, Z., Zhang, K., Du, B., Li, Y., & Li, W. (2007). Case study of the use of genuine progress indicator to measure urban economic welfare in China. *Ecological Economics* 63(2–3), 463–475.

Wilson, J., & Tyedmers, P. (2013). Rethinking what counts. Perspectives on wellbeing and genuine progress indicator metrics from a Canadian viewpoint. *Sustainability* 5, 187–202.

7

PURSUING SUSTAINABILITY IN EDUCATION AND RESEARCH

A sustainability approach does not provide what to think, but how to go about thinking—in the classroom, at home, in the laboratory … wherever.

(Marilyn Waite)

Introduction

The education and research field is large. Education encompasses our very first steps in life and follows us through to retirement. Education and research include early childhood, primary and secondary schooling, higher education, specialized training, and research and development. Across all educational and research institutions, improvements can be made so that day-to-day operations promote sustainable development. These improvements include workspaces that optimize human interaction and productivity, water use and recovery, energy savings, materials use, and waste management. Beyond the campus and tangible assets of education facilities, the purpose of the institutions should also be to help students and research activities move society along a sustainability pathway.

In conversations with individuals in the education profession (researchers, consultants, principals of schools, deans, board of education members, and professors), here is what came to mind when they thought about sustainable development and sustainability:

"In my private life, sustainability means …"

- Building lasting relationships with friends and family
- Having roots in the community
- Making choices that allow for the conservation of resources (such as recycling, reusing grocery bags, buying in-season, using mass transit)

DOI: 10.4324/9781032615844-7

- Acting responsibly ("it is difficult to separate your private and professional lives when you are a public figure")

"In my career in education and research, sustainability means ..."

- Working on topics that I care about for a long time
- Improving my workplace
- Learning more and continuing in a lifelong track of learning
- Understanding the changes impacting children and families
- Continuing the mission of education
- Understanding that I must change and that my surroundings must change
- Being aware of the environment around me
- Being able to utilize my skills and ability in more than one area
- Assisting students in having opportunity and options once they graduate

There is an eclectic group of responses from those working in education and research. However, there are common threads, which include continuity and preparing the next generation. As one person mentioned, separating private life and career can be nearly impossible when you are in a visible position such as professor or principal of a school. It would be embarrassing for a student to see his or her teacher littering at a grocery store, for example, if that principal teaches the practice of not littering at school. Therefore, a sustainability outlook is likely to have an impact on both spheres: private and public.

Research is intricately tied to the field of education since it entails the search and communication of new knowledge. There are two main schools of thought involving sustainability in education and research: one is that sustainability can be integrated into any subject matter or discipline and the other is that sustainability concepts should be a separate discipline. This chapter encompasses both approaches.

Education for sustainability (EfS)/education for sustainable development (ESD)

The five pillars of education according to UNESCO are learning to know, learning to do, learning to live together, learning to be, and learning to transform oneself and society (UNESCO, 2012a). Sustainability concepts can add purpose to education, give a common vision, provide relevance to the curriculum (a factor in school dropout), raise economic potential, help make abstract concepts more concrete, and save pupils' lives (e.g., in natural disasters) (UNESCO, 2012a). Education for sustainable development (ESD) is also called education for sustainability (EfS). The are four components of EfS: improving access and retention in quality basic education, reorienting existing educational programs to address sustainability, increasing public understanding and awareness of sustainability, and providing training to all sectors of the workforce (UNESCO, 2012a). EfS is a global initiative that develops learning practices needed to promote a sustainable development pathway. Authors Kennelly, Taylor, and Serow define EfS as, "Education that builds community capacity to shape a future that is more sustainable in biophysical, social, political and economic dimensions" (Kennelly et al., 2012).

The Australian EfS guide incorporates five rubrics for sustainability in education: *Culture, Understanding, Learning, Community*, and *Managing*. The guide outlines a path toward sustainability based on each rubric: *starting* (school realizes the need for change), *challenging* (school is actively involved in challenging practices and establishing processes for change), *committing* (EfS is integrated into life of the school and its broader community), and *transforming* (the school, with its community, is continuously learning and living) (Australian Government, 2007). In EfS schools, the culture of sustainability is reflected in areas such as the staff selection process. Thus, a checklist for interviewing a potential math teacher would include questions like "Is this candidate certified to teach geometry?" and "Is this candidate knowledgeable about sustainability?"[1]

The orthodox approach to education is for the curriculum to be broken down into a number of subjects or key learning areas; however, "the compartmentalized, piecemeal, disjointed learning that ensues can be inadequate to

TABLE 7.1 Sample list of adjectival education

Antiracist Education	Energy Education	Anti-Smoking Education
Disaster Prevention Education	Workplace Education	Life Skills Education
Vocational Education	Economics Education	Indigenous Studies
Gender Studies	Leadership Education	Earthquake Education
Water Education	International Studies	Values Education
Indigenous Peoples Education	Development Education	Human Rights Education
Drug Use Prevention Education	Tsunami Education	Heritage Education
Genocide Education	Self-Image Education	Sexuality Education
Consumer Education	Conservation Education	Health Education
Horticulture Education	Cooperative Education	Systems Thinking Education
Conflict Resolution Education	Religious Education	Global Education
Computer Studies	Recycling Education	Gender Education
Community Studies	Population Education	Civics Education
Family Studies	Futures Education	Permaculture Education
Entrepreneurship Education	Citizenship Education	Character Education
Biodiversity Education	Nutrition Education	Environmental Education
Equity Education	Outdoor Education	Experiential Education
Anti-Violence Education	Nature Studies	World Studies
Peace Education	Multicultural Education	Media Education

grasp the realities that are global, transnational, multidimensional, transversal, polydisciplinary and planetary" (Morin, 2001). According to Edwards, ESD must develop a more integrated and flexible curriculum that reconciles the tension between abstract academic knowledge and "the grounded knowledge acquired from everyday experience" (Edwards, 2006). There are numerous examples of how teachers can incorporate sustainability throughout the existing curriculum in an accessible way. In order to meet the learning needs of all pupils in the classroom and thus address the social equity pillar of sustainability, UNESCO proposes four teaching ESD techniques: simulations, class discussions, issue analysis, and story-telling (UNESCO, 2012a). To teach about graphs, a math teacher could use national population pyramids from population education; in history class when learning about World War II, the teacher can ask, "Why do you think war prevents countries from making progress towards sustainability?" In biology, predator–prey relationships can have a sustainability angle by explaining the consequences of the introduction of non-native species (UNESCO, 2012a).

Teaching teachers

In order for educators to teach about sustainability, they too must have a sound knowledge base. In many instances, curriculum evolves at the local, regional, or national level to include sustainability learning without adequate training for the teachers who are expected to deliver. In addition, for many current teachers, sustainability is a new concept and one that they were not taught during their pre-service training.

In a study completed in New South Wales University, recent graduates of the Bachelor of Primary Education program were questioned during their first year of teaching as to the effectiveness of a pre-service EfS training. Specifically, the following research question was asked: "What links did participant teachers make between pre-service EfS and their capacity to engage with EfS in their schools?" (Kennelly et al., 2012). The teachers interviewed cited the following as very valuable pre-service EfS training: content knowledge; the ability to source relevant information and use local resources and expertise from sustainability organizations and individuals; the experience of observing how hands-on projects were organized and how they were received by children; and the opportunity to connect practical and outdoor experiences with the curriculum through their own efforts (Kennelly et al., 2012).

As one teacher noted:

> When you try to explain something to children you really need to have a good knowledge of the science behind it. And even though you think that you do, you really don't. You might have knowledge that you're happy with yourself. But when the children ask "why," I really think you need those fundamental science principles behind you.
>
> (Kennelly et al., 2012)

This hints at the need for sustainability training for existing and upcoming teachers in the scientific principles behind sustainability if sustainability is to be part of a school curriculum.

Primary education and secondary education

Primary education, including early childhood education, is the first notion of formal education. It generally takes place in the daycare or caregiver environment, but some school systems also offer early childhood education programs for children starting at three years old. Worldwide, primary education is viewed as an absolute necessity so that students acquire basic numeracy and literacy skills needed for future learning. Incorporating sustainability at this level of learning is thus critical. Practices learned at this early age are likely to become habit and mainstreamed into larger societal norms.

Post-apartheid South Africa has embarked on incorporating sustainability in education. The education sector seeks to equip learners with the skills to "demonstrate an understanding of the world as a set of related systems by recognizing that problem solving contexts do not exist in isolation" (DoE RSA, 2012). The South African curriculum statement emphasizes the relationship among human rights, social justice, inclusivity, and a healthy environment. In geography class, students learn about conflicts surrounding resource use; in technology class, students learn about environmentally sustainable design; in natural sciences, students learn about biodiversity in South Africa; in life orientation class, the students learn about the link between the environment and health (Lotz-Sisitka, 2006).

So what is a sustainable school? According to the Australian EfS guide, it is a place that values a whole-school approach to EfS, community developed vision and values, the equality of all participants, respect for self, others, and the environment, student voices and student action, community partnerships and relationships, long-term thinking and decision making, health of ecological systems, diverse cultural perspectives, holistic thinking, and sustainable lifestyles (Australian Government, 2007). Whole-school programs are applied across the whole life of the school and diverge from approaches that isolate sustainability in the curriculum; whole-school programs reorient "school pedagogy and practice to address the complex and critical needs of sustainability, linking learners with teachers, school administrators, parents and the wider community" (Tilbury & Wortman, 2006).

Higher education and research

Institutions of higher education (IHE) are undergoing sustainability transformation in workplace and campus life infrastructure, in activities, and in curriculum development. Many IHEs hire sustainability coordinators, directors, and professors across many disciplines that specialize in a sustainability component.

Various specializations, such as environmental economics, environmental science, environmental engineering, social science, and humanities, come together to form new interdisciplinary branches, involving sustainability thinking and learning. The career opportunities are vast for those who know how to incorporate a quadruple bottom line (social, environmental, economic, and generational results) into their teaching, their homework assignments, their publications, and their field.

Research is the systematic investigation of proving or disproving existing notions and developing new ones. It touches upon every thinkable content area and is often the source of new disciplines. Research takes place in dedicated institutions (public and private) and is the cornerstone of academia and universities worldwide. Companies take part in research and development to compete, improve market share and profits, and survive. Likewise, government institutions undertake research to improve jurisdictional competitiveness and to support innovation. Therefore, many career sectors can overlap with research. There are researchers in health care, medicine, law, education, science, engineering, media, history, literature, and linguistics, just to name a few. The careers in research are thus tied to a subject area, sustainability now being one of them. Since research most often visibly takes place in an IHE, careers in research are closely linked with careers in education. Sustainability considerations can be brought into any field of research. For example, finding an alternative material that can perform the same function with less energy may be the work of a researcher in metallurgy. Or analyzing the trends in social, environmental, intergenerational, and economic writing in a certain century may be the work of a researcher in literature. Researchers in education may also use sustainability metrics to analyze the quality of education over time and the impact of education on society.

IHEs are playing an increasing role in bridging (1) sustainability and research and (2) sustainability and education. Over 200 universities have signed the Earth Charter, a declaration of fundamental ethical principles for building a just, sustainable, and peaceful global society, as an ethical framework for guiding education and research[2] (Earth Charter, 1997). Over 400 university leaders have signed the Talloires declaration,[3] a ten-point action plan for incorporating sustainability in higher education activities (UNESCO, 2012b). In addition to IHEs' commitment to education for sustainability, universities have also been ranked according to their sustainability efforts. In the United Kingdom, People & Planet's Green League annually issues a comprehensive and independent league table of universities ranked by environmental and ethical performance (People & Planet, 2023). A green ranking provides a means for education and research institutions to attract their clients—future students.

There are a growing number of business schools that are taking sustainability education seriously. These IHEs are preparing students for what the business world requires in terms of skills. Since the business world is engaged in corporate social responsibility, sustainability, environmental, social and governance integration, and diversity, equity, and inclusion initiatives, recruiters expect incoming talent to have relevant knowledge and practical approaches. To perform well in senior management and C-suites jobs, employees will likely need skills to deal with complex sustainability challenges. The Principles for Responsible Management Education (PRME) were developed in 2007 by an international task force of 60 deans, university presidents, and official representatives of leading business schools and academic institutions. Updated in 2023, the seven principles cover purpose, values, teach, research, partner, practice, and share[4] (PRME, 2023). Author Mabry suggests a "whole person" approach to integrating a sustainability paradigm into business education. This is an approach where the learner or user is "involved in affective, behavioral, and cognitive aspects of the learning experience" (Rogers, 1980); this approach could be practically administered by involving students in a team-based research project (Mabry, 2011).

Author Rusinko has created a matrix to integrate sustainability in management and business education. This matrix can be used for integrating sustainability at all levels of education (primary, secondary, post-secondary) and for different content-based subject matter. Quadrant I is the option of integrating sustainability into an already existing course as a new topic, case, module, or service learning project; Quadrant II is the option of integrating sustainability through a narrow discipline-specific focus by creating a new structure (example: stand-alone course on sustainability in management); Quadrant III is the option of integrating sustainability within existing structures through a broad cross-disciplinary focus within the curriculum; Quadrant IV is the option of integrating sustainability through new structures with a broad cross-disciplinary focus (can be pursued through transdisciplinary sustainability programs, majors, or minors) (Rusinko, 2010).

From Teach for America to principal of Mundo Verde—Dahlia's story

> All learning is service in some way.
>
> *(Dahlia Aguilar, principal at Mundo Verde)*

Mundo Verde is no ordinary primary school. In the heart of Washington, D.C., Mundo Verde shines as the first local school to be founded on sustainability principles. The school is bilingual Spanish–English and stresses expeditionary learning, sustainability, and stewardship.

As I entered the halls of Mundo Verde, I was greeted by children, parents, teachers, and support staff of all backgrounds. But there was one common thread among everyone—bright smiles and vibrant energy. I sat down on a modern bench in the brightly lit hallway. Before me was a wall demonstrating school projects, including "Why do animals look the way they look?" in English and "Características del ciclo de vida de la mariposa" (Characteristics of the butterfly life cycle) in Spanish. Pictures accompanied the life-cycle presentation wall. The students were getting a deeper meaning of nature beyond the classroom theory.

Charter schools were created in Washington, DC and other parts of the U.S. as a response to a perceived failure of traditional public education; parents and students wanted more choices and higher academic attainment. The U.S. Department of Education administers various grants under the Charter Schools Program. In the 2022–2023 school year, both DC Public Schools (DCPS) and the public charter school sector saw graduation rate increases; the four-year graduation rate for DCPS was 72.5%, an increase of about 2% from the previous year, while the four-year graduation rate for public charter schools was 80.1%, an increase of 3% from the previous year (DCPS, 2023).

Mundo Verde was thus established as a charter school allowing for flexible operations and a focus on high standards. But unlike others, Mundo Verde has a sustainability mission: "Purposefully diverse and culturally inclusive, Mundo Verde was founded to empower students to reach their full potential and give them the skills they need to work together to solve sustainability challenges" (Mundo Verde, 2013).

In comes in Dahlia, principal of Mundo Verde. We sit down in the teachers' planning room. Dahlia was raised in Texas and left to work as an English as a second language (ESL) teacher with Teach for America. After working as an elementary school teacher for four years, she moved back to Texas and worked in high school education. Teaching these two age groups gave Dahlia the opportunity to understand learning development and further motivated her commitment to social justice. "Teaching and schooling are different things," Dahlia affirmed. Dahlia became involved with the U.S. National Council of La Raza (NCLR), the largest Hispanic civil rights and advocacy organization in the U.S. that works to improve opportunities for Hispanic Americans; there are over 350 community-based organizations associated with NCLR. Dahlia also served as administrator and assistant principal of Bell Multicultural High School (now a part of the Columbia Heights Educational Campus). There, she learned that being undocumented is a real barrier to college acceptance, including financial aid.

Dahlia became committed to helping prepare students of all backgrounds to become productive members of society. Her biggest drive was to meet the needs of students whose first language was other than English, including students who are immigrants. She became involved first as a board member for Mundo Verde Public Charter School, founded with U.S. federal funding and a startup grant from the Walton Foundation. Then she was recruited for the position of principal. Dahlia not only became the leader of the new school, but also a parent, since her son also attends Mundo Verde. Now she experiences both the feelings of guilt and satisfaction when, at home, after dishing out a meal without green vegetables, her son asks, "Can something green be put on my plate?" Dahlia became hooked on the mission to create stewards for sustainability at Mundo Verde. In 2011, Mundo Verde opened its doors to students at pre-kindergarten through second grade levels. And it opened its doors for me to observe classroom learning, sustainable school lunches, and urban farming.

As I told Dahlia that I was impressed by the butterfly expo in the hall, she explained that the students learned about the Monarch butterflies' loss of habitat in both Washington, DC and Michoacán, Mexico. The students, with the help of their teachers and documentary film partner Meridian Hill Pictures, created a short film about the habitat, life cycle, and migration of Monarch butterflies. Spoken in Spanish, the students wrote the original content and designed and constructed the sets, props, and costumes. They presented their expedition on the Monarch butterfly to the Mexican Cultural Institute in Washington, DC, which helped to raise awareness about deforestation.

As I entered the classrooms, I noticed the school uniform: a Mundo Verde T-shirt or sweatshirt. The students (and teachers) had their choice of different colors. Since the other items of clothing were flexible, the Mundo Verde approach allowed people to maintain both a sense of individuality and the collective.

"*¿Qué es importante cuando conoces a un amigo?*" (What's important when you meet a friend?), the teacher in one of the pre-K classes asked his students. The students' responses clearly showed their understanding of friendship and community. I didn't remember having that kind of social sensibility lesson when I was in pre-K, but I was glad to see it happening at Mundo Verde.

In the next class, I saw student-constructed rules written on the board such as "*ser amable*" (be kind), which was a more refreshing, positive message compared to what I remember at that age (a lot of "don't" do this and "don't" do that ...). There was a peace corner where students could write their feelings (inspired by the book *Feelings* by Aliki).

Mundo Verde uses the U.S. Common Core standards for language, arts ,and math, Washington State standards for sustainability (taught in science and social studies), the U.S. Partnership for Education for Sustainable Development National Education for Sustainability K-12 Student Learning Standards, and Responsive Classroom (a research- and evidence-based approach to elementary education for greater teacher effectiveness, higher student achievement, and improved school climate). Student learning is not limited to the classroom and ready-made curriculums. In fact, teachers create their own curriculum, often with the help of the Australian Rubrics for EfS. Sustainability is integrated into the classroom throughout the curriculum and through co-curricular activities, including designing, planting, maintaining, and harvesting an organic garden; visiting local farms to explore food production and sustainable practices; investigating natural resources and alternative energy sources, such as solar and wind power; and separating trash into compost, recycling, and waste bins in conjunction with exploring the implication of our use of resources (Mundo Verde, 2012).

At Mundo Verde, social skills are just as important as the academic curriculum. For Dahlia, this is a huge paradigm shift from traditional learning, where the academic content is more valued than student learning of empathy and social responsibility.

The "garden to fork" concept of growing local organic produce to eat is reinforced by an on-site garden. Students learn the concept of seasonality in a hands-on manner. When I passed by the school lunchroom, something smelled appetizing. I had a quick flashback of my days in elementary school. I remember that I didn't eat much and I didn't like what I ate much. Things at Mundo Verde were different. The catering company, Graceful Affairs, provides nut-free, pork-free, red-meat-free, naturally grown, healthy food. The plates and utensils used are sustainable (compostable from 2012–2014; reusable from 2014), and the compost bins are on-site for students to understand the process first-hand. First graders studied trash, went to ECO City Farms (local farm and outreach center that converted previously vacant land into a productive farming enterprise that produces Certified Naturally Grown produce); as a result of this experience, the students launched their own composting campaign. Many classrooms now have their own worm bins for composting.

For Dahlia, "all learning is service in some way; the greatest expression of understanding is to create something for an authentic change." She encourages activities where students apply their knowledge, such as creating a "how to" book on composting. Pre-K students completed an expedition on health and took their "how to care for your body" brochures to a local clinic. "Students feel like they are solving a problem, and sometimes they really are," Dahlia stated. She added, "The students feel authentically part of a community of researchers, which is motivating college readiness."

Inclusion is also a part of the sustainability ethos of Mundo Verde. There is an extra commitment to help students performing at level, below level, or above level. The after-school team at Mundo Verde helps grow the sustainability identity of the school through movement, physical education, arts (re-envisioning sustainability), and healthy eating where students showcase recipes to parents. Mundo Verde Bilingual Public Charter School was named a winner of the 2013 Mayor's Sustainability Awards for outstanding achievements and leadership in sustainable practices. Mundo Verde is a part of the U.S. Department of Education's Green Ribbon Program, a recognition of schools and districts that are exemplary in reducing environmental impact and costs; improving the health and wellness of students and staff; and providing effective environmental and sustainability education, which incorporates STEM, civic skills, and green-career pathways (ED-GRS, 2014).

Dahlia went full circle: from her teaching roots as an elementary teacher to most recently principal of a startup elementary school focused on bilingual sustainability education. "Mundo Verde has transformed me," Dahlia expressed a sense of gratitude. "I am now much more conscious about sustainability and understand it within the realm of stewardship," Dahlia explained. Dahlia hopes that students will carry the sustainability values, which she noted are universally applicable, with them throughout life. "It's about being a good person, really," Dahlia stated. Dahlia did not start out her career incorporating a sustainability framework. She has learned many methods over the years, such as the Socratic method of teaching and learning by questioning, which she holds dear. Dahlia believes that teachers are models of what it is to learn (as opposed to being the experts); she has learned about sustainability through the opportunity to become the principal of Mundo Verde—an unexpected but fulfilling turn of a career path. For some teachers at Mundo Verde who were well versed in environmental sustainability, working with the students taught them how important cultural diversity, one aspect of social sustainability, is to overall sustainability. Dahlia believes sustainability being incorporated into primary, secondary, and tertiary education will continue to grow and the opportunities to use sustainability knowledge in careers will grow with it.

Mundo Verde has a waitlist of over 1,000 students.

From environmental studies to professor of music (and back again)—Aaron's story

> We do not just want a world to sustain; we want to sustain a beautiful world.
> (Dr. Aaron S. Allen, University of North Carolina at Greensboro)

It was unusually cold for the month of March in the state of North Carolina— hardly above freezing. February saw massive snowstorms, a state of emergency, and associated blackouts. As I drove through the city of Greensboro, I noticed the churches nearly on every corner, the lack of pedestrian crosswalks, barren trees, and signs of economic decline. As I pulled into 100 McIver Street, a modern mostly brick building awaited me: the School of Music, Theatre, and Dance at the University of North Carolina at Greensboro (UNCG). The mood immediately changed as I stepped into a nicely day-lit building with bamboo growing in the courtyard and wonderful instrumental sounds coming from the various music rooms. Day lighting has been shown to increase learning speed (an increase of 20–26% for test scores measured in primary and secondary schools) (Hopkins, 2009). A young man in a bow tie passed me by. A lady with an all-black outfit and violin in hand reminded me of the recitals and music concerts in which I once took part. Gray and pink motif flooring. I felt welcome.

As I searched for the office of associate professor of music, Dr. Aaron S. Allen, I smiled at the musical life coming from each direction. "Nice to meet you," Aaron and I reached his office simultaneously. We take a seat. I smile when the light remained off. "That's something I would do to save on electricity and use the natural light," I thought to myself.

Aaron's office was packed with books. To my left, there were books about classical music. To my right, there were modern books with words I didn't understand, like "Ecomusicology." "I grew up in rural Appalachia," Aaron began. Aaron's family is from West Virginia, a state with historically some of the poorest areas in the U.S. When his family realized that he had exceptional intellectual abilities, they decided that it would not be feasible to drive five hours each day to find a high-functioning school. They packed their bags and headed south for Key West, Florida. His family later relocated to his father's original hometown of Long Beach, Mississippi.

In West Virginia, Florida, and Mississippi, Aaron grew up hiking and camping. As he stated, "I had no nature-deficit disorder." By his last year of high school, he knew he wanted to be a teacher, but didn't know exactly in what or at what level. His close-to-nature upbringing led him to major in environmental studies at Tulane University. Tulane's nickname, "The Green Wave," probably sub-consciously enticed Aaron to attend. He thought of transferring to a more activist campus, but then decided to try to help transform Tulane. There, on scholarships and financial aid, Aaron was president of the Green Club, which advocated for environmental justice and promoted on-campus environmental responsibility. Little did he know then that the combination of music and environment would be his claim to career fulfillment and fame.

During university, Aaron wanted to make the most of the free and abundant education. He took extra classes, classes during the summer months, and classes that had nothing (so it seemed) to do with the environment. Before he knew it, the music minor turned into a major. Aaron earned a double degree: Summa Cum Laude and Phi Beta Kappa with a Bachelor of Arts in Music and a Bachelor of Science in Ecological Studies. His environmental thesis, entitled "Greening the Green Wave," was about making Tulane's campus more sus-tainable in terms of operations and education (Allen, 1999a, 1999b, 2000).

Then Aaron met with what he called "failure." He was a finalist for the Truman, Rhodes, and Marshall scholarships, but did not secure an award. He did, however, win the Morris K. Udall Scholarship in 1996 and 1997. During the interviewing process for one of the bursaries, someone pulled him to one side and said: "I wish you would have applied as a music student." "They saw something that I didn't," Aaron explained. Aaron had always isolated the environment and music; he lived two lives in parallel. But in October of that year, Aaron decided to apply to graduate school to study music. He had handed a few ideas to his advisor at Tulane, who told him to aim higher. Aaron was hesitant, citing his socio-economic background as an inhibitor. But his advisor, Anthony (Tony) Cummings, then dean of the college and professor of musi-cology at Tulane, said, "It's precisely because you are a poor kid from Appa-lachia that you should apply to top schools." Eventually, Aaron went to Harvard to study musicology, or music history. He wanted a break from working on the perils of the world as an environmentalist. He did propose a thesis on a music and nature topic, but it was most thoroughly rejected.

So, he studied the nineteenth-century Italian reception of Beethoven—because why not? After spending time in Italy and as a lecturer at Harvard, Aaron secured a tenure-track position at UNCG. He returned to his interests in environmental studies by joining the faculty committees for campus sustainability and for the small Environmental Studies Program. Soon thereafter, when his dean encouraged his interdisciplinary interests in music and environmental studies, he started working with the idea of ecocritical musicology, or ecomusicology.

Aaron laughed as he reflected. He explained, "My professional organization is called the American Musicological Society; when I first introduced the idea of ecocriticism in music, their knee jerk reaction was that I should get that tree-hugging stuff out of here." However, Aaron gathered enough support for his idea to launch the Ecocriticism Study Group of the American Musicological Society; he also was co-founder and chair of the Ecomusicology Special Interest Group of the Society for Ethnomusicology. Aaron, who was commissioned to write an entry on ecomusicology for the *Grove Dictionary of American Music*, defines ecomusicology as the study of music, culture, and nature; it involves the study of the connections between human sound worlds and non-human sound worlds. The *Grove Dictionary* goes on to state, "Ecomusicology considers musical and sonic issues, both textual and performative, related to ecology and the natural environment" (Allen, 2014).

In 2013, Aaron became a tenured professor at UNCG in the School of Music, where he taught classes in Beethoven, general music history, chamber music, musical instruments, ecomusicology, and many more subjects. In that same year, he also became UNCG's first academic sustainability coordinator. The mission of this position allows Aaron to work with professors and the provost to bring about sustainability transformation on campus. There is now a minor in sustainability studies at UNCG, which views sustainability as "Academics, operations, and outreach … conducted with careful attention to the enduring interconnectedness of social equity, the environment, the economy, and aesthetics" (UNCG, 2013). The emphasis on aesthetics is particularly suited to UNCG since its strengths are as an arts and culture institution of higher education. As Aaron put it, "At UNCG, we do not just want a world to sustain; we want to sustain a beautiful world."

Aaron uses sound and music to reach those who may not connect to the scientific language used to describe environmental challenges like climate change. "Sonification and musicalization can reach people you might not otherwise reach," Aaron enthused. Music can do a lot for collective action and listener communities are very diverse. Aaron has researched political rock, environmental leadership, natural resource use for instruments, and the representations of nature in music. Needless to say, Aaron was able to develop a career path in teaching and research revolving around sustainability in music, culture, and nature. As Aaron states in "Ecomusicology: Bridging the Sciences, Arts, and Humanities" (2012a), "Music, like history and literature, is a widespread phenomenon that can trigger powerful emotional responses, often quickly, making it a productive medium for environmental education messages."

Now well known as a founding father of ecomusicology, Aaron has a unique and visible position in the education marketplace. He has co-edited the first major volume on the subject, *Current Directions in Ecomusicology*. Not only does Aaron see the value of sustainability to his career and those of fellow faculty members and students, but also he has seen sustainability play a role in hiring decisions. UNCG's Bryan School of Business and Economics recently hired a faculty member in tourism and hospitality. For that position, the job specification stipulated the need for knowledge and interest in sustainability. And while a specific sustainability-oriented job description is not widespread for most faculty positions, the lack of knowledge, interest, and ability to connect one's role to the larger goals of sustainability would be insufficient.

Fast-forward to 2023, Aaron's role at UNCG had evolved, notwithstanding the obstacles that are inherent in educational systems.

In 2015, he became the director of the interdisciplinary Environment and Sustainability Program. In that role, Aaron helped to double the number of majors. Yet, without a specific academic home for the Program, the financial and human resources to support the work did not double. Being the director was a part-time position for Aaron, who was still expected to fulfill research and teaching duties in the School of Music. Aaron became the Program, which was not by any means sustainable. In 2017, an internal review found that there was indeed a need for change. The Program subsequently merged with the Geography Department and, in 2018, became the Department of Geography, Environment, and Sustainability (GES).

Although Aaron was relieved by the help and his now full-time status in GES, his new home brought additional complexities. He was still expected to be the advisor to all the students in the Program, and because he was tenured in a different discipline, music, he was not paid at the level of his peers in GES. "It's a structural injustice," Aaron lamented. In U.S. academia, one is assigned a CIP (Classification of Instructional Programs) code based on one's degree; in Aaron's experience, it is with this code and its associated pay grade that one remains—forever and ever. In addition, there is a general contraction of higher education in the U.S. that was accelerated by the COVID-19 crisis; there is less hiring and more budget cuts. Aaron explained that "ultimately, it's the students who suffer."

On the bright side, due to a hire in another department, Aaron was able to recruit a stellar associate director. He was thrilled to work with Dr. Plaxedes T. Chitiyo, whose PhD in natural resources and experience on the African continent were complementary to his skills. The Program has increasingly incorporated the concepts of justice, equity, diversity, and inclusion into its curricula. "The students have greatly benefited from our two perspectives: mine as a white guy steeped in the environmental justice issues of Appalachia and the U.S. South and hers as a Black woman steeped in agricultural science and the political economy of Africa," Aaron reflected. As Aaron reminded readers in his article "From Anthropocentrism to Ecocentrism," published in *Ethnomusicology,* since 1850 the Global North has emitted over 70 percent of greenhouse gases but represents less than 20 percent of the population (Allen, 2020). The Global South perspective on climate justice is thus an important one.

Aaron's experience is an example of how despite individual grit, talent, and execution, we work in systems that need to evolve if we are to achieve the best personal and collective outcomes. In that vein, work that improves educational policy and governance for sustainability-focused fields is most welcome. The Environment & Sustainability Program at UNCG is centered around a four-leaf clover: the planet (the biggest leaf), development and economics, social justice, and the arts and humanities. These four elements cannot progress in tandem if they sit on rigid rules that inhibit creative minds from flourishing.

Aaron leaves us with this silver lining: "When you plot a new path, a different path, you will be confronted with all kinds of obstacles. But overcoming them and effecting change will be worth it."

Separate lives, separate roles, same vision for sustainability

Neither Dahlia nor Aaron started their early careers as sustainability professionals. Aaron started out in college passionate about *environmental issues* and saw the value of teaching to reach that goal. Dahlia started out in college passionate about *social justice* and saw the value of teaching to reach that goal. However, both educators have used sustainability in their current roles and career path as a means of expressing their original passions and expanding their purpose. Aaron's path has led him to higher education and research. Dahlia's path has led her to primary and secondary school administration. They both have differentiated themselves in the workplace and remained committed to education and sustainability. Rural Appalachia and urban Texas, where Aaron and Dahlia started their own first learning adventures respectively, are miles apart. However, sustainability knows no boundaries. Educators make a significant difference in the lives of individuals; they can make the same difference in society through sustainability education.

SURF Framework for careers in education and research

Those charged with teaching sustainable practices must understand the theoretical and practical frameworks for implementing sustainability (McFarlane & Ogazon, 2011). The SURF Framework can be used to structure sustainable transformation of education and research and all the careers that it encompasses.

Education and research careers involving supply chain

Apart from the supply chain of the physical infrastructure of an educational institution, the heart of the supply chain is that of human resources. An educational institution's reputation and attractiveness is highly dependent on the quality of its students, teachers, researchers, and administrators. Potential employees who perceive the institution, work streams, and curriculum as unsustainable may be less likely to apply for positions or seek tenure and other opportunities. Likewise, the institution's main "product" is the wealth of knowledge it imparts to its students. The alumni are the proof of the institution's level of excellence. If these outgoing alumni leave without sustainability knowledge, the educational institution may also be perceived as outdated and irrelevant to the workforce.

Careers in the supply chain of education include textbook and other publication providers (writers, editors, printing, and online media specialists, etc.), programmers for innovative learning software (including gaming), purchasers for educational and laboratory materials, and online instructors who may help decarbonize the educational supply chain. Music professor and ecomusicology expert Aaron Allen teaches his students about the sustainability considerations in the supply chain of music, especially musical instrument purchasing decisions. Many violinists believe that "You are not a violinist unless you have a Pernambuco bow." However, Pernambuco is an endangered wood from Brazil (which students do not know, and thus learning about sustainable options is eye-opening for students).

On the other hand, the culturally engrained notion that spruce from the Italian Alps is superior for violin making helps sustainability. Antonio Stradivari is regarded as one of the best artisans of stringed instruments throughout the music world. He sourced from his nearby forest in the Italian Alps for spruce. "The community there today, partly because of their pride in the tradition, manages their forest sustainably in order to preserve nature and the tradition" (Allen, 2012b).

In the community rubric of the Australian Sustainable Schools Initiative (AuSSI), schools are encouraged to share their learning with each other. Communication strategies include invitations to school presentations and events, displays in local libraries, and media coverage that may lead to broader community participation (Australian Government, 2007). When a school becomes a sustainable place, the local supply chain also becomes important for supplying goods and services. Exchanges outside of the school but within the community can lead to new products (such as cleaning materials, gardening utensils, and school lunches) that are mutually beneficial for a sustainable school and the local community. There are numerous roles and jobs that are intertwined in a locavore community, including purchasing and sustainability managers. Authors Rands and Starik present the amalgam "glocal" for the phrase "think globally, act locally" (2009). Making both global and local connections can be a challenge for sustainability management educators (Collins & Kearins, 2010). One way to make these connections in education is through the supply chain, explaining global, ethical, and environmentally conscious trade and using local goods and services.

Education and research careers involving the user

Careers intimately linked to the "user" in education and research include teachers and tutors at various levels. The sub-fields include special education, primary and secondary school, higher education, test preparation, and vocational education. The specialization includes instructional specialists, curriculum developers, and behavioral specialists, and mental health specialists. Imparting sustainability knowledge requires a behavioral change for the user (or learner), which requires emotional engagement and passionate commitment (Shrivastava, 2010). This is a specialty of psychologists, behavioral consultants, coaches, mindfulness instructors, and more.

Passion is described by career consultant Sigmund Ginsburg as "The energy that comes from bringing more of *you* into what you do"; passion means doing work as a natural extension of who you are (Shrivastava, 2010). Sustainability education has the goal of bringing about a passion for sustainability for everyone in any career path. It is well documented that students who have a favorable attitude toward a subject also engage more; in addition, motivation to learn and actual learning are correlated (Erskine & Johnson, 2012). There are careers in ensuring a passion and ardor for sustainability through education.

In the learning rubric of the AuSSI, an EfS program integrates curriculum, learning processes, and pedagogies; it values hands-on learning. "The educator becomes a facilitator who ensures that all students have opportunities to be listened to and participate in actions for sustainability" (Australian Government, 2007). In a sample of over 150 business students in the U.S., the perceived effectiveness of learning about sustainability was measured. The researchers found that the six most effective learning approaches for sustainability are sustainability-related scholarships, integrating sustainability into various classes, internships related to sustainable business practices, using sustainability-related business simulations in class, sustainability-related practices implemented at the university level, and international opportunities to learn about sustainability (Erskine & Johnson, 2012). Most of these approaches involve a hands-on, interactive approach. Educators who view the user/learner with this in mind will be more successful and perceived as effective by their students.

Education and research careers involving relations

Career roles closely related to stakeholder relations in education and research include counselors (e.g., career and guidance counselors), administrators, principals, superintendents, deans, university presidents, and teachers.

In the culture rubric of the AuSSI, "educators are challenged to consider the purpose of education and their own role in sustainable communities" (Australian Government, 2007). Jobs for staff include educators, school service officers, administrators, and more. Teachers are charged with the task of helping to create a learning culture—a passion for learning. Adding sustainability to the agenda helps bring meaning to the learning and also helps improve relations with stakeholders who may be interested in different components of the learning experience (e.g., road safety in school zones, healthy school meals, and diverse pedagogical tools).

A teacher may maintain positive relations with parents through parent–teacher conferences, participation in parent–teacher associations, and regular communication via an online newsletter. The teacher may also maintain open communication with students through after-school tutoring and office hours. Wider community outreach may be obtained through school events open to the public (such as science fairs, plays, and concerts) and through targeted communication in public areas such as libraries.

Education and research careers involving the future

The Association of University Leaders for a Sustainable Future (2015) states that from an education perspective, sustainability "implies that the critical activities of a higher education institution are ecologically sound, socially just and economically viable, and that they will continue to be so for future generations." The emphasis on the future is made explicit in this understanding of sustainability. The "F" component of the SURF Framework is especially tied to the education sector (charged with the task of preparing future generations), and to the research sector (charged with the task of improving the future through discoveries and knowledge creation).

Careers tied to future generations are present throughout the education and research sector since, a priori, the purpose of education and research is always linked to future discoveries and/or future generations of workers. Research assistants, principal investigators, professors, and teachers are especially involved in critical thinking about the future.

In the understanding rubric of the AuSSI, inquiry is valued: "questioning is an effective way to start and encourage inquiry into the nature and implications of sustainability" (Australian Government, 2007). Various reflections on future generations and the future in general can be supported using a questioning approach, including backcasting. Teachers and researchers connect to the future through inquiry.

Conclusion

Careers in education and research that incorporate sustainability are not only forward thinking, but also increasingly mandatory. As sustainability continues to shape curriculum development, teacher training, grants for research, and more, individuals who understand sustainability and how to apply it to their job will be higher-valued professionals. The anthropologist Margaret Mead once said, "Children must be taught how to think, not what to think." This nicely summarizes sustainable education and research, and it applies not only to children, but also to all generations. A sustainability approach does not provide what to think, but how to go about thinking—in the classroom, at home, in the laboratory ... wherever. At all levels of education, from early childhood to advanced doctoral studies, sustainability learning is pertinent and can help awaken new ways of tackling a subject matter. Some practical tips for professionals in the education and research sector include:

- Use frameworks to gauge sustainability progress:

  - Apply the SURF Framework to the educational establishment, to the job and career trajectory
  - Commit to the Earth Charter
  - Use the Sustainability Tracking, Assessment & Rating System (STARS) by AASHE
  - Apply the seven Principles for Responsible Management Education.

- Use local, national, and international sources for curriculum development and teaching resources. Examples include:

  - The Education for Sustainable Development Toolkit
  - The Australian Rubrics for Education for Sustainability
  - Aspen Institute's Case Place, for cases, syllabi, and different teaching resources
  - AoM, Organizations and the Natural Environment (ONE), for cases, syllabi, sample assignments, and different teaching resources
  - CO_2nnect for sustainable transportation teaching
  - The Center for Green Schools.

- Read and contribute to academic journals. Examples include:

  - *The Journal of Management Education Special Issues* (Greening and Sustainability Across the Management Curriculum; Teaching About the Natural Environment in Management Education)
  - *Journal of Education for Business* (Sustainability-focused articles)
  - *Journal of Sustainability Education*
  - *Journal of Education for Sustainable Development*
  - *International Journal of Sustainability in Higher Education*
  - *Journal of Teacher Education for Sustainability*.

- Benchmark whole-school programs. Examples include:

  - ENSI Eco-Schools in Europe
  - Foundation for Environmental Education (FEE) Eco-Schools worldwide
  - Green Schools Alliance worldwide
  - Green Ribbon Schools in the U.S.
  - Enviro-schools in New Zealand.

- Join professional associations dedicated to sustainability in education and research, such as:

  - Association for the Advancement of Sustainability in Higher Education (AASHE)
  - Alliance for Research on Corporate Sustainability (ARCS)
  - Association of University Leaders for a Sustainable Future (ULSF)

- BEST Education Network (international consortium of educators committed to furthering the development and dissemination of knowledge in the field of sustainable tourism).

- Join the conversation through various platforms, such as:

  - Second Nature (Education for Sustainability)
  - The U.S. Partnership for Education for Sustainable Development
  - The Center for Green Schools.

Notes

1 ESD teaches all spheres of sustainability, whereas environmental education focuses more on the environment. Core disciplines in primary and secondary education generally consist of mathematics, science, language, and social studies (UNESCO, 2012a). Adjectival educations, also known as second tier subjects, are also part of the curriculum depending on resources and priorities; these adjectival educations include art, music, health, life skills, and technical and vocational education and training (UNESCO, 2012a). ESD guides and transforms both the core and adjectival educations so that they can contribute to a more sustainable future (UNESCO, 2012a).

2 The Earth Charter includes the following principles (Earth Charter, 1997):
  1. Respect Earth and life in all its diversity.
  2. Care for the community of life with understanding, compassion, and love.
  3. Build democratic societies that are just, participatory, sustainable, and peaceful.
  4. Secure Earth's bounty and beauty for present and future generations.
  5. Protect and restore the integrity of Earth's ecological systems, with special concern for biological diversity and the natural processes that sustain life.
  6. Prevent harm as the best method of environmental protection and, when knowledge is limited, apply a precautionary approach.
  7. Adopt patterns of production, consumption, and reproduction that safeguard Earth's regenerative capacities, human rights, and community well-being.
  8. Advance the study of ecological sustainability and promote the open exchange and wide application of the knowledge acquired.
  9. Eradicate poverty as an ethical, social, and environmental imperative.
  10. Ensure that economic activities and institutions at all levels promote human development in an equitable and sustainable manner.
  11. Affirm gender equality and equity as prerequisites to sustainable development and ensure universal access to education, health care, and economic opportunity.
  12. Uphold the right of all, without discrimination, to a natural and social environment supportive of human dignity, bodily health, and spiritual well-being, with special attention to the rights of indigenous peoples and minorities.
  13. Strengthen democratic institutions at all levels, and provide transparency and accountability in governance, inclusive participation in decision making, and access to justice.
  14. Integrate into formal education and lifelong learning the knowledge, values, and skills needed for a sustainable way of life.
  15. Treat all living beings with respect and consideration.
  16. Promote a culture of tolerance, nonviolence, and peace.

3 The Talloires Declaration includes the following ten principles (ULSF, 1990):
   1. Increase Awareness of Environmentally Sustainable Development
   2. Create an Institutional Culture of Sustainability
   3. Educate for Environmentally Responsible Citizenship
   4. Foster Environmental Literacy For All
   5. Practice Institutional Ecology
   6. Involve All Stakeholders
   7. Collaborate for Interdisciplinary Approaches
   8. Enhance Capacity of Primary and Secondary Schools
   9. Broaden Service and Outreach Nationally and Internationally
   10. Maintain the Movement

4 The seven principles of PRME are as follows (PRME, 2023):
   1. Purpose: We advance responsible management education to foster inclusive prosperity in a world of thriving ecosystems.
   2. Values: We place organizational responsibility and accountability to society and the planet at the core of what we do.
   3. Teach: We transform our learning environments by integrating responsible management concepts and practices into our curriculum and pedagogy.
   4. Research: We study people, organizations, institutions, and the state of the world to inspire responsible management and education practice.
   5. Partner: We engage people from business, government, civil society, and academia to advance responsible and accountable management education and practice.
   6. Practice: We adopt responsible and accountable management principles in our own governance and operations.
   7. Share: We share our successes and failures with each other to enable our collective learning and best live our common values and purpose.

References

Allen, A. S. (2020). "From Anthropocentrism to Ecocentrism," in SEM President's Roundtable 2018 "Humanities Response to the Anthropocene" [with Ruth Hellier, Mark Pedelty, Denise Von, Jeff Todd Titon, and Jennifer Post], edited by Timothy Cooley. *Ethnomusicology* 64(2), 304–307 (301–330). https://doi.org/10.5406/ethnomusicology.64.2.0301.

Allen, A. S. (1999a). *Greening the Campus: Institutional Environmental Change at Tulane University*. New Orleans, LA: Tulane University.

Allen, A. S. (1999b). Institutional Change and Leadership in Greening the Campus. In W. L. Filho (ed.), *Sustainability and University Life* (pp. 105–127). Frankfurt am Main: Peter Lang.

Allen, A. S. (2000). Institutional Change and Campus Greening at Tulane University. In *Proceedings of a Conference on Sustainability of Wetlands and Water Resources, Oxford, Mississippi. General Technical Report SRS-50* (pp. 4–13). Asheville, NC: United States Department of Agriculture.

Allen, A. S. (2012a). Ecomusicology: Bridging the Sciences Arts and Humanities. In D. R. Gallagher (ed.), *Environmental Leadership: A Reference Handbook* (pp. 373–381). SAGE Publications.

Allen, A. S. (2012b). Fatto Di Fiemme: Stradivari's Violins and the Musical Trees of the Paneveggio. In L. Auricchio, E. H. Cook, & G. Pacini (eds.), *Invaluable Trees: Cultures of Nature, 1660–1830* (pp. 301–315). Oxford: Voltaire Foundation.

Allen, A. S. (2014). Ecomusicology. In *The Grove Dictionary of American Music*. New York: Oxford University Press.

Association of University Leaders for a Sustainable Future. (2015). About. https://ulsf.org/about.

Australian Government. (2007). *Education for Sustainability*. Australian Sustainable Schools Initiative, South Australia. Adelaide: Australian Government.

Collins, E. M., & Kearins, K. (2010). Delivering on Sustainability's Global and Local Orientation. *Academy of Management Learning & Education* 9(3), 499–506.

DCPS. (2022). OSSE Announces 2022 Graduation Rates. https://osse.dc.gov/release/osse-announces-2022-graduation-rates.

DoE RSA. (2012). *Basic Education Question and Answer Booklet*. Pretoria: Republic of South Africa Department of Education.

Earth Charter. (1997). The Earth Charter Initiative. https://earthcharter.org/read-the-earth-charter.

ED-GRS. (2014). U.S. Department of Education: Green Ribbon Schools. www2.ed.gov/programs/green-ribbon-schools/index.html.

Edwards, G. (2006). Beyond the Separate Subjects: Towards a Post-Disciplinary Approach to Environmental Education. In J. Lee, & M. Williams (eds.), *Environmental and Geographic Education for Sustainability: Cultural Contexts* (pp. 109–121). Nova Science Publishers.

Erskine, L., & Johnson, S. D. (2012). Effective Learning Approaches for Sustainability: A Student Perspective. *Journal of Education for Business* 87, 198–205.

Hopkins, M. (2009). What Executives Don't Get About Sustainability (and Further Notes on the Profit Motive). *MIT Sloan Management Review* 51(1), 35–40.

Kennelly, J., Taylor, N., & Serow, P. (2012). Early Career Primary Teachers and Education for Sustainability. *International Research in Geographical and Environmental Education* 21(2), 139–153.

Lotz-Sisitka, H. (2006). Enabling Environmental and Sustainability Education in South Africa's National Curriculum: Context, Culture and Learner Aspirations for Agency. In J. Lee & M. Williams (eds.), *Environmental and Geographic Education for Sustainability: Cultural Contexts* (pp. 323–335). Hauppauge, NY: Nova Science Publishers.

Mabry, S. (2011). Tackling the Sustainability Dilemma: A Holistic Approach to Preparing Students for the Professional Organization. *Business Communication Quarterly* 74(2), 119–137.

McFarlane, D. A., & Ogazon, A. G. (2011). The Challenges of Sustainability Education. *Journal of Multidisciplinary Research* 3(3), 81–107.

Morin, E. (2001). *Seven Complex Lessons for the Future*. UNESCO. Paris: UNESCO.

Mundo Verde. (2012). Sustainability. www.mundoverdepcs.org/sustainability.

Mundo Verde. (2013). Mundo Verde wins 2013 Mayor's Sustainability Award. https://doee.dc.gov/page/mundo-verde-case-study-mayors-2013-sustainability-awards.

People & Planet. (2013). People & Planet Green League. https://peopleandplanet.org/university-league.

PRME. (2023). The Principles for Responsible Management Education (PRME). www.unprme.org/what-we-do.

Rands, G., & Starik, M. (2009). The Short and Glorious History of Sustainability in North American Management Education. In C. Wankel, & J. A. F. Stoner (eds.), *Management Education for Global Sustainability* (pp. 19–50). Charlotte, NC: Information Age Publishing.

Rogers, C. (1980). *A Way of Being*. Houghton Mifflin.

Rusinko, C. A. (2010). Integrating Sustainability in Management and Business Education: A Matrix Approach. *Academy of Management Learning & Education* 9(3), 507–519.

Shrivastava, P. (2010). Pedagogy of Passion for Sustainability. *Academy of Management Learning & Education* 9(3), 443–455.

Tilbury, D., & Wortman, D. (2006). Whole School Approaches to Sustainability. In J. Lee & M. Williams (eds.), *Environmental and Geographic Education for Sustainability: Cultural Contexts* (pp. 95–107). Hauppauge, NY: Nova Science Publishers.

ULSF (University Leaders for a Sustainable Future). (1990). Talloires Declaration. https://ulsf.org/talloires-declaration.

UNCG. (2013). UNCG Sustainability. https://sustainability.uncg.edu.

UNESCO. (2012a). *Education for Sustainable Development Sourcebook 2012.* United Nations Educational, Scientific and Cultural Organization. Paris: UNESCO.

UNESCO. (2012b). *Shaping the Education of Tomorrow 2012 Report on the UN Decade of Education for Sustainable Development, Abridged.* Paris: UNESCO.

8

PURSUING SUSTAINABILITY IN MEDIA AND ENTERTAINMENT

The sustainability mindset enables the professional to find one's place in the crazy world of media and entertainment.

Introduction

Media and entertainment are both about communicating through different platforms. There are professionals who seek to primarily inform, professionals who seek to primarily entertain, and those that combine the two in order to convey messages to an audience, often with the expectation of obtaining an intended response from such audience. The positions in media and entertainment include journalists (print, broadcast, online), screenplay and scriptwriters, producers, actors, musicians, dancers, performers, and various support function professionals such as image consultants, event planners, and media marketing managers.

Over the years, there has been an increasing presence of socially and ecologically responsible themes throughout the media and entertainment sectors. Concert organizers implement sustainable practices such as recycling on-site, waste reduction, sustainable procurement requirements for vendors, energy efficiency in lighting and equipment, carbon offsets for attendees, and more. The We Love Green festival in France, for example, incorporates eco-design and sustainability practices by using recycled and recyclable inputs for the scenography, solar panels for on-site electricity, potable water fountains that reduce the use of bottled water, local, organic, and plant-based restaurants, a composting supply chain, and on-site awareness building for festival goers (WeLoveGreen, 2014).

Despite these efforts, there is still room for advancement. The infrastructure and operations of media and entertainment outlets, small and large, can be

DOI: 10.4324/9781032615844-8

made more sustainable. This opens up opportunities for more professionals such as builders, architects, engineers, and urban planners to incorporate sustainability into their roles. Reverb, a non-profit based in the U.S., educates and engages musicians and their fans in sustainability; they help put on greener concerts and venues. The greening of the media and entertainment sectors has also opened up the opportunity for those professions directly involved in communications to incorporate sustainability into their work. Daily and weekly newspapers and magazines are increasingly including a climate change, diversity and inclusion, or other sustainability-focused theme in their columns. Radio shows and podcasts of a variety of topics often cover topics related to sustainability. For example, Freakonomics Radio, focused on the hidden side of economics, hosted a show on *Weird Recycling* in which nuclear waste, medical waste, and chicken feet all made a debut.

As is the case in many career fields, specialists and generalists alike in media and entertainment can incorporate sustainable development into their roles. Doing so can help the professional stay abreast of an important, current topic and/or provide a new niche in which to develop a career.

Media

Media is a collective noun that has a broad meaning. It describes the collection of mass communication sources where people obtain information that shapes and informs their opinions and decisions (Morse & Agopian, 2012). These communication sources include television, newspapers, blogs, newsletters, podcasts, radio, and more. Digital media and social media are on the rise with the widespread use of the Internet, especially on mobile devices. Norris assigns three functions to the media: a civic forum, a mobilizing agent, and a watchdog (Norris, 2001). All three functions can incorporate sustainability.

The results of a longitudinal sustainability themed analysis of 115 national newspapers worldwide between 1990 and 2008 revealed that (1) there was a significant, incremental increase in media coverage of sustainability-related concepts and (2) certain global events triggered a substantial amount of media coverage, including the Earth Summits, Conference of the Parties to the UNFCCC, and the Nobel Peace Prize for sustainability-oriented actions (Barkemeyer et al., 2009). The probability of the terms sustainability or sustainable development appearing in an article rose from around 10 percent in the 1990s to around 30 percent for sustainable development and 50 percent for sustainability toward the end of 2008. This indicates that the vocabulary of sustainability is becoming more engrained in media, notwithstanding the peaks associated with major events.

News and journalism

News, the definition of which is still the subject of debate, is a component of media and entertainment. News can be personal, professional, or organizational, and has temporal and spatial qualities; the news is influenced by economic, political, historical, and cultural factors (Lester, 2010). According to Lester in *Media & Environment*, news is "a mediated version of reality but with significant and real consequences." Lester draws inspiration from Brian McNair's paradigm, which is as follows:

> News is still what news always was: a socially constructed account of reality rather than reality itself, composed of literary, verbal and pictorial elements which combine to form a journalistic narrative disseminated through print, broadcast or online media. No matter how "live" the news is, and regardless of how raw and visceral the account of events being brought into our living rooms appears to be, it is still a mediated version of reality.
>
> *(McNair, 2006)*

In a seminal 1965 publication, Johan Galtung and Mari Ruge (as cited in Harcup and O'Neill, 2010) listed the following criteria, or values, for events to be considered "newsworthy":

1. *Frequency*: An event that unfolds at the same or similar frequency as the news medium is more likely to be selected as news than is a social trend that takes place over a long period of time.
2. *Threshold*: The bigger an event, the more likely it is to be recorded, and a threshold exists that the event has to pass before it is recorded at all.
3. *Unambiguity*: The less ambiguity the more the event will be noticed.
4. *Meaningfulness*: The culturally similar is likely to be selected because it fits into the news selector's frame of reference.
5. *Consonance:* How much a person predicts or wants an event to happen affects his or her capacity to register it.
6. *Unexpectedness*: Providing some correction to the previous two points, events that are regular and institutionalized, continuing and repetitive, will not attract much attention.
7. *Continuity*: Once defined as news, it is more likely to stay in the news even when its connection to other news values declines.
8. *Composition*: If a news bulletin is dominated by foreign news, it will be harder for a foreign news event to become news.

(Harcup & O'Neill, 2010)

Harcup and O'Neill examined samples of the United Kingdom press and developed a contemporary set of values that determines newsworthiness as follows:

1. *The Power Elite*: Stories concerning powerful individuals, organizations, or institutions.
2. *Celebrity*: Stories concerning people who are already famous.

3. *Entertainment*: Stories concerning sex, show business, human interest, animals, an unfolding drama, or offering opportunities for humorous treatment, entertaining photographs, or witty headlines.
4. *Surprise*: Stories that have an element of surprise and/or contrast.
5. *Bad News*: Stories with particularly negative overtones, such as conflict or tragedy.
6. *Good News*: Stories with particularly positive overtones such as rescues and cures.
7. *Magnitude*: Stories that are perceived as sufficiently significant either in the numbers of people involved or in potential impact.
8. *Relevance*: Stories about issues, groups, and nations perceived to be relevant to the audience.
9. *Follow-up*: Stories about subjects already in the news.
10. *Newspaper Agenda*: Stories that set or fit the news organization's own agenda.

This new paradigm of news may also signal a shift for news that is more likely to incorporate sustainability as newsworthy. Good news could be about a climate tech entrepreneur making a difference. Bad news could be about increased natural disasters due to climate change. In many stories, celebrities are featured for sustainability initiatives (musicians holding concerts to raise awareness about a particular social or environmental challenge; actors narrating documentaries on a pressing environmental issue). Al Jazeera's Climate Crisis section. Caixin's Green Insight. All of these are examples of how sustainability has gone mainstream. In doing such, generalist journalists and those with support function roles must also embrace, or at least understand, the sustainability and ESG paradigm.

In "Reporting Sustainable Development: A Broadcast Journalist's View," Harrabin said it well when he pointed out that "Sustainable development is not a story—it is an idea, and what is more, an idea which has already been expressed" (Harrabin, 2000). In other words, the role of sustainable development in media and entertainment is often one that is incorporated within a story as opposed to the story itself. As John Eck, media executive, stated, "People want great stories told to them, to have their hearts touched, and to laugh or cry" (Dalton, 2006). Extreme weather events systemically caused by climate change may bring about more sad stories, whereas an innovative green business that has solved a long-standing problem may bring about a cheerier story. In either case, the stories are both opportunities to communicate notions of sustainability.

While traditional media outlets create more of a one-way flow of information, social media has positioned the world in a two-way communication stream through online commentary outlets such as LinkedIn, and what can be called participatory journalism. McNair identifies four kinds of online journalists:

1. Professional-institutional actors; the websites of newspapers and national broadcasters; and the websites of Internet-only journalistic organizations.
2. Professional-individual actors, which number in the thousands for English language outlets.
3. Non-professional-institutional actors, including government agencies, political parties, campaigning and lobby groups.
4. Non-professional-individual actors, or private bloggers, numbering in the tens of millions.

(McNair, 2006)

Author Anthony Downs described five stages of the "issue attention cycle," which are especially potent in sustainability-related matters (Downs, 2013). As a media or entertainment professional, it's helpful to first situate the issue at hand along this cycle to bring about the best outcomes for people and planet:

1. **Stage 1: The pre-problem stage.** Some highly undesirable social condition exists but has not yet captured much public attention, even though some experts or interest groups may already be alarmed by it.
2. **Stage 2: Alarmed discovery and euphoric enthusiasm.** As a result of some dramatic series of events, or for other reasons, the public suddenly becomes both aware of and alarmed about the evils of a particular problem.
3. **Stage 3: Realizing the cost of significant progress.** Gradually spreading realization that the cost of "solving" the problem is very high (e.g., money and major sacrifices by large groups in the population may be warranted).
4. **Stage 4: Gradual decline of intense public interest.** Gradual decline in the intensity of public interest of the problem; some people get discouraged, others feel threatened, and others become bored. Some other issue has entered Stage 2.
5. **Stage 5: The post-problem stage.** An issue that has been replaced at the center of public concern moves into a realm of lesser attention. May sporadically recapture public interest. Problems that have gone through the cycle almost always receive a higher average level of attention, public effort, and general concern than those still in pre-discovery stage.

Entertainment

Some argue that entertainment is one of the main functions of journalism, while others argue that entertainment programs and informational programs are not alike (Lieb, 2001). Regardless, entertainment has a role to play in how people interpret the world and their community and is therefore an important career trajectory in which to apply sustainability concepts. Author Peter Vorderer gives the following definition of entertainment:

[Entertainment] is an experience that helps media users to cope with their everyday life. For some, it's pleasure seeking in boring situations or compensation in burdening situations; for others it's compensation in a depriving situation, fulfillment of needs in unsatisfactory situations, and self-enhancement or even self-realization when they are—for whatever reason—ready for it. In any case, it's playing and it helps [one] cope with life. It's what media users seek very often, and to their own advantage.

(Vorderer, 2001)

Music entertainment has been a core component of various social and environmental movements and points of progress. For example, songs such as Marvin Gaye's "Mercy Mercy Me (The Ecology)" and Joni Mitchell's "Big Yellow Taxi" helped raise awareness of environmental pollution and disappearing green spaces, respectively. U.S. Folk singer Pete Seeger's "My Dirty Stream," which referred to the polychlorinated biphenyl (PCB) dumped by General Electric in the Hudson River, inspired the creation of Clearwater Story, an organization that promoted environmental education and eventually helped advocate for the Clean Water Act of 1972 (Chally & Seely, 2022).

Authors Bartsch and Viehoff support a multi-level appraisal framework of media entertainment where emotions can be associated with pleasurable feeling qualities (arousal, positive valence, etc.) and can be functional within the broader context of social and cognitive need gratification; audiences pursue different concerns with varying priorities at a time (Bartsch & Viehoff, 2010). Based on a research experiment, Bartsch, Viehoff, and Mangold identified seven factors that represent audience gratification in media entertainment: *emotions* (fun; thrill; being moved) and *social* and *cognitive* needs (thought-provoking experiences; vicarious experiences; social sharing of emotions; acting out emotions that have no room in everyday life) (Bartsch & Viehoff, 2010). The first narrative in this media and entertainment chapter touches on all of these factors, first through audio and then through visual presentations.

From traffic radio host to sustainable business anchor—Nathalie Croisé's story

In the heart of the media and entertainment hub of the Paris region sits the headquarters of BFMTV. As I approached the building, a serious-looking security officer blocked the entrance. As the fourth estate, media centers are unfortunately often the target of attacks and raids. Journalists and anchors themselves are also attacked, kidnapped, and, in extreme cases, tortured and killed. The Al Jazeera network launched the "Journalism is Not a Crime" (or #FreeAJStaff) campaign after a number of their journalists were arrested in Egypt for peacefully exercising their profession.

I could understand the enhanced security measures at BFMTV. I waited for Nathalie and we walked to a nearby café.

Nathalie Croisé is a television anchor on BFMTV, France's most-watched news network, with 10 million daily viewers. She intervenes for BFM Business. But she didn't start off in the limelight. At the age of 11, Nathalie knew she wanted to be a journalist. She was curious. She wanted to share what she had learned. From the start, she saw journalism as an effective means of communicating a positive message and being of service for those who have positive stories to tell. In today's world of mass negative media, Nathalie Croisé has remained loyal to these ideals of her childhood.

What followed for Nathalie was a rather traditional education in literature and journalism. She studied at the Institut Pratique du Journalism (IPJ) in Paris. After graduating, she first thought of entering the print media market. She interned with *Le Parisien*, a daily newspaper in France covering both international and national news. Shortly afterwards, a former professor was recruiting radio hosts for France Info, a radio station of the Radio France Group. Nathalie seized the opportunity, trained to become a radio host, and fell in love with the vocal and auditory form of delivering messages. She hosted radio shows on Autoroute-Info and RFI (Radio France Internationale).

In 1997, Business FM (known as BFM) recruited Nathalie for its radio programs. BFM was bought in 2002 to exclusively focus on economic and financial issues. Nathalie quickly adapted to covering many different aspects of the financial and business worlds. She then migrated from radio to television and once again trained in-house to be in front of the camera. She hosted the morning shows and filled in for a program on green business that was launched by Nicolas Lespaule at the time. "I came across *Green Business* completely by accident," Nathalie stated. She was editor in chief, creating articles and papers on the green business topics. When the financial crisis hit in 2008, Nicolas Lespaule had to lead a program dedicated to the crisis. This gave Nathalie the opportunity to become the anchor for *Green Business* in March 2008.

"In the beginning the idea of *Green Business* was a bit blurry," Nathalie admitted. "It gave the impression of small and medium-sized enterprises who were run by environmental hippies. Now, sustainable business is core business for small to large companies alike," Nathalie explained. *Green Business* has been rebaptized *Business Durable* (*Sustainable Business*) and has no shortage of requests. Those featured on the show include chief sustainability officers and vice presidents of sustainability of CAC 40 companies, entrepreneurs with innovative startups, and collaborative economy businesses.

Nathalie had to delve into the very transversal nature of sustainable business. She had to become an expert in transportation, energy, water, infrastructure, products, manufacturing, impact investment … and the list continues. This challenged her and pleased her simultaneously. "It's not easy. Each time you must take a deep dive into someone's story," Nathalie mentioned. She was able to fuse her wish to deliver positive news with the paradigm of sustainable business. "Through my role as anchor and managing editor of *Sustainable Business*, I better understand the stakes and challenges of sustainable development," Nathalie acknowledged. "It would be nice if the topic of sustainability were introduced in the curriculum for journalism," Nathalie added.

Nathalie has worked exclusively as a journalist, media expert, managing editor, and anchor in sustainable business for over three years. She envisions staying the course because sustainable business is about the "economy of tomorrow." "It's cutting edge and I want to continue to highlight all of the great things that are happening," Nathalie explained.

"I'm not an environmental activist," Nathalie clarified. Indeed, she rather fell into the topic of environmental and social responsibility as a means to improve business. She is a great example of how anyone in any sector can incorporate sustainability into their work—and how it can lead to a more fulfilling career. The most motivating factor of Nathalie's work is meeting new people and knowing that her work adds value and has a positive impact. Nathalie is happy with what she does and the sustainability mindset has enabled her to find her place in the crazy world of media and entertainment.

From organic farmer to environmental journalist—Winifred's story

As I stepped off the bus at Matsumoto Inter, a slight feeling of desertion fell upon me. There was not much around, just cars swooping past. I didn't speak a word of Japanese. I stood out like a sore thumb. Not ethnically Japanese and not in Tokyo. Within five minutes, however, a van pulled up to help. "Hi, Marilyn? Get in," Winifred said. I thanked her for agreeing to be interviewed and agreeing to fetch me in rural Japan.

Winifred Bird began to explain where we were: Nagano Prefecture. This region is mountainous, serene, and far from the coast as far as Japan goes. I learned that the different regions of soba noodles were important in Japan, so we stopped at one of the best soba mills and shops on our way to Winifred's farm.

I noticed the charms hanging in the car. "What are these?" I asked. "Oh, those are my husband's Omamori. He is religious. The Shinto charms in the car are for road safety, protection from ill, and … oh, I can't remember all of them," Winifred explained. I started to ask Winifred many questions while she took us through the beautiful hills of Nagano.

Winifred was born in Philadelphia and raised in California. "I had a hippie and intellectual upbringing," Winifred reminisced. She had lived in Haight-Ashbury, a district of San Francisco. Her parents were both painters, which may have helped to spark a creative outlook to Winifred's career choices. After studying political science at Amherst and working on organic farms in Western Massachusetts, she decided to volunteer with Worldwide Opportunities on Organic Farms (WWOOF) for a year in Canada and the U.S.

She met her husband while they both were volunteering on an organic farm in Canada. Originally from the Mie Prefecture in Japan, Winifred's future husband was learning post and beam construction. Eventually, Winifred and her husband moved to rural Japan because they both had friends there who were already doing organic farming.

Winifred had started to serve as an English instructor in her transition from West to East. When she was not teaching, she was writing about the many farms she had visited in the U.S. and Canada. "I had written about all of the farms that I visited," Winifred stated. She enjoyed writing. "I don't hate kids, but teaching was not my calling" Winifred joked. "Some people really have a calling to teach, and those people should be teaching," Winifred further explained. Winifred enrolled in an online freelance journalism class, which, although she claimed was not particularly good, gave her enough confidence and motivation to pursue journalism.

Winifred and family then moved to a more remote location in Japan, Mihama, for organic farming and construction opportunities. She still taught part- time, and during a serendipitous moment at her boss's dinner party, she met a Turkish underwater archaeologist who was studying a shipwreck. She called the *Japan Times* to cover the story, and the rest is history. She then started to write more and more, focusing on the environment because that was her interest. She joined the Society of Environmental Journalists and received a very inspiring mentor. "My mentor was a real career strategist; she taught me how to make better pitches … and I liked her Quaker beliefs and back-to-the-land lifestyle," Winifred affirmed. They joined forces to write about Fukushima and Chernobyl after successfully obtaining a grant. The article about forest management in Fukushima and Chernobyl won first prize in the feature category of the Society of Environmental Journalists awards competition in 2014.

As Winifred gradually started to cut back the teaching hours, she moved to Nagano Prefecture to pursue organic farming close to friends. "We help each other out; we share equipment, for example," Winifred explained in a calm voice. Winifred and her husband grow rice, wheat, beans … and, as she mentioned, "We've got some ducks roaming in the rice field." The ducks keep Winifred grounded from June to August because they eat weeds in the rice fields and "We need to put them away at night to protect them from predators." Such closeness to nature and concern for its well-being is reflected in her writing. Understanding nature on different levels, including the practical level, helps in Winifred's journalistic endeavors. Her husband works as a carpenter, and they both host WWOOF volunteers to help maintain their organic farm. In the winter, mid-December to April at least, Winifred cannot do much outside so she focuses on her writing.

Winifred has a unique sustainability outlook after having lived for about a decade in Japan. For her, "We need to think about how to shrink, sustainable shrinkage. There is barely enough room for wildlife in Japan. We also need to ask: are we undermining future generations?" Winifred sees a parallel between 3/11 in Tohoku (where the tsunami hit) and Hurricane Katrina in New Orleans. "These events are tragic; yet they provide a chance to do things a different way," Winifred expressed a glimmer of hope. According to Winifred, "sustainable" and "development" should not go together in highly economically developed countries. "Wealthy countries like Japan should think about a circle—not a trajectory," Winifred wisely noted. She recognized that a path, or trajectory, is still a useful concept for countries whose citizens still do not have access to education, enough to eat, shelter, and the basics. "Most people are interested in maintaining their lives; unless it's easy to do so, people will not choose sustainability as a top factor, so we need incentives," Winfred declared.

At the time of the interview, Winifred was completing a book about agriculture in Japan: the relationship between farms and the natural environment, the philosophies of farming, and the connection between farms and democracy. When Douglas MacArthur, then supreme commander for the Allied Powers, introduced land reform in 1945 during the U.S. occupation of Japan, the idea of small farm holdings was solidified in order to reduce inequality in rural settings. Now, Japan is going through a period of consolidation and trade liberalization. When I asked about what constitutes unsustainable journalism, Winifred stated that it included repeating the line (corporate or government) without questioning, advertising, and not looking at the issue through a sustainability lens. As Winifred said:

> Farm size is a buzz word in Japan. But many journalist do not look at it from a sustainability perspective. What happens to community farms if they are ten times bigger? More monocrops, diseases, and pests? People leaving the land? Is that what we want? Policies are being made without anyone thinking about that word: sustainability.

Winifred was able to find the right balance of career and family through her passion for sustainability-oriented journalism in an organic farm setting. She focuses on long-term features and environmental writing for the general public. "Unless you want to be a breaking news reporter, you need to have a specialty," Winifred explained. A bilingual English–Japanese speaker is certainly useful in journalism in Japan. The environmental niche pays well for more scientific articles. "The market price is about two dollars per word for scientific journals, but for a newspaper, it is 20 cents per word," Winifred said. "The other route to an economically sustainable career in journalism is to break into the large outlets that also value sustainability-focused journalism like Nat Geo," Winifred stated. Since "eco" and "sustainability" are important buzzwords now, there is more and more demand for journalists who wish to incorporate the sustainability concepts within genres such as technology, business, and even gadgets.

Different paths lead to sustainability in the media

Winifred was raised in an environmentally conscious and active setting; Nathalie was not. Nathalie knew that she wanted to be a journalist from a young age; Winifred did not. Nevertheless, they both found that incorporating sustainability into their media careers would be rewarding. Winifred was able to live in the geographical location of her choice—rural Japan—while nourishing her appetite for environmental storytelling. Nathalie was able to anchor and lead a popular sustainable business show in one of the most-watched French television news stations. If one is contemplating a career in media and entertainment, whether one specializes in environmental and social issues or not, being versed in sustainability will help. Sustainability knowledge certainly helped Winifred and Nathalie.

SURF Framework for careers in media and entertainment

Media and entertainment careers involving supply chain

Physical infrastructure, equipment, and various supplies enable the success of media and entertainment. From handheld microphones to hands-free voice amplifiers, technology has played an important role in the progression and impact of various media outlets. Printing presses can use vegetable-based inks, chlorine-free paper, paper from sustainably managed forests, recycled paper, and more. Music, radio, and television studios contain specialized equipment that can be more energy efficient and made from sustainable materials, in addition to sustainable office supplies and furniture. Temporary exhibitions and concert venues come with their own set of sustainable supply chain challenges and solutions.

The roles involved in the supply chain of media and entertainment include purchasing managers, supply chain managers, environmental engineers and architects, event planners, travel planners (to minimize emissions for travel for photo shoots, news gathering, filming, etc.), stage and costume designers, and any role that addresses the materials and infrastructure needed to deliver a text, visual, or sound through entertainment or media.

Advertisements have ripple effects in the media and entertainment supply chain. By advertising more sustainable products on media outlets, consumers are made more aware and able to support sustainable development. CBS, for example, encourages users to look for the EcoAd, EducationAd, and WellnessAd program logos on commercials. They indicate that the advertiser has provided funding for a number of urgent yet underfunded projects such as energy-efficiency retrofits and mobile health clinics (CBS EcoMedia Inc., 2012). Positions in advertising and creative solutions that link sustainable products and media are also within the realm of supply chain careers in media and entertainment.

Media and entertainment careers involving the user

Although the agendas of the press, television, and radio can differ, and within these mediums there can be differences (wake-up programming versus late-night programming), sustainability themes can be relevant to all. Text, sound, and the visual: these are the three elements that can be used to communicate by different professionals such as writers, radio hosts, and photographers. The users in these careers are listeners, watchers, readers, moviegoers, concertgoers, etc. Users may require social and environmental responsibility for deciding whether to patronize an event or media outlet. Users may also want to be knowledgeable and entertained around sustainability problems and solutions.

All careers in media and entertainment involve the "U" component of the SURF Framework. Careers that are intimately linked to the user include "behind the scenes" content roles (like producers, screen writers, and public relations campaign managers,) and "end-user facing" (the journalist that can receive comments from readers; the anchor delivering the green business special on television; the radio host interviewing people and setting the tone for discussion; the flutist performing in front of a live audience, etc.).

New media has created a shift in the balance of power between the sender and receiver of information. New media, such as social media, podcasts, and newsletters, has contributed to "horizontal media" where users have more control over the production and distribution of content (Morse & Agopian, 2012). In many cases, breaking news emanates from citizen bloggers, (photo) journalists, and other contributors through tech platforms. The user can become a photojournalist, breaking news journalist, and more—simply by taking a snapshot with their smartphone and uploading it with commentary to online platforms. The user may even send the story to more traditional media outlets. In turn, professional journalists crowdsource ideas, photographs, opinions, and stories from new media. The new media outlets can provide a tool for maintaining, and in some cases improving, traditional print, broadcast, and online platforms.

Podcasts are on-demand audio or video programs made available for downloading (Waters et al., 2012); they have made conventional radio programs more accessible by allowing the user to decide when they will listen to a program. In a study by authors Waters et al., more than 50 environmental podcasts were studied for popularity. The researchers found that a podcast's *content, communication style,* and *openness about organizational affiliation* have the most significant impact on popularity. As such, workers in broadcast media must address the user's needs for effective delivery, vivid and memorable messages, and credible sources.

Media and entertainment careers involving relations

The media and entertainment industries (especially in today's world of global access to even the most local of stories) have a far-reaching stakeholder list. It would not be odd to say that everyone with the auditory or visual capacity to receive and interpret information is a part of this sector's stakeholder list. If a local radio host creates a podcast about a local music trend, that podcast could be downloaded, listened to, commented on, shared, and blogged about, and spur a ripple effect—at the complete opposite end of the Earth. New careers such as community manager or social media manager are dedicated entirely to forming, maintaining, and increasing relationships with customers and the larger community of those interested and/or impacted by the communicator's work. Reports of hundreds of pages are communicated using a handful of characters.

The "R" component of the SURF Framework is thus indispensable for careers in media and entertainment. Even when catering a message to a particular audience, professionals in this sector must be aware of its wider implications in the community. In addition to awareness, creating and maintaining positive stakeholder relations can be gained through participating in community forums, abiding with laws or taking steps to ensure that content inappropriate for children is not provided, using social media to maintain dialogue with the public, and using stakeholder management guidelines such as ISO 26000.

The Media Sustainability Index (MSI) was first designed in 1999 by the International Research & Exchanges Board (IREX). Their definition of sustainable media is "a media sector able to serve the public as the fourth estate and show resilience to pressures that would undermine that mission" (Morse & Agopian, 2012). There are five indicators used to measure a media system's overall sustainability:

1. Legal and social norms protect and promote free speech and access to public information.
2. Journalism meets professional standards of quality.
3. Multiple news sources provide citizens with reliable, objective news.
4. Media are well-managed enterprises, allowing editorial independence.
5. Supporting institutions function in the professional interests of independent media. *(IREX, 2011)*

Cinépolis, owner of over 2,000 movie screens and the largest movie theatre chain in the Spanish-speaking part of the Americas, launched a successful sustainability campaign aligned with its core business and purpose. Showing movies is, of course, highly visual; the 2011 release of the black-and-white silent film *The Artist* helps to capture the moviegoer experience as being a primarily *visual* one. Cinépolis was able to help create a social conscience for visual health issues and raise money for eye surgeries that benefit the lower socio-economic class of Mexican society (Laasch & Conaway, 2011). Movie theatre advertising has been shown to engender a better recall than television by as much as 20 percent, as well as provide a greater proximity to purchasing actual goods, since 69 percent of people combine movie going with shopping (Laasch & Conaway, 2011). Cinépolis employees were made aware of the "Love Gives Birth to Eyesight" campaign (frontline employees placing buttons on their uniforms), and Cinépolis has successfully established itself as a socially responsible company. There are a number of roles involved in making a CSR campaign successful, from strategy and marketing to employee training and operations management. Careers in media and entertainment can incorporate sustainability and thus improve wider community stakeholder relations.

Media and entertainment careers involving the future

Media professionals need to broaden their search for insights in framing sustainability messages—to future generations. Media and entertainment content makers tend to focus on a particular audience that includes age demographics. Whether you gear a book or a show to an elderly or young audience, understanding different generations and the interactions among generations will be important for effective delivery. How is the silver age group portrayed in the work? How about teenagers? Intergenerational equity is an important component of sustainability that is equally important in careers in entertainment and media. Does the newspaper staff have members of diverse age groups to reflect the different perspectives that can be brought about by including different generations? Has the journalist interviewed different generations to write about the impact of a new plant in the neighborhood?

Careers involving the future in media and entertainment include executives that must create a long-term vision. This vision is expected to include greater attention to sustainability concepts and ideas that have not been considered much before. Other future-oriented media careers include content development and planning for events that will host multiple generations. Even social media, which is known for instantaneous updates and a "now" culture, must be tuned into future generations as they become connected and voice their opinions through social media outlets.

Conclusion

Author Kolandai-Matchett studied the impacts of a campaign on sustainable consumption in New Zealand and found that: (1) public understanding about sustainability terminologies should not be presumed; (2) sustainability may be considered a buzzword "often cited with little reference to its meaning or its implications"; (3) it is necessary to address the idea of needs in association with well-being; and (4) it is necessary to engage a wider range of communication channels and appropriately repeat messages to increase the probability of exposure (Kolandai-Matchett, 2009). If the results of this study can be generalized for many media and entertainment situations, then building a career in this field while incorporating sustainability involves communicating effectively on what is meant by sustainability and related concepts; directing messages to the user so that there is a mutual understanding of needs; and building content (such as news programs and sections of a magazine) that addresses stakeholder needs for sustainability communication.

Some practical tips for professionals in this sector include:

- Use frameworks to gauge sustainability progress:
  - Apply the SURF Framework to the business establishment, to the job, and to the career trajectory.
- Use reference guides and reports, such as:
  - Industry Green from Julie's Bicycle
  - Institute for Sustainable Communication
  - Green Film Making Toolkit
  - Media Sustainability Index (MSI).
- Refer to existing best practices, such as:
  - UNEP Music and Environment Initiative
  - Guardian News and Media Sustainability Report.
- Join professional networks that address sustainability in media and entertainment, such as:
  - Society of Environmental Journalists
  - Earth Journalism Network
  - Various country-based networks for journalists (environmental journalists, science journalists, sustainability journalists, etc.)
  - Green Music Alliance
  - Media Entertainment & Arts Alliance (Journalist Code of Ethics)
  - Green Planet Films
  - Green.tv.
- Attend conferences and festivals that address sustainability in media and entertainment.
- Apply for fellowships that address sustainability in media and entertainment, such as:
  - Ted Scripps Fellowships in Environmental Journalism
  - Green Film Making Competition.
- Tune in to sustainable media and entertainment outlets.

References

Barkemeyer, R., Figge, F., Holt, D., & Hahn, T. (2009). What the Papers Say: Trends in Sustainability a Comparative Analysis of 115 Leading National Newspapers Worldwide. *Journal of Corporate Citizenship* 33, 69–86.

Bartsch, A., & Viehoff, R. (2010). The Use of Media Entertainment and Emotional Gratification. *Procedia Social and Behavioral Sciences* 5, 2247–2255.

CBS EcoMedia Inc. (2012). CBS EcoMedia Inc. Broadens Reach With Launch of "Wellness" and "Education" Ads. PR Newswire. www.prnewswire.com/news-releases/cbs-ecomedia -inc-broadens-reach-with-launch-of-wellness-and-education-ads-146975905.html.

Chally, B., & Seely. P. (2022). Ecomusicology: Examining Environemntal Messages within Modern Music. In E. Dobbins, M. Piga, & L. Manca (eds.), *Environment, Social Justice, and the Media in the Age of the Anthropocene* (Ch. 15). Lexington Books.

Dalton, C. M. (2006). The Business of Entertainment: An interview with John Eck, President, Media Works, NBC Universal. *Business Horizons* 49, 9–15.

Downs, A. (2013). Up and Down with Ecology: The Issue Attention Cycle. In A. Hansen (ed.). *Media and the Environment, Volume I: Environment, Media and Environmental Communication*. Routledge.

Harcup, T., & O'Neill, D. (2010). What Is News? Galtung and Ruge Revisited. *Journalism Studies* 2(2), 261–280.

Harrabin, R. (2000). Reporting Sustainable Development: A Broadcast Journalist's View. In J. Smith (ed.), *The Daily Globe: Environmental Change, the Public and the Media*. (pp. 49–63). Earthscan Ltd.

IREX. (2011). Media Sustainability Index (MSI) Methodology. www.irex.org/resource/m edia-sustainability-index-msi.

Kolandai-Matchett, K. (2009). Mediated Communication of "Sustainable Consumption" in the Alternative Media: A case study exploring a message framing strategy. *International Journal of Consumer Studies* 33, 113–125.

Laasch, O., & Conaway, R. N. (2011). "Making It Do" at the Movie Theatres: Communicating Sustainability in the Workplace. *Business Communication Quarterly* 74(1), 68–78.

Lester, L. (2010). *Media & Environment*. Polity Press.

Lieb, C. (2001). Entertainment. An examination of functional theories of mass communication. *Poetics* 29, 225–245.

McNair, B. (2006). *Cultural Chaos: Journalism and Power in a Globalised World*. Routledge.

Morse, L., & Agopian, E. V. (2012). Measuring Press Freedom and Media Sector Performance: How Social Media Have Affected the Media Sustainability Index. *Journal for Communication Studies* 5(1), 29–43.

Norris, P. (2001). *Digital Divide: Civic Engagement, Information Poverty and the Internet Worldwide*. Cambridge University Press.

Vorderer, P. (2001). It's All Entertainment—Sure. But what exactly is entertainment? Communication research, media psychology, and the explanation of entertainment experiences. *Poetics* 29, 247–261.

Waters, R. D., Amarkhil, A., Bruun, L., & Mathisen, K. S. (2012). Messaging, Music and Mailbags: How technical design and entertainment boost the performance of environmental organizations' podcasts. *Public Relations Review* 38, 64–68.

WeLoveGreen. (2014). We Love Green Festival. www.welovegreen.fr.

9

PURSUING SUSTAINABILITY IN CLIMATE-RELATED CAREERS

> It will take the masses—in every job, in every sector, and at all levels of power—to turn the ship around.
>
> *(Marilyn Waite)*

Within the big tent of sustainability-related careers, careers that involve climate change are worth special mention. Unlike any other problem, issue, or topic, climate change is unique in that it threatens our ability to inhabit Earth and thus our ability to make progress on a number of environmental, economic, intergenerational, and social goals.

The rapid rise of greenhouse gas emissions, which started in the Industrial Revolution and vastly accelerated in the post-World War II economy, has already led to a number of devasting impacts on people and planet. If not quickly abated, the loss of people and ecosystems will increase due to extreme and frequent floods, droughts, heatwaves, and a host of other harms. Entire communities may be wiped out, such as small islands in the Caribbean and the Pacific. Realizing that his country of 33 coral atolls and reef islands was at risk of disappearing, former president of the Republic of Kiribati, Anote Tong, purchased 6,000 acres of Fiji land for $US 8 million (Robinson, 2018).

The greenhouse effect had been identified in 1824, illustrated in a lab by 1859, and quantified by 1896; the connection between increased carbon dioxide and global average temperature warming was made by 1938 (Wagner & Weitzman, 2015); public reporting on climate change accelerated in the 1970s, and, in 1988, the Intergovernmental Panel on Climate Change (IPCC) was established to provide policymakers with scientific assessments on climate change (IPCC, 2023). In short, we've had time to act and have failed to sufficiently do so. It will take the masses—in every job, in every sector, and at all levels of power—to turn the ship around.

DOI: 10.4324/9781032615844-9

This is not a book about climate change science or solutions. There are tons of resources—books, podcasts, films, games, and people from whom one can learn about climate change. What I provide here is an acknowledgment of how much human beings are actively addressing climate change, and, as the overall thesis of this book posits, that means leveraging the workplace, work, and career trajectories.

Every imaginable industry and field of work has a role to play in mitigating the worst of climate change impacts and adapting to what has already unfolded. For example, ABET, the U.S. accreditation board for engineering, has acknowledged the need to teach engineering students about climate change (ABET, 2018). In a 2018 survey of over 4,500 senior engineering students studying at the undergraduate level at ABET universities, researchers found that the greatest predictor of students wanting to address climate change in their career was whether the issue was personally felt. "Feeling a responsibility to deal with environmental problems and global warming being an important issue to them personally" outweighed all other predictors such as engineering sub-discipline; respondents acknowledged collective societal responsibility while expressing a personal connection (Shealy et al., 2021).

The healthcare industry is also no stranger to climate change. Researchers analyzed over 30,000 jobs from publichealthjobs.org from 2003–2019 and found a statistically significant increase in jobs that mentioned either "climate change" or "global warming." Furthermore, in a survey of 97 mostly U.S. public health employers, over 90 percent of respondents believed that there might be a need for climate change-trained public health professionals in the future (Krasna et al., 2020).

One of the largest sectors in terms of employment—agriculture—is also increasingly recruiting for climate-smart capabilities. There are roughly 1.2 billion workers employed in farming, fishing, and forestry, and while climate change is threatening livelihoods, climate solutions also present an opportunity for work in land restoration, biodiversity conservation, and carbon sequestering agriculture (Sofiah, 2023). Climate-related agriculture careers include those in commerce, public policy, land management, and research. For example, agricultural economists have an important role in analyzing the impacts of climate change on agriculture and communicating the implications (Norton, 2020). Researchers in Australia found that professional development in applied climate education improves agricultural and natural resource management (Georgea et al., 2009).

Climate justice

Climate change is not only an environmental problem. Limiting climate change to the "E" of ESG is not only a misread of the root causes of climate change and the harms climate change produces, but doing so has also inhibited progress for decades. Climate change is what I call an "everything bagel"[1] problem: it's a humanitarian problem, a technological problem, an economic problem, a financial problem, a social problem, an ecological problem, and more.

The current climate injustice has its roots in underlying inequities both within countries at the domestic level and among countries at the international level. Relying on extractive, polluting industries to fuel an inequitable society has been normalized. Systems of racism, sexism, classism, ableism, and other "isms" continue to exist and render those at the top of a socially created caste hierarchy better able to cope with climate change impacts. An increase of the neoliberal form of capitalism ("neoliberalism"), which favors deregulation, reduced government spending, and privatization, has exacerbated social and economic inequality, increased corporate dominance, and disincentivized more sustainable, eco-friendly practices (Longley, 2021).

Society has already witnessed the consequences of dramatic changes in climate from which we can collectively learn. During the Little Ice Age of the 1500s in Europe, when frozen rivers such as the Scheldt and Seine melted and caused heavy flooding, when a global influenza pandemic devasted communities, and when low harvests provoked famines, ethno-religious communities were scapegoated—expelled, purged, and confined to tightly regulated areas (Jenkins, 2021). This period also corresponds to the beginnings of Western European colonialism, which brought devastation to people around the globe while enabling inequitable wealth accumulation in a small number of countries. The small-scale climate change in the form of the Little Ice Age had treacherous consequences not only for where it occurred in Europe but also for the world.

The practice of rendering a population inferior and scapegoating that same population in times of upheaval is a long-standing trend and one that the current global climate crisis is exacerbating. In *Reconsidering Reparations*, philosopher Olúfemi O. Táíwò explains how the twenty-first-century world has been fundamentally shaped by slavery and colonialism; drawing on the work of philosopher Charles Mills, Táíwò calls on readers to witness our society as foundationally shaped by the past five hundred years' consolidation of global white supremacy (Táíwò, 2022). Indeed, the constant failures to achieve climate justice for the Global South (or the Global Majority) illustrate just how stuck we are with the legacies of the past few hundred years. It's fitting that the University of California's Center for Climate Justice defines climate justice as the recognition of "the disproportionate impacts of climate change on low-income communities and communities of color around the world, the people and places least responsible for the problem" (Center for Climate Justice, 2023).

Táíwò urges us to adopt a constructive view of reparations: that is, to approach reparations as a future-oriented world-remaking project, a project to build a better social order. As Táíwò elucidates:

> Does being Deaf mean that you can't thrive in public school? Does using a wheelchair mean that you can't fly a plane? The answers depend not on the individual but on what kind of world we live in, and how we've built it.
>
> (*Táíwò*, 2022)

For climate action, this implies that our ability to solve climate change, and do so in a just and equitable manner, will require reconstructing the way the current world is built. Colette Pichon Battle provides an elegant framing in *All We Can Save*:

> Climate change is not the problem. Climate change is the most horrible symptom of an economic system that has been built for a few to extract every precious ounce of value out of this planet and its people, from natural resources to the fruits of our human labor. This system has created this crisis.
>
> *(Battle, 2020)*

All of this means that there is a lot of work to do to bring about climate justice. Remaking the world order so that all people and the planet can prosper is no small feat, yet it is also an exciting prospect for the younger and older generations alike. Policymakers and those that control the purse are most in the driver's seat to enact this change, and the transformation will not occur without artists, musicians, creatives, writers, and a plethora of other professions.

From linguist to climate champion—Geneviève Yéhounmè's story

Geneviève Yéhounmè is like a fish in water in West Africa—breezily crossing borders set up by Europe's colonial interventions. Having spent some of her childhood in Nigeria and currently residing in Togo, Geneviève is a Beninese national who identifies linguistic ability as vital to individual and collective prosperity.

Geneviève received her first degree in Applied Linguistics of English from the University of Abomey-Calavi in Benin. Initially, she sought to study medicine, but at that time, the medical field was out of reach for middle-income families like her own that had neither the social capital nor the financial capital for the medical school gatekeepers. She acknowledges that the situation has improved in Benin; there is now greater access to all professions for all people. Looking back, Geneviève views this door being closed as a blessing in disguise, for many medical professionals today in Benin experience a salary cap, while her climate-related profession allows her to better support her family.

"Being a French-speaking country, Benin is way behind in terms of opportunities. Since English is the global lingua franca, it is easier for people and institutions to forge partnerships when they speak English. In addition, we use the CFA franc, which means we neither print nor control our own money. This is problematic," Geneviève explained. In 2015, Geneviève went to study for a master's degree in international environmental policy at the Middlebury Institute of International Studies at Monterey on a Fulbright Scholarship. It was there that she further developed her inkling that business was important for Benin and West Africa's future. She concentrated on the nexus among business, sustainability, and economic development, and when she returned to Benin, she started to work in for-profit business.

Green Keeper Africa, a company that turns an invasive species—water hyacinth—into a natural absorbent, attracted Geneviève. The absorbent is a fibrous substance that has many applications, including cleaning up oil spills and absorbing humidity. She started at Green Keeper Africa as a fundraising associate and worked for four years in several roles. In her last role as sales manager, she serviced Benin, Togo, Nigeria, Côte d'Ivoire, and Ghana. Her time at Green Keeper Africa allowed her to illustrate environmental leadership through action as opposed to words. "I don't go around telling people not to litter; what I try to do is show the way; for example, I bring my own reusable bags to the supermarket," Geneviève explained.

After working at Green Keeper Africa, Geneviève joined Climate Analytics, a research institute that supports Global South countries with climate science and related analysis. As a project manager, she integrates sustainability into her current work by supporting Climate Analytics in advising governments and other institutions on climate impacts, climate finance, and climate action plans. She uses her business acumen in understanding client needs to better interact with local stakeholders.

For Geneviève, one of the most important aspects of justice, equity, diversity, and inclusion in Benin is gender equity. "Even though women can legally buy land, there are still many who believe that women should not have access to land ownership in my hometown," Geneviève lamented. Upon further reflection, she admitted that, like Ghana, the southern part of Benin was more economically developed than the north, partly due to colonial preferences; it is therefore important to become intentionally inclusive of regions that have been historically overlooked.

Geneviève's father passed away in 2022, which caused her to approach life with even more deliberate consciousness. This consciousness is acute for those of her generation—generation Z—especially when it comes to addressing the climate crisis.

From computer scientist to climate startup founder—Alpha Wang's story

Alpha Wang led me to his office on the umpteenth floor of a SOHO commercial building in Beijing's Chaoyang district.

"We need nuclear fusion, and I don't mind that having this technology may put us out of business one day," Alpha explained. "Technology like fusion has the ability to reduce wars sparked by oil and gas reliance," he continued.

Despite Alpha's enthusiasm, he is not in the nuclear fusion business. He is the founder and CEO of TerraQuanta (大地量子), which focuses on geospatial analytics, using artificial intelligence to access and evaluate climate-related physical risk data. The company currently has two offices—one in Beijing and one in Chengdu, Alpha's hometown.

Alpha experienced a rather typical upbringing in a period of rapid economic growth in China. He studied for the national college entrance exam known as the Gao Kao (高考) and was admitted to one of the top schools—Shanghai Jiaotong University. His parents were engineers who worked for one of the electricity transmission and distribution companies, State Grid (国家电网公司); Alpha followed in their footsteps and studied electrical engineering. Alpha then went to the United States to pursue a PhD in computer science at the University of Southern California. Although he contemplated becoming a professor at times during his PhD program, Alpha knew from childhood that he wanted to be an entrepreneur. He built his own personal website at the age of 11 and created a small social networking website for his peers during high school. "It felt like a natural choice for me to start my own business," Alpha expressed.

TerraQuanta does not have any explicit sustainability objectives, though perhaps after my nudge Alpha may express some of the company's policies in terms of the United Nations sustainable development goals (SDGs). For example, TerraQuanta hires women and other underrepresented workers in the Chinese tech field and views them as equally efficient and productive. If he were a policy maker, he would prioritize job creation over most other ESG factors. Alpha explained, "There is not much value today in being a carbon-neutral small and medium-sized enterprise (SME) in China, though that may change in five years; there needs to be some kind of financial incentive for smaller companies to take on net-zero goals." Larger companies in China have both reputational and financial motivation to become carbon neutral. The European Union's Carbon Border Adjustment Mechanism (CBAM), whereby imports on certain goods are priced according to embedded carbon emissions, is partly motivating large Chinese manufacturers to reduce carbon emissions.

Given its small operational size with 30 employees, TerraQuanta focuses rather on the positive impact that the company can have through its product. "We serve the power generation companies and large consumers of energy; we are helping renewable power integration into the grid by providing valuable weather prediction data for wind and solar projects," Alpha explained. That said, Alpha still acquiesces to requests for pro-bono environmental services; for example, TerraQuanta helped a local newspaper gather evidence of illegal deforestation that led to real change on the ground.

Alpha's advice to his 16-year-old self would be to "follow your heart," and given the economic slowdown in China, he reminds himself that many companies, such as Yahoo and Google, were founded during economic downturns in their industries. Alpha is not what many would call an environmentalist. Yet, if the world is going to get out of the climate crisis, then the task of implementing climate solutions cannot be left to only one perspective or demographic.

Since we need all hands on deck, Alpha's work through TerraQuanta provides a useful place for the techno-optimists to meet the tree huggers. And who knows, maybe Alpha is subconsciously motivated by those pandas, native to his hometown of Chengdu.

From mechanical engineer to energy efficiency CEO—SaLisa Berrien's story

"Legacy is what drives me. I have children, and I want to leave behind a climate-friendly economy where future generations can live, work, play, and thrive," SaLisa Berrien explained.

SaLisa is a seasoned energy expert and the CEO of COI Energy, a U.S. based company that helps customers detect, eliminate, and monetize energy waste in buildings to drive efficiency and optimize the electric grid.

Although SaLisa is now at ease in the electricity world, her first interactions with the sector were devastating. "I grew up in energy poverty in Allentown, Pennsylvania. My family couldn't pay the bills when I was young and I experienced a lot of dark nights," SaLisa reflected. Shaped by this experience, SaLisa decided to study mechanical engineering at the University of Pittsburgh and obtained her first job in technical sales at Pennsylvania Power & Light—the very same electric utility that had served (and not served) her family growing up.

SaLisa worked in several roles with progressive responsibility in the electric utility space: promoting technologies like absorption chillers for a vertically integrated utility, procuring federal energy management contracts for a deregulated utility, and eventually starting a consulting company focused on reducing energy inefficiencies in the built environment. For the latter, the timing could not have been worse—SaLisa launched the business officially on September 5, 2001. Days later, a major terrorist attack would disrupt economic activity and lead to the cancelling of contracts. Nevertheless, SaLisa did not let the bleak context stop her mission. She went on to work for four energy-related startups. She remembered, "I loved witnessing first-hand the impact my contributions made on the success of the businesses. As hectic as the startup environment could be, it feels more like home for me."

In 2016, SaLisa founded COI Energy. By then, her whole career had been customer facing. She developed a reputation in the industry for both valuing the customer and having a deep understanding of energy efficiency and the electric grid. It was in her last startup role that she experienced an aha moment in meeting customer needs. SaLisa explained metaphorically, "We were offering a luxury car when what the customer actually wanted was an economy vehicle." She decided to break out on her own to provide sharp attention in meeting specific customer demands.

With COI Energy, SaLisa leads a team and product that responds to market needs in energy efficiency and carbon management. COI Energy won their first contract because they narrowly focused on the specific customer asks, rather than providing unwanted bells and whistles. Today, COI Energy serves over 240 commercial, industrial, and utility customers, helping eliminate energy waste in buildings while often serving vulnerable populations such as the elderly and those living in affordable housing.

As CEO, SaLisa sees the mission of COI Energy as closely tied to its original meaning: circle of influence (COI). "Iron sharpens iron," SaLisa recounted. "If you are not working together to take care of the environment and people, then you will not be sustainable." The ethos of developing and supporting one another extends beyond staff and close stakeholders. For example, during the COVID pandemic, COI Energy used funds collected from their kW for Good program to provide personal protection equipment to communities.

SaLisa identifies justice, equity, diversity, inclusion, and sustainability as one and the same. COI Energy's commercial objectives are very much aligned with SaLisa's life journey from energy poverty to energy wealth. SaLisa wants others to benefit, including monetarily, from energy savings, all while supporting a healthy planet and a better climate.

Intersecting the SURF Framework and climate change for sustainability pursuits

The SURF Framework proves useful when pursuing climate-related careers.

Climate-related careers involving supply chain

The crux of climate-related careers involving the supply chain can be found in what is known as "scope 3 emissions." The Greenhouse Gas Protocol (GHG Protocol) defines scope 3 emissions as "all other indirect emissions that occur in a company's value chain"; scope 1 emissions are direct emissions from owned or controlled sources; scope 2 emissions are indirect emissions from the generation of purchased energy consumed by the reporting company (GHG Protocol, 2011b).

There are many jobs that support supply chain decarbonization. The tools used include identifying and choosing climate-friendly suppliers (e.g., purchasing sustainably harvested paper products instead of petrol-based plastic products), working with existing suppliers on decarbonization plans, and selecting local suppliers and thereby reducing transport-associated emissions. Sometimes a company's carbon neutrality or net-zero goal is arbitrarily set by company leadership, and sometimes the goal is based on scientific scenarios to keep global warming under 1.5 degrees C. Over 430 companies across 56 industries and 38 countries have signed The Climate Pledge, which calls on companies to do three things: measure and report GHG emissions on a regular basis, implement decarbonization strategies in line with the Paris Agreement, and neutralize any remaining emissions with additional, quantifiable, real, permanent, and socially beneficial offsets to achieve net-zero annual carbon emissions by 2040 (Amazon, 2023).

In addition to the physical supply chain, the GHG Protocol also identifies the financial supply chain as a part of Scope 3. Under Scope 3, Category 15 of the GHG Protocol, "emissions from investments should be allocated to the reporting company based on the reporting company's proportional share of investment in the investee" (GHG Protocol, 2011b). The Partnership for Carbon

Accounting Financials (PCAF), whose methodologies are built on the GHG Protocol and have been verified by the Protocol, enables financial institutions such as banks and asset managers to "assess and disclose greenhouse gas emissions associated with financial activities"; there are over 440 financial institutions that represent over $93 trillion of assets under management that have joined PCAF to measure and disclose financed emissions (PCAF, 2023).

Retirement savings are one of the most climate-harming investment tools in the marketplace. In the United States, retirement assets are valued at more than US $37 trillion. Defined contribution (DC) plans, plans where employees contribute part of their salary to an account with optional employer matching, total over US $10 trillion; on average, these plans finance carbon emissions at 64 tons of carbon dioxide equivalent per US$1 million in retirement assets invested (tCO2e/$mm invested) (CFA Institute, 2022). There are therefore roles to help companies align their employee retirement benefits with sustainability, including reducing climate risk and taking advantage of climate opportunities in investments.

Even more impactful than retirement accounts, bank savings pose significant harm when those savings spend the night in a carbon-intensive bank. A rule of thumb is that for every one U.S. dollar in a bank account (or credit union), the bank (or credit union) leverages that amount by ten in order to make loans; those loans can either help or harm people and planet. The world's 60 largest banks have financed at least US$5.5 trillion worth of fossil fuels in the seven years since the adoption of the Paris Agreement (Rainforest Action Network, 2023). On a positive note, there are a plethora of banks and credit unions in most countries that offer fossil fuel-free, deforestation-free, climate-friendly banking; these include ethical banks and neo fintech banks.

Researchers found that the average carbon intensity by fossil fuel banks in the U.S. is around 126 kilotons of carbon dioxide equivalent per US$1 billion in cash deployed (ktCO2e/$bn in cash deployed); so for each US$1 billion deployed, these banks generate emissions comparable to about 30,000 internal combustion engine cars running for a year; researchers also found that the cash holdings of many U.S. companies, including Alphabet, Microsoft, and Salesforce, are their largest source of emissions and, when accounted for, increase total emissions by 91 to 112 percent when compared to most recently reported emissions (Vaccaro & Moinester, 2021). In other words, there is a lot of work to be done in cleaning up the financed emissions of companies and banks, as well as helping the climate-friendly banks and credit unions, such as those that are B Corporation certified or a part of BankForGood, scale their climate lending.

Questions that one could answer in roles that combine the supply chain and climate-related careers include:

- What are our scope 3 emissions, including financed emissions?
- How can we reduce our scope 3 emissions, especially in ways that create a net positive for the planet and do not simply transfer the carbon burden onto another owner?

- Do we bank with a fossil fuel-free and deforestation-free bank? Does our bank's carbon footprint represent the lowest possible available to us?
- Have we decided to bank with a sustainable bank as determined by a national mission designation, B Corporation status, Benefit Corporation status, membership and adherence to principles such as those set out by the Global Alliance for Banking on Values (GABV) or the European Federation of Ethical and Alternative Banks and Financiers (FEBEA), or inclusion in BankForGood and similar initiatives?
- Do our employee retirement benefits default to sustainable, climate-friendly options?
- Have we used third-party resources (such as Morningstar Globes, As You Sow's values investing databases, Ask Sustainable, or China's Climate Friendly Invest database) to determine if our investment products are sustainable?
- Have we completed a supply chain audit for climate justice, including any negative impacts of our supply chain on marginalized communities? Have we developed an action plan to rectify any negative impacts?

Climate-related careers involving the user

In addressing climate change, end users have been historically scapegoated by the fossil fuel industry. "We have to work on the demand side of fossil fuels to solve climate change"—so goes the mantra of an industry that clearly has a conflict of interest in making change.

Nevertheless, there are plenty of user-oriented climate-related careers that do not center scapegoating consumers or greenwashing. For example, one could support improving consumer goods to render them less carbon intensive and circular. One could design and lead campaigns to increase consumer action for climate-friendly retail banking and investing. One could create processes that make consumer decisions easier and/or remove the need to make a decision altogether, in favor of default climate-friendly options. Public works that make taking an electric train more convenient than taking an electric car would be one such example.

In a global survey of 58,000 people in 23 countries that cover 70 percent of the planet and 80 percent of GHG emissions, researchers found that the most important emotion for climate action was love and care for future generations (Potential Energy, 2023). When users (clients, consumers, constituents) ask what they can do for climate change, they are essentially expressing love. Having a concrete, scientific, and impactful response to that question is not playing into the hands of extractive industries, but rather responding to humanity's need to express love.

Project Drawdown, an organization that seeks to help the world stop climate change as quickly, safely, and equitably as possible, found that while 70–75 percent of global emissions can be reduced directly by business, utility, and government decisions, "individual and household actions have the potential to produce roughly 25–30 percent of the total emissions reductions needed to avoid dangerous climate change (>1.5°C rise)" (Frischmann & Chissell, 2021).

Questions that one could answer in roles that combine the user and climate-related careers include:

- Does the end user have sufficient climate information about a product/service/process to make an informed decision? Is there transparency and comparability in climate information for products/services/processes?
- How can the information burden, or expertise burden, be removed from the end user to render climate-friendly products/services/projects the default choice of end users?
- How can ideas and feedback from end users be used to drive better design and manufacturing of climate-friendly products?
- What structure and/or mechanisms can be put in place for end users to share in the profits of an enterprise (e.g., a cooperative dividend structure)?

Climate-related careers involving relations

Stakeholder relations are everything—including in climate-related careers. Siting large-scale renewable energy projects, such as wind and solar farms, requires just as much stakeholder engagement, environmental and social impact assessment, and community-driven decision making as dirty energy projects. Legitimate concerns over the negative environmental and social footprint of materials needed for climate solutions have increased in recent years. For example, the mining of cobalt, a key ingredient in many lithium-ion batteries used for electric vehicles, has been linked with increases in farmland loss, food and water insecurity, violence, substance abuse, and physical and mental health challenges (Northwestern University, 2021).

Questions that one could answer in roles that combine stakeholder relations and climate-related careers include:

- What are the justice, equity, diversity, and inclusion (JEDI) ramifications of the proposed climate product/service/process? How can more equity be embedded?
- What structures and processes have been put into place for community-driven input, decision making, and opportunities to build collective wealth in a proposed climate project?
- Have tools such as environmental and social impact assessments, and/or environmental life cycle assessment (E-LCA) or social life cycle assessment (S-LCA) been used?
- What risks, opportunities, and impacts does the proposed climate project present to all stakeholders?
- How are two-way communications maintained for a proposed climate intervention?
- How are the voices of those furthest from power centered in communications and decision making?

Climate-related careers involving the future

A future without climate action workers looks bleak.

At 4 degrees Celsius of warming by 2100, there is intolerable heat stress across most of the world, agriculture deprivation due to expanding desert and severe droughts, rainforest turned to grassland due to increased fires, and scarce freshwater (Vince, 2022). Reaching 2 degrees Celsius of warming is also dreary: flooding will impact over 130 cities, causing more than $1.4 trillion in annual damages by the end of the twenty-first century; 3.3 billion people will be exposed to deadly heatwaves; and 1.5 billion people will be forced into migration by 2050 (Vince, 2022).

Homo sapiens cannot physically survive at wet bulb temperatures[2] above 35 degrees C; at this level, people overheat and die within six hours; a few places in Asia crossed the wet bulb threshold in 2020, and even during the 2003 European heatwave when a wet bulb temperature of 28 degrees C was reached, more than 70,000 people died (Vince, 2022).

To avoid this future, the world must stop producing and using fossil fuels, deforestation, and greenhouse gas-emitting agriculture, and start producing and using climate solutions in all areas of the economy.

Climate-related careers are inherently future oriented as climate change most acutely threatens humanity's ability to have a viable future. Nevertheless, there are some economic activities that may reduce greenhouse gases in the short term while posing long-term harms. It's therefore important to also be mindful of the systemic impacts of climate solutions and constantly push ourselves to enshrine long-lasting future benefits to any climate solution.

Questions that one could answer in roles that combine a future orientation and climate-related careers include:

- How does the product/service/process help create not only GHG reduction, but also long-term social, economic, and intergenerational benefits?
- What are the future risks, opportunities, and impacts of a solution that reduces GHG emissions?
- How can circular and regenerative outcomes be generated with the product/service/process in question?

Table 9.1 provides a number of career-focused resources for finding jobs, networking, learning, and expanding thinking in climate-related careers; Table 9.2 provides a list and summary of newsletters, podcasts, videos, and other media on climate-related careers and topics.

Conclusion

Climate-related careers are a natural extension of sustainability-related careers. The climate crisis has made clear that the environment, society, economy, and future generations are inextricably linked. In this chapter, I introduced some of

TABLE 9.1 Non-exhaustive examples of climate-related career resources

Resource	One-sentence summary
Climate Action Tech	A community of practice of tech workers that provides support and guidance for systemic change in the tech field to face the climate crisis.
Climate Base	A platform for jobs at thousands of organizations working on climate solutions.
Climate Change Careers	Platform where one can search for jobs at organizations solving climate change and the latest courses in climate science, renewable energy, electric vehicles, and more.
Climate Designers	Provides the knowledge, skills, and professional network to support designers to be climate leaders.
Climate Diversity	Resources for climate-related equity, diversity, inclusion, and belonging.
Climate Draft	Platform that provides climate tech information and opportunities to connect with climate startups looking for advisors, investors, and team members.
ClimateEU	Slack community and platform that brings together climate tech startups, investors, talent, and corporates in Europe.
Climate Investing Club	Slack community that focuses on ways to save, spend, invest, and donate money in ways that are climate-friendly and value aligned.
Climate People	Technology recruiting firm that is dedicated to decarbonizing the global economy by placing mission-driven talent into ClimateTech careers.
Climate Solutions Lab	Distributes solution-oriented climate knowledge, including a climate jobs board and a climate change syllabus bank.
Greentech Noir	Slack network for the Black diaspora creating systemic change in industries including clean energy, smart cities, clean transportation, infrastructure, water, circular economy, agriculture, conservation, investment, policy, environmental justice, climate tech, and beyond.
Leafr	Climate organizations post jobs on Leafr and are matched with applicants from the Leafr network.
My Climate Journey	Slack platform that enables the flow of information, ideas, and capital to accelerate individual climate journeys and advance collaboration.
New Energy Network	Open Slack community hosted by New Energy Nexus for those working on bringing clean energy to 100% of humanity.
Open Door Climate	Community of climate professionals available to chat with climate career seekers.
Out in Climate	A community for LGBTQ+ professionals in climate.
TeamClimate	Slack community for people looking for tips and knowledge exchange around climate transformation for businesses.
Terra.do	An organization that provides immersive learning programs that train individuals to transition into climate.
Tofu	Slack community for climate tech marketers.

Resource	One-sentence summary
Women in Climate	Platform for climate conference and event organizers to find women speakers for any event and a slack community to collaborate and communicate.
Work on Climate	An action-oriented Slack community for people serious about climate.
Zopeful	14-day Intro to Climate email course that provides 5–10-minute easy-to-read emails that covers the basics of climate change.

TABLE 9.2 Newsletters, podcasts, videos and other media on climate-related careers and topics

Resource	One-sentence summary
All We Can Save	A book that centers women of different backgrounds in climate action, as well as an organization built to nurture the leaderful climate community.
A Matter of Degrees Podcast	Covers stories about what drives climate change and the tools to fix it.
Chartbook Newsletter	A newsletter on economics, geopolitics, and history that sometimes explicitly covers the climate crisis but otherwise includes relevant information for understanding the climate context.
China Cleantech (生态创新) Podcast	Podcast that features China-connected cleantech innovations and innovators.
Climate Finance Podcast	Podcast that covers a number of climate finance topics and whose website has a lot of climate-related resources, including Slack groups.
Climate Now Podcast	Presents the research of climate change experts (climate science, economics, policy, clean energy, and negative emissions technologies).
Climate One Podcast	Engages advocates, influencers and policymakers in empowering conversations that connect all aspects of the climate emergency.
Drilled Newsletter	Focused on climate accountability and the drivers of climate action delay.
Energy Iceberg Newsletter	Covers China's renewable and clean power market with policy and industry insights.
Global South Climate Tech Podcast	Shares the challenges and triumphs of climate tech innovators in Global South economies to attract better investment, perspectives, and economic prosperity.
Green Rock Newsletter	Focuses on mining and its connection to clean energy.
Heated Newsletter	Offers original reporting and analysis on the climate crisis.
How to Save a Planet Podcast	Discusses climate change in a way that leaves listeners feeling energized.

Resource	One-sentence summary
Inside Climate News	A non-profit, nonpartisan news organization that provides reporting and analysis on climate change, energy, and the environment.
Inside the Movement (ITM) Newsletter	Assembles, each week, what is happening in the climate movement and ways to take action.
Invested in Climate Podcast	Shares optimistic conversations about climate action.
New Economy Now Podcast	Highlights the leaders who are taking a regenerative, bio-regional, equitable, transparent, racially just, and whole-systems approach to creating the new economy.
New Climate Capitalism Podcast	Covers the change-makers working at the intersection of finance, climate, and activism.
NextGen Banker Podcast	Covers the future of finance for more equitable, environmentally conscious, and transparent banking.
The Long Run	Covers money, power, and politics and thus the foundations of the climate economy.
Project Drawdown	A book and an ongoing resource that presents over 80 climate solutions and coming attractions using science and narrative.
Shuang Tan Newsletter	Provides policy analysis, data insights, and interviews on China from a decarbonization perspective.
SpaceshipOne Podcast	Shares stories of Earthlings who work on climate change, clean energy, public health, and environmental justice.
Su$tainable Mobility Newsletter	Describes where the money resides in all things related to sustainable mobility, transportation, and logistics.
Sustainable Nation Podcast	Interviews global corporate sustainability leaders.
Think 100% Podcast	Offers conversations that reimagine how Black, Indigenous, and Brown people thrive in our environment and solve climate change.
Watt Matters Podcast	Covers the shift to a decarbonized economy, focusing on Europe, North America, and the global context.
Yale Climate Communications	A platform for research and media dissemination on public climate change knowledge, attitudes, policy preferences, and behavior.

the momentum for climate that various industries are experiencing and told stories of professionals who are pursuing sustainability in climate-related careers on different continents. Importantly, the underpinnings of climate justice are explained, as well as how using the SURF (supply chain, end user, relations, future) Framework specifically in the climate context can help orient people towards new roles and approaches.

Notes

1 The everything bagel is a type of bagel popular in the United States; it contains many ingredients such as garlic flakes, onion flakes, poppy seeds, and sesame seeds. The

metaphor of the everything bagel was made popular in the 2022 film *Everything Everywhere All at Once*.
2 Wet bulb temperature is the lowest temperature at which air can be cooled by the evaporation of water into the air (at a constant pressure). www.sciencedirect.com/top ics/engineering/wet-bulb-temperature.

References

ABET. (2018). Sustainable Education: Readying Today's Higher Ed Students to Tackle the World's Grand Challenges. www.abet.org/wp-content/uploads/2018/11/ABET_ Sustainable-Engineering_Issue-Brief.pdf.

Amazon. (2023). Everything you need to know about The Climate Pledge. www.abou tamazon.com/news/sustainability/what-is-the-climate-pledge.

Battle, C. P. (2020). An Offering from the Bayou. In A.E. Johnson & K.K. Wilkinson (eds.), *All We Can Save* (pp. 329–333). One World. www.allwecansave.earth.

Center for Climate Justice. (2023). What is Climate Justice?https://centerclimatejustice. universityofcalifornia.edu/what-is-climate-justice.

CFA Institute. (2022). The Carbon Impact of U.S. Company Sponsored 401(K) Plans. www. businessclimatefinance.org/_files/ugd/d008b0_6cd63c0a59d340338371c43f9be0af06.pdf.

Frischmann, C. & Chissell, C. (2021). The powerful role of household actions in solving climate change. Project Drawdown. https://drawdown.org/news/insights/the-power ful-role-of-household-actions-in-solving-climate-change.

Georgea, D., Clewettb, J., Birchc, C., Wright, A., & Allene, W. (2009). A professional development climate course for sustainable agriculture in Australia. *Environmental Education Research*, 15(4), 417–444. https://doi.org/10.1080/13504620902946978.

GHG Protocol. (2011a). Corporate Value Chain (Scope 3) Accounting and Reporting Standard. World Resources Institute and World Business Council for Sustainable Development. https://ghgprotocol.org/sites/default/files/standards/Corporate-Value-Cha in-Accounting-Reporing-Standard_041613_2.pdf.

GHG Protocol. (2011b). Technical Guidance for Calculating Scope 3 Emissions. Cate- gory 15: Investments. https://ghgprotocol.org/sites/default/files/standards_supporting/ Chapter15.pdf.

IPCC (Intergovernmental Panel on Climate Change). (2023). History of the IPCC. www. ipcc.ch/about/history.

Jenkins, P. (2021). *Climate, Catastrophe, and Faith: How Changes in Climate Drive Religious Upheaval*. Oxford University Press. https://global.oup.com/academic/p roduct/climate-catastrophe-and-faith-9780197506219.

Krasna, H., Czabanowska, K., Jiang, S., Khadka, S., Morita, H., Kornfeld, J. & Shaman, J. (2020). The Future of Careers at the Intersection of Climate Change and Public Health: What Can Job Postings and an Employer Survey Tell Us? *International Journal of Environmental Research and Public Health*, 17(4), 1310. https://doi.org/10. 3390/ijerph17041310.

Longley, R. (2021). What Is Neoliberalism? Definition and Examples. ThoughtCo. www. thoughtco.com/what-is-neoliberalism-definition-and-examples-5072548.

Northwestern University. (2021). Understanding cobalt's human cost. *ScienceDaily*, 17. www.sciencedaily.com/releases/2021/12/211217113232.htm.

Norton, G. (2020). Lessons from a Career in Agricultural Development and Research Evaluation. *Applied Economic Perspectives and Policy*, 42(2), 151–167. https://doi.org/ 10.1002/aepp.13052.

PCAF. (2023). The Partnership for Carbon Accounting Financials. https://carbonaccoun
tingfinancials.com.

Potential Energy. (2023). Climate Week & The Ultimate "Why."https://medium.com/@
ThatsInteresting_PE/climate-week-the-ultimate-why-38c5b1ab7675.

Rainforest Action Network (RAN), BankTrack, Indigenous Environmental Network
(IEN), Oil Change International (OCI), Reclaim Finance, the Sierra Club, and Urge-
wald. (2023). Banking on Climate Chaos. www.bankingonclimatechaos.org.

Robinson, M. (2018). *Climate Justice: Hope, Resilience, and the Fight for a Sustainable
Future*. Bloomsbury. www.bloomsbury.com/us/climate-justice-9781632869289.

Shealy, T., Katz, A. & Godwin, A. (2021). Predicting engineering students' desire to
address climate change in their careers: An exploratory study using responses from a
U.S. National survey . *Environmental Education Research* 27(7), 1054–1079. https://
doi.org/10.1080/13504622.2021.1921112.

Sofiah, A. (2023). How climate change is affecting the working world: Expected jobs to be
created and displaced. Human Resources Online. www.humanresourcesonline.net/how-
climate-change-is-affecting-the-working-world-expected-jobs-to-be-created-and-displaced.

Táíwò, O. (2022). *Reconsidering Reparations*. Oxford University Press. https://global.
oup.com/academic/product/reconsidering-reparations-9780197508893.

Vaccaro, J., & Moinester, P. (2021). The Carbon Bankroll: The Climate Impact and
Untapped Power of Corporate Cash. The Climate Safe Lending Network, The Outdoor Policy Outfit, and BankFWD. www.carbonbankroll.com/.

Vince, G. (2022). *Nomad Century How Climate Migration Will Reshape Our World*.
Flatiron Books. https://us.macmillan.com/books/9781250821614/nomadcentury.

Wagner, G., & Weitzman, M. (2015). *Climate Shock: The Economic Consequences of a
Hotter Planet*. Princeton University Press. https://doi.org/10.2307/j.ctv7h0rzq.

10

PURSUING SUSTAINABILITY THROUGH JUSTICE, EQUITY, DIVERSITY, AND INCLUSION

> While solving climate change requires "all hands on deck," the impacts of climate change do not impact all hands equally.
>
> *(Marilyn Waite)*

Introduction

Since the first edition of *Sustainability at Work* was released, one of the major trends and qualifiers of sustainability has been that of justice, equity, diversity, and inclusion, sometimes denoted JEDI or DEI-J. The variations of this concept are many. Sometimes only "DEI" or "D&I" is used; sometimes there are additions such as "B" for "belonging" or "SJ" for "social justice." Regardless of the exact variation, the core message is that dismantling systemic disparities should be centered when pursuing sustainability.

Professions occur within the real world, where there is a real history of how we arrived at the unsustainable policies and practices that we have today. It is not by accident that there are movements for LGBTQIA+ pride, racial justice, gender equity, disability inclusion, and the intentional inclusion of various marginalized identities. The movements are a response to the unconscious and conscious bias, prejudice, and discrimination that negatively impacts both the associated identities and all people alike. The social movements are the results of years, decades, and centuries of systemic and systematic exclusion and inequities perpetuated by government and business policies, practices, and culture.

In pursuing ecological regeneration, social unity, intergenerational equity, and economic well-being, it becomes negligent to ignore a JEDI lens, especially if we would like the outcomes of our efforts to be, well, sustainable.

DOI: 10.4324/9781032615844-10

So what do each of these concepts mean? JEDI, as defined by the Avarna Group and used by the Public Lands Alliance, can be broken down as follows (Avarna Group, 2023):

- Justice: Dismantling barriers to resources and opportunities in society so that all individuals and communities can live a full and dignified life. These barriers are essentially the "isms" in society: racism, classism, sexism, etc.
- Equity: Allocating resources to ensure everyone has access to the same resources and opportunities. Equity recognizes that advantages and barriers—the "isms"—exist. Equity is the approach and equality is the outcome.
- Diversity: The differences between people based on which we experience systemic advantages or encounter systemic barriers to opportunities.
- Inclusion: Fostering a sense of belonging by centering, valuing, and amplifying the voices, perspectives, and styles of those who experience more barriers based on their identities.

The practice of JEDI in the workplace necessitates an understanding of each of the concepts that goes beyond how they might be (mis)used in everyday language. Author Mor Barak has called out the specificity of the concepts applied to the work environment; for example, workplace diversity is defined as the division of the workforce into distinction categories that (1) have a perceived commonality within a given cultural or national context, and that (2) impact potentially harmful or beneficial employment outcomes such as job opportunities, treatment in the workplace, and promotion prospects—irrespective of job-related skills and qualifications (Mor Barak, 2022).

With some form of diversity and inclusion training now being a global, multi-billion-dollar business with mixed outcomes, many organizations and professionals are seeking greater clarity on what works and what does not. Author Jessica Nordell, in *The End of Bias: A Beginning. The Science and Practice of Overcoming Unconscious Bias*, describes best practices, including the scientific observations that (1) curtailing biased behavior requires paying attention to differences—the very opposite of trying to be "blind" to them—and 2) developing a better understanding of history leads to a greater grasp of present-day prejudice, which is in consistency with the Marley Hypothesis that group differences in perception of racism reflect dominant-group denial of and ignorance about the extent of past racism (Nordell, 2021).

Tactically, developing a JEDI mindset is like a muscle that needs to be exercised. Author Ruchika Tulshyan introduced the BRIDGE Framework, which some professionals may find practical when pursuing sustainability goals with an inclusion lens (Tulshyan, 2022):

Be uncomfortable
Reflect (on what you don't know)

Invite feedback
Defensiveness doesn't help
Grow from your mistakes
Expect that change takes time

Inclusion connotes an organizational culture that keeps changing to reflect a diversity of values and norms, while exclusion connotes conformity to pre-established organizational values and norms that reflect the "majority" or "mainstream" (Mor Barak, 2022). Underpinning a culture of inclusion is the idea of cultural competency, which can be defined as "the awareness, knowledge and skills needed to work with others who are culturally different from self in meaningful, relevant, and productive ways" (Pope et al., 2004).

Professor Kimberlé Crenshaw coined the term "intersectionality" in her 1989 academic article, "Demarginalizing the Intersection of Race and Sex: A Black Feminist Critique of Antidiscrimination Doctrine, Feminist Theory and Antiracist Politic," where she contrasts the "multidimensionality of Black women's experience with the single-axis analysis that distorts these experiences" (Crenshaw, 1989). According to the Center for Intersectional Justice, intersectionality can be defined as "the ways in which systems of inequality based on gender, race, ethnicity, sexual orientation, gender identity, disability, class and other forms of discrimination 'intersect' to create unique dynamics and effects" (CIJ, 2023). Even those with entrenched biases towards the "other" have been found to largely agree that intersectionality "accurately describes the way people from different backgrounds encounter the world" (Coaston, 2019).

The environmental and climate change imperatives of a JEDI lens

The climate crisis has exacerbated inequities and brought to the fore the reality that much of our present-day systems are designed to extract and divide. Many parts of the world are already experiencing climate-disaster migration and displacement. One such example is in Miami, Florida, where the wealthy are displacing the lower-income and immigrant communities in the higher-ground areas as coastal erosion occurs (Battle, 2020). There is a long history of environmental injustice in many parts of the world, as those in power greenlight "sacrifice zones," or populated areas with high levels of pollution and environmental hazards, to place vulnerable groups in harm's way for the economic benefit of privileged groups (The Climate Reality Project, 2023). The Global Atlas of Environmental Justice (EJAtlas) is an interactive online platform, managed by a team of researchers, that portrays and documents social conflicts around environmental issues.

Some of the starkest examples of environmental racism and structural inequities can be found on the European continent. Three examples are highlighted here, taken from the European Network Against Racism (ENAR) groundbreaking work on climate justice. More than 90 percent of the population in France's majority Black provinces of Guadeloupe and Martinique are contaminated with cancer-causing chlordecone (Ramanujam & Asri, 2021). This chemical, which had been banned in most places, including the United States and mainland France, was granted an extension to be used on fruit plantations in these French regions with a legacy of chattel slavery. In essence, the European Union and its member state France created a sacrifice zone of racialized communities by permitting a toxic substance to be used in one location and not others. Italy's neofascist group CasaPound used environmental sustainability as a rationale to keep one of Europe's largest ethnic minorities, the Roma, from being housed in a district of Rome (Ramanujam & Asri, 2021). This is an example of how unless sustainability progress intentionally uses a JEDI lens, socially inequitable decisions can be made under the guise of environmental protection. For Ireland's Irish Travellers, 80 percent of whom are unemployed, the climate crisis is exacerbating an already precarious situation. Many Travellers live in trailers with poor insulation and experience fuel poverty. The EU's reliance on fossil gas, with prices skyrocketing in recent years, has only added to the energy burden of Irish Travellers. Without a justice and inclusion lens on energy investments and policies, communities such as the Irish Travellers will continue to be disproportionately burdened (Ramanujam & Asri, 2021).

Climate change mitigation is a rare opportunity to drive JEDI outcomes, especially when it comes to reducing wealth gaps and building an economy that works for the 100 percent. Although trillions of dollars in green investments are being mobilized, those that have been historically disadvantaged in the dirty economy currently remain so in the clean economy. For example, in the United States, women and Black workers in energy-efficiency jobs greatly lag national workforce averages, and solar firm senior executives are 80 percent men and 88 percent white (Waite, 2021). As author Garrett Neiman points out using Credit Suisse data, due in large part to such internationally synchronized bigotry, the U.S., Canada, and Europe hold 57 percent of the world's wealth—over $200 trillion—while representing just 17 percent of the global population (Neiman, 2023). Given the newness of many climate solutions, such as building and scaling renewable energy, regenerative agriculture, and electric transportation, climate mitigation presents an opportunity for a more just and equitable economy. Unfortunately, the world is currently falling short on delivering such a brighter future.

As capital is mobilized for climate-friendly projects, there is also an opportunity to ensure that the infrastructure is inclusive of people with disabilities. According to Harriet Larrington-Spencer and colleagues:

> The concept of disability is very broad, and can relate to a wide range of impairments, including autism spectrum conditions, long-term health conditions, mental health conditions, physical or mobility impairments, sensory impairments (e.g. deafness and blindness) and learning difficulties.
>
> (Larrington-Spencer et al., 2023)

Environmental and climate action has often lacked the intention of disability inclusion and therefore has projected problematic ableism. While one of the most visible ways that climate infrastructure can be inclusive is by designing and implementing transit systems that are accessible for those with mobility impairments, there are many other ways that climate-friendly systems can move from ableist to anti-ableist. In "Disabled Environmentalisms," Larrington-Spencer et al. define a few disability-inclusive pathways, including qualifying what it means to be an eco-friendly shopper (e.g., pre-chopped produce, sometimes derided by environmentalists, supports people with limited hand dexterity); creating disability-inclusive spaces for activism (e.g., ensure that fully accessible toilet facilities are available at protests); and designing disability-inclusive climate finance (e.g., subsidizing adapted cycles, which are generally more expensive than standard two-wheel bicycles) (Larrington-Spencer et al., 2023).

The environmental and climate movements have also failed the LGBTQIA+ community, especially by perpetuating heteronormativity in communications. Here, I use Emma Foster's definition of using LGBTQIA+ as the overarching term to describe "marginalized sexualities and genders, including lesbian, gay, bisexual, transgender, transsexual, queer, questioning, intersex, a-sexual, a-gender and their allies, as well as those who do not neatly correspond to the acronym, such as gender-queer, pansexual and polysexual" (Foster, 2023). Some of the historical issues with respect to a lack of LGBTQIA+ community inclusion in ecologically focused initiatives are rooted in a discourse that same-sex sexualities are "crimes against nature," which automatically pits sexuality against environmental progress (Foster, 2023). Climate impacts such as extreme heat and flooding disproportionately impact unhoused people, and in places like the United States, the LGBTQIA+ is disproportionately discriminated against in access to housing (Reta, 2022).

From Ken Saro-Wiwa, who was executed in 1995 for standing up to the oil and gas company Shell and leading a peaceful movement for the environmental and human rights of the Ogoni people in the Niger delta, to Chico Mendes, the Brazilian labor leader and conservationist, who was assassinated by local ranchers in 1988 while fighting to save the Amazon Rainforest, pursuing sustainability with an eye towards justice has been met with violence and oppression (Satheesh, 2023). The acceleration of institutional diversity, equity, inclusion, and justice initiatives has provided a new opportunity for a peaceful pathway for simultaneously solving environmental and social challenges.

While solving climate change requires "all hands on deck," the impacts of climate change do not impact all hands equally. It's thus imperative to center the voices of the most climate impacted, people and communities that represent marginalized identities, so that equitable and just solutions can be developed and implemented.

Know your history (KYH)

The investment industry follows the principle of "know your customer" (KYC) to comply with anti-fraud mandates and to provide tailored products to clients.

I've argued that policymakers creating rules for the financial industry should follow the principle of "know your history" (KYH), in order to set regulations that acknowledge the harm of past policies and bring about improved, historically adjusted outcomes for people and planet (Waite, 2023). KYH can also be generally applied to every professional incorporating sustainability in their career trajectory. Consistent with the Marley Hypothesis, the necessity of KYH becomes apparent when applying a lens of justice, equity, diversity, and inclusion.

One example of why KYH is vital can be found in unpacking the historical makings of the racial wealth gap in the United States. The roots of the banking industry can be found in the trading of African and Indigenous flesh. Wall Street started in 1711 as the first official slave market of the country, an activity that made New York City wealthy as the city received 40 percent of the slave-driven cotton revenue through money in its financial firms and shipping businesses. The US$8 trillion insurance industry also made its wealth from slaves, as slave owners purchased life insurance on slaves and could be paid three-fourths of their market value upon death. The Homestead Act of 1862 provided 160 acres of land stolen from Indigenous communities for free to U.S. residents, but only if they were white immigrants according to the 1790 Naturalization Act. The 1865-founded Freedman's Bank had a goal of providing banking access to newly freed Black people, but the Bank, mismanaged by white trustees, disproportionately lent millions in unsecured loans to white business-people, leading to its failure. The 1900s continued with a racism-first approach, and the New Deal era of the 1930s brought forth government-sanctioned red-lining, the practice of not providing home loans to communities of color. The 2022 Inflation Reduction Act's Greenhouse Gas Reduction Fund explicitly excluded depository institutions, such as minority depository institutions that serve those harmed by the legacy of racist policies, from directly benefiting from the public funding (Waite, 2023).

China's current inequities of coastal–inland, east–west, and urban–rural disparities can also be traced back to historical policies and economic development strategy. While the average annual economic growth rate was 9.4 percent from 1978 to 2018, this rate was spatially unbalanced within China (Guo, 2023). This is partly due to policies that favored the comparative advantages of coastal cities, such as the establishment of coastal special economic zones in the early 1990s. For example, provinces like Guangdong were able to take advantage of proximity to Hong Kong and Macao in ways that were not available to other locations (Guo, 2023). Established in its modern form in 1958, the Chinese *hukou* system, which determines where citizens can receive public services such as education and public housing, has left the approximately 400 million Chinese migrants in a situation where they cannot access services in the city where they work (Storey, 2023). Justice, equity, diversity, and inclusion work in China is more commonly known to fall under the banner of the government's shared prosperity (共同富裕) framework; the framework and a number of other policies incorporate JEDI elements and make clear the importance of understanding China's unique history in order to create sustainability-oriented policies. China has over US$3.2 trillion in green loan balances (Cash & Yao, 2023), the most common means for green development in the economy; ensuring that green investments reach places that reduce the current disparities is thus one avenue that using the JEDI lens can be helpful for sustainable development.

Sustainability, from poetry to venture capital—Taj Ahmad Eldridge's Story

While some prefer a different ordering of the words behind JEDI because they prefer not to risk making indirect references to *Star Wars*, Taj Ahmad Eldridge is on the opposite side of the spectrum: he named his kids Luc and Lea after the protagonists in *Star Wars* and fully embraces the associations. Taj's career journey is one of the most eclectic in the climate movement—having moved from poetry to banking to startup acceleration. Incorporating sustainability and a lens of justice, equity, diversity, and inclusion is not something that required a special chapter in Taj's biography, for the concepts have been interwoven at each step of his life. Usually dressed to the tee while wearing a hat that is eco-friendly and socially responsible, Taj likes to joke that he wears many hats literally and figuratively. At the time of this writing, Taj co-founds a green economy network called GreenTech Noir, leads on climate innovation at Ares-backed Jobs for the Future (JFF), and is a partner at Include Ventures.

How did Taj come to wear these hats? He listened to his parents—at least on some level.

Taj wanted to become a musician—specifically a rapper. His immigrant parents, who voluntarily came from Sudan and the Dominican Republic to the United States, had a different plan for him: become a doctor. In a very circuitous journey, he would fulfill his parents' wishes while still using words to incite social change.

Taj's first step was majoring in poetry and literature at university. When Taj graduated with his degree in the mid-1990s, many local newspapers were closing, and it seemed the most obvious place to apply his knowledge was not hiring. He therefore asked, "Who else employs people who understand expression and persuasion?" It turns out banks do.

Taj obtained his first job in retail banking in 1996 when banks were trying to test whether they could be more successful by operating from grocery stores, closer to and more convenient for the customer. During his time at Wells Fargo in Dallas, Texas, Taj decided to take a study break to pursue an international MBA degree. He would crisscross the world—from Hong Kong, China, to Santiago, Chile—learning about both how historical events shaped the present and the rise of technology.

After eight years at Wells Fargo and the MBA, Taj wanted a more permanent geographical shift. Los Angeles eventually beckoned him where he remains until this day. It was in LA that Taj decided to work for the asset management division at UBS. There, he helped managed OPM (other people's money) at scale; the few years of experience managing institutional capital served as a gateway to venture capital.

Taj decided to leave asset management for angel investing—and a PhD. Taj was not about to disappoint his parents' wishes for him to become a doctor, one way or another. He also genuinely thought a PhD in geopolitical economics would help him become a better investor. Maybe he was right. Soon after graduating and thus becoming Dr. Eldridge, Taj went into angel investing full-time and experienced his first exit 16 years later when marketing agency Xtopoly was acquired by Vincit.

During his angel investing years, Taj navigated diverse industries—from wine making to high-end textiles. At every step, he observed the lack of sustainability. Water quality and quantity were major issues—often called risks—impacting the wine industry. The fashion industry was in general hugely wasteful, and Taj focused on a niche to fit professional basketball players in fashionable clothes using China-based manufacturing. The problem was this: not many people in the world are sized like NBA athletes and the clothes were only worn once.

Eventually, Taj was poached by the University of California in Riverside to lead their startup accelerator. He helped build the reputation of Riverside as a center of excellence and an ecosystem where Latinos and African Americans could thrive. He also served on several startup boards that specialized in solving a sustainability challenge, including FarmSense (food protection) and KIGT (electric vehicle charging). From Riverside, the Los Angeles Cleantech Incubator (LACI) made Taj an offer to join them as an investment director. LACI presented an opportunity for Taj to express his intersectionality like never before. He was excited to put to work his sustainability experience, his track record for diversity and inclusion, and his investment chops.

Yet life has a way of balancing the yin and the yang. On Taj's first day of work at LACI, he was diagnosed with a kidney disease called focal segmental glomerulosclerosis (FSGS). He later found out that three of his cousins died of the same disease and traced the cause not to genetics, but rather to environmental hazard. Growing up in an area of Texas polluted with agrochemical runoff, lead and mercury pollution in the water were so elevated that Taj's grandparents were eventually entitled to compensation. But no monetary payment could prevent Taj from facing this life-threatening hurdle. The damage had already been done. To make matters worse, doctors indicated that the local air pollution may have also exacerbated the condition.

Comprehensive medical studies have shown the negative effects of pollutants such as toxic metals (especially cadmium, lead, and mercury) and particulate matter (PM) on the kidneys. For example, people living within 2 kilometers of industrial plants in the United Kingdom were found to have excess kidney disease mortality; climate change is believed to contribute to the increased incidence of a chronic kidney disease called MesoAmerican nephropathy (MeN) (Afsar et al., 2019). In short, the same industries that are causing climate change are also contributing to immediate public health crises.

FSGS caused severe kidney damage so that Taj had to undergo dialysis for ten hours at a time for seven days a week until he was able to have a transplant. Taj is alive today thanks to his donor Emilee McGowan, wife of his fraternity brother Rob McGowan. With this "new life," Taj is more than ever determined to invest in both climate narrative and capital allocation changes. His personal experience has allowed him to identify the climate crisis as one of public health, justice, equity, diversity, inclusion, and ecological dimensions.

"Faith without work is dead," Taj explained to me. "My kidney donor not only prayed but also acted—literally allowing for life to flourish." When thinking about the SURF Framework, it's clear that each aspect—supply chains, end users, relationships, and future generations—is present in Taj's career pathway. Nevertheless, Taj finds that relationships are the most vital for his line of work. Taj added, "Venture capital is the only asset class where relationships matter to the extreme," and "my roles are centered on the four Cs: capital, connections, customers, and culture."

When I asked Taj about whether he had any advice for his 16-year-old self, he stated, "Trust the unknown process. I see now how poetry is the possibility of language and economics is the possibility of quantifying our decisions. Our climate industry needs a new language to influence the decisions of more than a few to combat the crisis in the time we need."

From brand promotions to solar equipment manufacturing—Li Xia's Story

Li Xia (李霞) is no stranger to adventure. Self-described as "a village girl who left for the big city and then onto the international stage," she mostly balances her time between China and numerous Global South economies.

It was in China's northernmost province of Heilongjiang (黑龙江), where the winters are cold and the economic activity is comparatively low, that Li Xia spent her childhood. She experienced poverty as a child and dropped out of middle school to help her family earn more income. At the age of 18, Li Xia went to Beijing to work to support her younger brother's education. She taught herself English and took advantage of government programs to pursue part-time education.

In 2001, Li Xia went to Shenzhen (深圳) for her first corporate job. At the time, Shenzhen was transforming from a fishing village into a megacity, rivaling Shanghai and Beijing in terms of GDP. She worked in electronics for three years and then decided to start her first company at the age of 23. Her first foray into entrepreneurship was offering promotional services to a wide array of brands, including airlines and cosmetics companies. She flew to many high-income countries selling promotional products. Although the business was successful by many metrics, Li Xia was not very satisfied with the endeavor. Sure, she could buy a house and car on her own, but ultimately, she didn't wake up with a sense of purpose.

It was on a trip to India in 2007 that Li Xia experienced an aha moment. In visiting the Indian slums at that time, Li Xia listened to stories about how a lack of lighting provided the conditions for rape to fester and how fires occurred due to cramped living conditions combined with a reliance on kerosene. These observations got her thinking, "My promotional business is not a necessary business; people who really need certain products are being denied them, while those who do not really need products are being offered them." She thought back to her own upbringing and decided she would start a new business, this time working for people at the "bottom of the pyramid" (BOP) in terms of wealth.

Li Xia went back to Shenzhen and leveraged the already well-developed manufacturing ecosystem there to design and manufacture affordable solar products. It took her three years to pilot and test products for product–market fit. There was no roadmap to show Li Xia how to create and execute; even most entrepreneurship curricula steered students away from the global poor.

Through perseverance, Li Xia's company Shenzhen Power Solutions has become a multi-million-dollar business serving over four million households across 63 countries. The products include solar lanterns, off-grid home lighting systems, and solar-powered appliances. Shenzhen Power Solutions has offices in Shenzhen, Lagos, and Addis Ababa.

When I finally met Li Xia in person, we were neither in China nor in one of her main Global South markets. She had come to France to team up with a few French companies that had operations on the African continent. She brought along coffee and tea from her travels, as well as two miniature statues—the popular stone lions, or shishi (石狮). Lions are not native to China, and according to some historians, Chinese people learned about them through interactions along the Silk Road. It was thus fitting for Li Xia to lug the shishi around as a token of interconnectedness.

Shenzhen Power Solutions' peers include the likes of d.light and Sun King (formerly Greenlight Planet), both of which have deeper pockets and are backed by high-income countries and institutions such as the European Investment Bank and Citi. Li Xia is not deterred by competition, however. She believes Shenzhen Power Solutions is uniquely positioned to scale this example of "South–South Cooperation," or cooperation among where most people live and work on the planet—the Global South. "I knew the day would come when Africa would be ready to manufacture green goods on its own home turf and that day is arriving," Li Xia explained. "China's manufacturing experience in rapidly becoming the world's go-to place for manufacturing may thus prove useful," she added. Li Xia recently signed their first contract to help an Ethiopian state-owned company manufacture, from raw components to finished product, a solar home system in East Africa.

When reflecting on the meaning of sustainability, Li Xia's perspective is one of both the lived experience of poverty and of helping others to more prosperity. "Sustainability for whom?" Li Xia questions. "Who is benefiting from the product or service? If the answer is not the environment, the end user, the community, and the company, then the offer is not sustainable," she explained. Li Xia also asserts that affordability is a pre-condition for sustainability, and she is a fan of the pay-as-you-go model since the model has enabled the masses to access important goods and services.

The traditional "3 Rs"—reduce, reuse, recycle—do not work well in many low-income settings according to Li Xia. She prefers a framework of "reduce, reuse, replace." From her experience, creating products where the components are easily replaceable is often better for the environment and more adapted to limited infrastructure realities than recycling processes.

In the future, Li Xia would like to list Shenzhen Power Solutions on the stock exchange to illustrate that serving the masses can be scalable and profitable. She is interested in leaving her company to the next generation as soon as possible. "I trust someone will do a much better job than me," Li Xia said encouragingly. Her advice for others who seek to incorporate the pillars of sustainability into their work is to rely on oneself and trust that there is always a way out: "Think big, start small, keep observing and persisting."

Intersecting the SURF Framework and JEDI lens for sustainability pursuits

The SURF Framework also proves useful when applying a JEDI lens for reaching sustainability outcomes.

JEDI careers involving supply chain

A JEDI lens shows up in supply chains in several ways, including through diversity-oriented procurement programs, policies that seek to ensure that principles of social justice are adhered to for suppliers, and specific mandates such as carbon neutrality goals combined with community benefits. The Association for Supply Chain Management (ASCM) and Gartner found that three-quarters of supply chain organizations report focusing on some dimension of diversity, and the top reason why supply chain organizations saw progress in DEI outcomes for people of color is that these organizations "equipped leaders to think and act more inclusively" (Gartner, 2022).

Questions that one could help answer in roles that combine the supply chain, justice, equity, diversity, and inclusion include:

• What are the main forms of inequities in the national or cultural context where the product or service is being manufactured, created, or delivered?

How can my company, product, or service help to bring about equity in this instance?

- What goals and targets can be created to ensure greater supplier diversity and inclusion?
- Do existing procurement policies pigeonhole underrepresented demographics to remain small and underrepresented? Is so, how can my company change such policies for better inclusion and equity?
- Does our organization issue request for proposals (RFPs) or similar asks that enable a level playing field in the supply chain? Are JEDI components part of the criteria?
- How can the organization build in the intentional inclusion of under-represented supplier demographics?

JEDI careers involving the user

The user aspect of the SURF Framework has been one of the most widely used tools for JEDI. The user of a product or service, known as the consumer, customer, or client, is a rather powerful lever for engendering equitable, just, and inclusive outcomes. The user-related benefits of incorporating a JEDI lens include increased brand loyalty, customer satisfaction, and understanding customer needs.

Consumers represent different demographics, and in order to respond to customer needs, the organization also needs to represent those demographics. The common logic framework is as follows: how can a product appeal to a certain community if the product was not designed by members of that community and in close collaboration with the community?

Nevertheless, author Jessica Nordell finds that pursuing diversity for only narrow business interests does not work and nor does pursuing diversity as only a matter of ethics. A third approach, where diversity is pursued as necessary because different skills and viewpoints are considered crucial for the institution itself to evolve, works best (Nordell, 2021).

One way to better incorporate justice, equity, diversity, and inclusion in sustainability pursuits is to center the user voice in ways that build community power and prosperity. The cooperative structure, which features democratic ownership and decision making, is one means by which users of a product or service can also reap additional benefits. Examples of user cooperatives include banking cooperatives, also known as credit unions (such as the Clean Energy Federal Credit Union), and consumer cooperatives (such as REI).

Questions that one could help answer in roles that combine the user, justice, equity, diversity, and inclusion include:

- Has a landscape been conducted to understand the current demographics of users of a product/service/product and potential future users? What does the landscape reveal?

- What steps is my organization taking to ensure that the demographics of various users are represented in the decision-making processes of the organization, including the board and senior levels?
- What equitable processes are in place to receive user feedback and how is an equity and justice framework used to make decisions based on the feedback?

JEDI careers involving relations

Applying a JEDI lens to one's career and work generally enables better relationships with a diverse group of people, which in turn widens the types of roles that one can succeed in and the complexity of situations that one can handle. JEDI competence is useful in any workplace situation, including in contexts where JEDI may be taken as a given. For example, in the United States, Historically Black Colleges and Universities (HBCUs) were created to educate newly liberated Black people who were denied formal education at the time. Research has shown that certain identities, such as foreign-born individuals and members of the LGBTQIA + community, however, have felt excluded as faculty members on many HBCU campuses. Therefore, even in a workplace context that seeks to address one form of historical exclusion, being intentionally inclusive about other marginalized identities is also needed to foster belonging (Hiatt et al., 2019).

There are a number of common pitfalls that leave professionals feeling stuck when addressing JEDI. Since relationships are foundational for most career and work progress, it is imperative to develop skills to navigate JEDI conversations. Authors Yoshino and Glasgow offer seven principles to have better JEDI conversations as follows (Yoshino & Glasgow, 2023):

- Principle 1: Guard against the four conversational traps of avoiding, deflecting, denying, and attacking.
- Principle 2: Build resilience by adopting strategies to manage emotional discomfort.
- Principle 3: Cultivate curiosity by adopting a learning posture, conducting research, questioning your gut reaction, and adopting a working hypothesis that it's you who doesn't understand.
- Principle 4: Disagree respectfully, recognizing where the conversation is located on the controversy scale (from least to most controversial: tastes, facts, policies, values, equal humanity).
- Principle 5: Apologize authentically using the four Rs: recognition, responsibility, remorse, and redress.
- Principle 6: Apply the Platinum Rule to help people as they wish to be helped, rather than as you wish to help them, and be an ally because it's the right thing to do, not because you expect to receive praise.
- Principle 7: Be Generous to the Source by separating the behavior from the person.

Questions that one could help answer in roles that combine relationships, justice, equity, diversity, and inclusion include:

- Are workers, including senior leadership and board members, trained in the theory and practice of applying JEDI frameworks such as Yoshino and Glasgow's seven principles and Tulshyan's BRIDGE Framework?
- Has an equity audit been performed to determined where there are gaps and areas of improvement for justice, equity, diversity, and inclusion? What does the audit reveal and what steps are being taken to respond to the audit?
- Are the voices that are most removed from power, both systemically in your cultural or national context and institutionally, centered and given influence? If so, how? If not, what steps can be taken to drive more equity?

JEDI careers involving the future

What are the links between future-oriented careers and a JEDI lens? The response hinges on justice. While many or perhaps all forms of justice require a deep, honest look at the past, we are also called to plot a brighter future when pursuing justice. Identifying the root causes of the injustice is the first step. For example, in seeking to correct climate injustice, the first step is to recognize that it is not a coincidence that greenhouse gas emissions accelerated during the Industrial Revolution and especially in the post-World War II economy: the colonial, imperial, and neoliberal pursuits are tied to an extractive economy that permits the pursuit of financial gains at all costs to people and planet. It should come as no surprise that some of the most climate-impacted people and places, such as those in low-income countries and marginalized communities in high-income countries, have contributed the least to increasing emissions.

The second step is to develop solutions driven by the most impacted. There are many myths that hold us back from a just future. One myth revolves around what passes for good leadership. In his book *Rich White Men*, author Garrett Neiman urges readers, especially rich white men who hold disproportionate power and wealth globally as of writing this book, to ditch stereotypically masculine leadership qualities such as narcissism, psychopathy, and Machiavellianism, for more stereotypically feminine leadership qualities such as empathy, vulnerability, humility, inclusiveness, generosity, flexibility, balance, and patience; "gender equity requires that every leader—male, female, and nonbinary—be free to pursue the leadership style that fits them personally and meets the needs of all affected stakeholders, unshackled from gender norms" (Neiman, 2023).

In the process of shedding myths and developing new paths forward, the Adaptive Leadership Framework by Heifetz, Grashow, and Linsky may be helpful. The framework seeks to help people thrive in the midst of challenges; the framework turns to evolutionary biology for understanding how beings need to *preserve*, *discard*, and *innovate* in order to thrive.

Successful adaptation has three characteristics: it preserves DNA essential for the species' continued survival; it discards the DNA that no longer serves the species' current needs; and it creates DNA arrangements that give the species' the ability to flourish in new ways and in more challenging environments.

(Heifetz et al., 2009)

Letting go of the myths is thus an essential step in flourishing and innovating for a future self, a future organization, and, by extension, a future career.

Questions that one could help answer in roles that combine the future, justice, equity, diversity, and inclusion include:

- How if at all does the product/service/process exacerbate existing disparities and/or create new ones?
- How can the product/service/process help close social gaps, drive equity, create a more inclusive society, and promote diversity?
- What about this product/service/process should be preserved for JEDI outcomes?
- What about this product/service/process should be discarded for JEDI outcomes?
- How can we innovate on this product/service/process for JEDI outcomes?

Table 10.1 provides practical resources for further applying a JEDI lens to sustainability.

As author Karen Bell states in *Diversity and Inclusion in Environmentalism*:

Diversity is essential because the presence of members of marginalized groups helps to ensure that the tactics, messages and solutions proposed reflect the interests of the marginalized group. At the same time, the visible participation of members of marginalized groups in actions and deliberations increases the trust in the movement by other members of the oppressed group.

(Bell, 2023)

Table 10.2 provides a sample of affinity groups which are organizing various marginalized groups in the climate and environmental movements.

Conclusion

In this chapter, I introduced the concepts of justice, equity, diversity, and inclusion (JEDI) to create a sense of shared vocabulary for readers. Best practices, tools, and frameworks for developing an inclusion mindset and JEDI skills were summarized. The JEDI imperative for sustainability and careers was further elaborated using the SURF Framework and career narratives of

TABLE 10.1 Non-exhaustive examples of JEDI resources

Resource	Source	One-sentence summary
Just Transition Principles	Climate Justice Alliance	A framework for a just transition that provides a place-based set of principles, processes, and practices that build economic and political power to shift from an extractive economy to a regenerative economy.
Diversity, Equity & Inclusion in the workplace	World Business Council for Sustainable Development (WBCSD)	The Future of Work working group has developed information regarding DEI in the workplace.
What is JEDI Investing?	2X Global, a global membership and field-building organization for investors, capital providers, and intermediaries	The Justice, Equity, Diversity, & Inclusion ("JEDI") Community of Practice promotes the incorporation of gender, racial, and ethnic justice in global investment decision making.
Due Diligence 2.0	Brent Kessel, Rachel J. Robasciotti, Tracy Gray, and Erika Seth Davies, with input and contributions from other asset managers	To catalyze movement of capital to BIPOC managers, the asset owners, consultants, and financial intermediaries that sign on to commit to making shifts in the due diligence processes as outlined in the commitment.
EJAtlas (Global Atlas of Environmental Justice)	Institute of Environmental Science and Technology (ICTA) at the Universitat Autònoma de Barcelona	The environmental justice atlas documents and catalogues social conflict around environmental issues.
The Green 2.0 Movement Podcast	Green 2.0	A podcast where activists and leaders in the environmental movement discuss issues related to diversity, equity, inclusion, and justice.
The Joy Report Podcast	Arielle King	A podcast by an intersectional environmentalist about climate solutions and environmental justice through the lens of intersectionality, optimism, and joy.
People Over Plastic (PoP) Podcast	Shilpi Chhotray and Patrice Simms	PoP focuses on uplifting Black, Indigenous, and People of Color (BIPOC)'s environmental justice stories in a way that is nuanced, sensitive, and in-depth.
Think 100% Podcast	The Hip Hop Caucus	Offers conversations that reimagine how Black, Indigenous, and Brown people thrive in our environment and solve climate change.

TABLE 10.2 Climate, environmental, and sustainability-related affinity groups for targeted diversity

Name of group	Affinity
Wildability	People with disabilities
Disability Awareness Around the Climate Crisis (DAAC)	People with disabilities
SustainedAbility	People with disabilities
International Disability Alliance	People with disabilities
Diversity in Sustainability	BIPOC
Intersectional Environmentalist	BIPOC
Les Impactrices	BIPOC and women (France focused)
Diverse Sustainability Initiative	BIPOC and LGBTQIA+
Greentech Noir	Black
Black Oak Collective	Black
The National Black Environmental Justice Network (NBEJN)	Black (U.S. focused)
Outdoor Afro	Black (U.S. focused)
Seeding Sovereignty	Indigenous
Indigenous Climate Action	Indigenous
Indigenous Environmental Network	Indigenous
Green Latinos	Hispanic/Latino/Latina/Latinx
Corazon Latino	Hispanic/Latino/Latina/Latinx
Latinx in Sustainability	Hispanic/Latino/Latina/Latinx
The Filipino American Coalition for Environmental Solidarity (FACES)	Asian (U.S. focused)
Asian Pacific Environmental Network (APEN)	Asian (U.S. focused)
Sustainability Africa	Global Majority (Global South)
Queer Out Here	LGBTQIA+ (UK focused)
The Gay Outdoor Club	LGBTQIA+ (UK focused)
Queers X Climate (QXC)	LGBTQIA+
Out in Climate	LGBTQIA+
OUT for Sustainability	LGBTQIA+
The Venture Out Project	LGBTQIA+
Women and Climate	Women
Women in Cleantech and Sustainability	Women
Women in Climate Tech	Women
Women of Color Collective in Sustainability	Women
HerValue	Women (China focused)

professionals working in climate action and economic empowerment. The rationale for KYH (Know Your History) was introduced, as well as how using JEDI can help an institution itself to evolve for the better.

References

Afsar, B., Asfar, R., Kanbay, A., Covic, A., Ortiz, A., & Kanbay, M. (2019). Air pollution and kidney disease: Review of current evidence. *Clinical Kidney Journal* 12(1), 19–32. https://doi.org/10.1093/ckj/sfy111.

Avarna Group. (2023). Justice, Equity, Diversity and Inclusion (JEDI). Public Lands Alliance. www.publiclandsalliance.org/what-we-do/jedi.

Battle, C. P. (2020). An Offering from the Bayou. In A.E. Johnson & K.K. Wilkinson (eds.), *All We Can Save* (pp. 329–333). One World. www.allwecansave.earth/.

Bell, K. (ed.). (2023). *Diversity and Inclusion in Environmentalism*. Routledge. https://doi.org/10.4324/9781003099185.

Cash, J., & Yao, K. (2023). China's green loans exceed $3.2 trln, central bank chief says. Reuters. www.reuters.com/world/china/chinas-green-loans-exceed-32-trln-central-bank-chief-says-2023-03-29.

Center for Intersectional Justice (CIJ). (2023). What is intersectionality? www.intersectionaljustice.org/what-is-intersectionality.

Coaston, J. (2019). The intersectionality wars. When Kimberlé Crenshaw coined the term 30 years ago, it was a relatively obscure legal concept. Then it went viral. Vox. www.vox.com/the-highlight/2019/5/20/18542843/intersectionality-conservatism-law-race-gender-discrimination.

Crenshaw, K. (1989). Demarginalizing the Intersection of Race and Sex: A Black Feminist Critique of Antidiscrimination Doctrine, Feminist Theory and Antiracist Politics. *University of Chicago Legal Forum* 1(8). http://chicagounbound.uchicago.edu/uclf/vol1989/iss1/8.

Foster, E. (2023). Environmentalism and LGBTQIA+ politics and activism. In K. Bell, (ed.) *Diversity and Inclusion in Environmentalism*. Routledge. https://doi.org/10.4324/9781003099185.

Gartner. (2022). Supply Chain DEI in 2022: Benchmark your diversity, equity and inclusion efforts with Gartner-ASCM DEI survey data. www.gartner.com/en/supply-chain/trends/supply-chain-diversity-equity-inclusion-ascm.

Guo, Y. (2023). Evolution and stages of China's economic inequality from 1978 to 2018. *PLoS One* 18(7). https://doi.org/10.1371/journal.pone.0288873.

Heifetz, R., Grashow, A., & Linsky, M. (2009). The Theory Behind the Practice: A Brief Introduction to the Adaptive Leadership Framework Excerpted from *The Practice of Adaptive Leadership: Tools and Tactics for Changing Your Organization and the World*. Harvard Business Press. www.ccresa.net/wp-content/uploads/2018/06/The-Theory-Behind-the-Practice-Heifetz-Grashow-Linsky.CLEAN-SHORT.pdf.

Hiatt, M. A., Letchie, A. M., Bagasra, A. B., Laufersweiler-Dwyer, D. L., & Mackinem, M. (2019). Perceptions of Diversity, Inclusion, and Belongingness at an HBCU: Implications and Applications for Faculty. In R. Jeffries (ed.). *Diversity, Equity, and Inclusivity in Contemporary Higher Education*. University of South Carolina. IGI Global.

Larrington-Spencer, H., Fenney, D., Middlemiss, L., & Kosanic, A. (2023). Disabled Environmentalisms. In K. Bell (ed.) *Diversity and Inclusion in Environmentalism*. Routledge. https://doi.org/10.4324/9781003099185.

Mor Barak, M. (2022). *Managing Diversity Toward a Globally Inclusive Workplace*, 5th Edition. Sage Publications. https://us.sagepub.com/en-us/nam/managing-diversity/book259165.

Neiman, G. (2023). *Rich White Men: What it takes to Uproot the Old Boys' Club and Transform America*. Hachette Book Group. www.hachettebookgroup.com/titles/garrett-neiman/rich-white-men/9780306925573.

Nordell, J. (2021). *The End of Bias: A Beginning. The Science and Practice of Over-coming Unconscious Bias.* Metropolitan Books. https://us.macmillan.com/books/9781250186188/theendofbiasabeginning.

Pope, R., Reynolds, A., & Mueller, J. (2004). *Multicultural Competence in Student Affairs.* Jossey-Bass/Wiley.

Ramanujam, A., & Asri, N. (2021). *The Climate Crisis is a (Neo)Colonial Capitalist Crisis: Experiences, responses and steps towards decolonising climate action.* European Network Against Racism (ENAR). www.enar-eu.org/wp-content/uploads/2022_report-climatechangeandrace_final.pdf.

Reta, M. (2022). How Environmental and Climate Injustice Affects the LGBTQI+ Community. Center for American Progress. www.americanprogress.org/article/how-environmental-and-climate-injustice-affects-the-lgbtqi-community.

Satheesh, S. (2023). Environmental Movements in the Global South. In K. Bell (ed.) *Diversity and Inclusion in Environmentalism.* Routledge. https://doi.org/10.4324/9781003099185.

Storey, H. (2023). Is China finally getting serious about hukou reform? The Interpreter by the Lowy Institute. www.lowyinstitute.org/the-interpreter/china-finally-getting-serious-about-hukou-reform.

The Climate Reality Project. (2023). Sacrifice Zones 101. www.climaterealityproject.org/sacrifice-zones.

Tulshyan, R. (2022). *Inclusion on Purpose: An Intersectional Approach to Creating a Culture of Belonging at Work.* The MIT Press. https://mitpress.mit.edu/9780262548496/inclusion-on-purpose.

Waite, M. (2021, January 18). The case for buying climate tech from BIPOC and women-owned suppliers. GreenBiz. www.greenbiz.com/article/case-buying-climate-tech-bipoc-and-women-owned-suppliers.

Waite, M. (2023, March 29). Climate financing is finally here, but will there be equity? *The Boston Globe.* www.bostonglobe.com/2023/03/29/opinion/climate-financing-is-finally-here-will-there-be-equity.

Yoshino, K., & Glasgow, D. (2023). *Say The Right Thing: How to Talk About Identity, Diversity, and Justice.* Atria Books.

11

CONCLUSION

Careers and the quadruple bottom line

> Start by asking the question: how does my current role directly or indirectly help the four pillars of sustainable development (society, economy, environment, and future generations)?

As stated by authors Krueger and Gibbs (2007), "It's really quite difficult to find anyone who isn't in favor of sustainability." For this reason, sustainability is the subject of much debate, admiration, and sometimes even animosity. Sustainability is not a perfect concept. In many cases, sustainability and sustainable development will be challenging, a seeming oxymoron. But it is this challenge that makes it an exciting and worthwhile paradigm to adopt in one's career.

As the field of human resources expands, human resource managers are increasingly looking for sustainability skills at all levels of the organization, across all sectors. The talent paradigm is shifting so that HR managers ask, "Do we make excellent decisions about the talent resources that are pivotal to sustainable strategic success?" (Boudreau & Ramstad, 2005). Organizational effectiveness is moving beyond the traditional financial and shareholder outcomes to incorporate values such as governance, transparency, ethics, diversity, social responsibility, environmental protection, community contribution, and employee rights (Boudreau & Ramstad, 2005). Fittingly, organizations are looking for workers who will match those values and improve a complex multiple bottom line.

Whether you work in an office space or in a factory, you will use products to get your job done, and those products can be made sustainable through supply chain management. The coffee and tea in the corner of the office can be organic and fair trade. The ink in the pen and the pulp in the paper can also be purchased "green" and "socially responsible." Work with partners that exemplify justice, equity, diversity, and inclusion. Choose sustainability-minded companies. Buy the A++ rated dishwasher for energy and water savings.

DOI: 10.4324/9781032615844-11

As one person mentioned to me once, "It's dangerous when someone is blaming the consumer." Consumers need information and means to go about making sustainable decisions. There are numerous career fields that directly deal with the user, including policy and public service, public relations within corporations, and product designers. There is room for life-cycle analysis consultants to turn a linear economy problem into a circular economy solution.

Stakeholder relationship careers are growing, as the need for maintaining positive relations and two-way communication channels beyond shareholders is growing. These careers involve being an entrepreneur, a business owner, and a CEO. They involve being a communications specialist and community organizer. There are now firms that specialize in stakeholder engagement and community building.

"Short termism is a huge problem" is a phrase that I often heard during the interviews I conducted across different sectors. Careers that enable organizations to move beyond myopia involve those that change systems—through policy making, through being a market leader independent of size, and through mass mobilization of people.

There are hundreds of thousands of different career trajectories, roles, fields, and positions. It is therefore not possible to discuss every sector and sub-sector, every possibility for incorporating sustainability within careers. But there are two final stories that I wish to impart that cover a multitude of sectors—agriculture, tourism, business, and social entrepreneurship.

Creating opportunity—Esteban Polanco's story

The Blanco Mountains are one of the most lush and fertile areas of the Dominican Republic. That's where I met Esteban Polanco, a lifelong community organizer and proponent of sustainable development.

On the drive to the Rio Blanco Ecotourism Complex, I was given a brief history of the Dominican Republic, including tense relations with its Haitian neighbors, the agricultural industries of sugar cane, coffee, and cacao, and the tourism boom in the northeast (Punta Cana).

As one flies over the Hispaniola peninsula, one can visualize the stark difference in forestation between Haiti and the Dominican Republic. As explained in Jared Diamond's book *Collapse*, about 28 percent of the area of the Dominican Republic is covered in forest as compared to 1 percent in Haiti (Diamond, 2005). Although at least a quarter of the Dominican Republic is protected in natural reserves, some still cut down trees and strip the forest cover. Many who participate in forest destruction do so to sell charcoal to survive.

As Esteban and I sat down to cups of locally grown organic coffee and fresh papaya, mango, and pineapple, we were surrounded by an entire ecological community complex. The Rio Blanco Ecotourism Complex is closest to the major town of Bonao—a nickel-mining area. "I was born here," Esteban said, pointing to the remote mountains in the distance. Esteban explained how, for him, sustainability means maintaining and preserving the ecosystem on which the community depends, maintaining and improving the quality of life of the people, and sustaining livelihoods through a vibrant economy. The nearby river is a major source of sustainability. "We have the responsibility to protect the most important lake of the country—the Rio Yuna—which serves many provinces," Esteban explained.

Esteban leads the Federación de Campesinos hacia el Progreso (referred to here as the Federation), which oversees a number of sustainability initiatives in the Rio Blanco area. He builds the institution to "commit the least errors as possible," meeting with delegates regularly to discuss and resolve issues. The Federation has formed a sustainable agriculture cooperative, with more than 150 member farms. The coop promotes and pools their produce together to sell. The coop also helps its members to use organic and natural farming practices.

The Federation also established a school for bamboo furniture making on-site; some students travel three to four hours by foot just for the opportunity to learn the trade. Of the furniture sales, 20 percent goes to the project to purchase more materials, 40 percent goes to the Federation, and 40 percent goes to the workers as salary. "Right now, the demand for the high-quality bamboo furniture is much greater than supply. We have a backlog," Esteban said.

The Federation has also built a rural and volunteer tourism complex, where visitors can meditate, learn about the community and farming practices, and connect with nature. "We need to take advantage of our strategic position in central DR, halfway between the two main cities and airports of Santiago and Santo Domingo," Esteban passionately expressed. The ecotourism project has had great success, with local and foreign visitors who are there to help, live, and learn by living with local families and contributing to the local economy.

Esteban was not always the head of the Federation. He was raised in an agricultural setting, and proudly stated that he has been a farmer all his life. He studied at the university level and soon became a school teacher. But after two years, the public school system experienced budget cuts and Esteban had to find his way otherwise. Esteban worked with the local community and outside institutions such as the European Union, USAID, and the CODESPA Foundation, to raise funds to establish the Federation officially in 1992. "We now have a track record of over 20 years of reforestation," Esteban stated. "Sustainable development means that we can use a resource permanently without destroying it; this means conserving the soil and not participating in deforestation." The Federation has also been able to launch basic health services for the local community. "Without health, education, electricity, and recreation, what is a human being?" Esteban asked rhetorically. In 1993, three kids in the community died of a simple health problem. "We now have a clinic that helps to prevent these kinds of deaths; and the local schools have improved—social sustainability is just as important as environmental sustainability," Esteban explained.

In 1998, Hurricane Georges ravished the Dominican Republic. But this was also an opportunity to rethink the development. Since then, the Federation has emphasized diversity, in both what is grown and in the economic activities. When I asked Esteban why he left teaching all together, he said, "I never left being a teacher; I consider many members of the community my students." Esteban has been able to support himself, his family, and his community through sustainable agriculture, sustainable furniture manufacturing, and eco-tourism. He has incorporated sustainability in every initiative that he has led. A real inspiration and role model to the community of Rio Blanco, Esteban shows that it is possible and, moreover, beneficial, to incorporate sustainability into a career in rural and developing economies.

Social entrepreneurship—Adnane Addioui's story

It was at the 2014 Global Entrepreneurship Summit in Marrakesh, Morocco, that I met an inspiring social entrepreneur—Adnane Addioui. I made my way through the stylistically Moroccan temporary tents and the teapots filled with green tea with mint. I found Addioui standing before a booth, with a welcoming smile and a demeanor that spoke "can do." Adnane is popular to say the least, constantly surrounded by passers-by and media cameras. But let's start from the beginning.

Adnane was born and raised in Rabat. He knew from an early age that he wanted to work with people, as opposed to within a cubicle in isolation. He worked hard and attended one of the best universities in the country, the National School of Business and Management in Settat (ENCG-Settat). He studied marketing and wanted to go into general business at the time. But that all changed in 2005 when he joined Enactus (formerly SIFE, Students in Free Enterprise). Enactus is a global non-profit present in more than 30 countries whose mission is to enable progress through entrepreneurial students.

It was through the Enactus program that Adnane learned that there was more to business than the financial bottom line. He became involved in small projects and became passionate about social entrepreneurship. He went to France to do a Master's at the University of Versailles, but it was during a short exchange in the U.S. at Georgetown University that he became exposed to a different way of thinking. "I went to a business ethics class at Georgetown, and with no notebook in hand, the professor asked us what we wanted to learn," Adnane explained. "It was out of this world." This gave Adnane the motivation to travel more and learn different approaches to business.

After finishing his Master's in France, Adnane worked for a few corporations. At Danone, he was in charge of implementing a new organizational strategy as the company changed its focus to health. "It was OK, but I was not creating enough impact," Adnane emphasized. He returned to Morocco to do just that. Adnane co-founded the Moroccan Center for Innovation and Social Entrepreneurship, which incubates and accelerates innovative startups in Morocco. "We mentor, coach, fund, and launch products and services," said Adnane. Since January 2013, Adnane is also the Moroccan Country Director for

Enactus. He oversees country operations and has led projects in water, energy, and more. Morocco ranked second in the global Enactus World Cup in 2014 for developing and delivering an innovative water filtration system.

Adnane describes social entrepreneurship as business that addresses a specific need or issue, has a sustainable business model, creates change by being innovative, and improves as many lives as possible. Adnane cites Muhammad Yunus, a famous social entrepreneur, as a big inspiration in his endeavors. Adnane would like to develop similar social entrepreneurship ecosystems in other countries, especially those in North Africa such as Algeria and Tunisia. His advice to students and professionals is to "surround yourself with like-minded people, and if you do not find what you are looking for, create it."

Final thoughts

Chuang-Tzu, a Taoist thinker once said this about the mind: "pour into it and it is never full, dip from it and it never runs dry." Author Jaimal Yogis says that, in this way, the mind is like the sea (Yogis, 2009). I would extend this to the framework of sustainability. It is all-encompassing; sustainability perhaps can never be completely "full" or accomplished. When we enter the career period of our lives, we face many choices such as work and life balance, specialization versus generalization, and remote versus on-site working. As we search for more meaning, purpose, and impact in our careers, incorporating sustainability is not an either/or choice. As illustrated in the various chapters, people all around the world are incorporating sustainability concepts in their daily activities and in their strategic career planning. One does not have to be an environmental or social non-profit activist to contribute to sustainable development through their career.

Start by asking the question: how does my current role directly or indirectly help the four pillars of sustainable development (society, economy, environment, and future generations)? How can my future roles move the human race and the ecosystems on which we depend along a sustainable development path while providing value to my organization? As you deepen your sustainability career reflection, use the SURF Framework and other resources presented in this book for further guidance. Actions such as saving energy and water in the home are part of sustainability 1.0; aligning one's bank and retirement savings with social and environmental justice is part of sustainability 2.0. Sustainability 3.0 includes taking sustainability into the workplace and the workforce. In terms of sustainability-related career action, as the saying goes, the best time to start was yesterday.

The next best time is now.

References

Boudreau, J. W., & Ramstad, P. M. (2005). Talentship, Talent Segmentation, and Sustainability: A New HR Decision Science Paradigm for a New Strategy Definition. *Human Resource Management* 44(2), 129–136.

Diamond, J. (2005). *Collapse: How Societies Choose to Fail or Succeed.* Viking Press.

Krueger, R., & Gibbs, D. (2007). *The Sustainable Development Paradox: Urban Political Economy in The United States and Europe.* The Guilford Press.

Yogis, J. (2009). *Saltwater Buddha: A Surfer's Quest to Find Zen on the Sea.* Wisdom Publications.

INDEX

Printed in the United States
by Baker & Taylor Publisher Services